Cinema of Crushing Motherhood

Cinema of Crushing Motherhood

A New Feminist Cinema

OLIVIA LANDRY

UNIVERSITY OF ILLINOIS PRESS
Urbana, Chicago, and Springfield

© 2025 by the Board of Trustees
of the University of Illinois
All rights reserved
1 2 3 4 5 C P 5 4 3 2 1
♾ This book is printed on acid-free paper.

Library of Congress Cataloging-in-Publication Data

Names: Landry, Olivia author
Title: Cinema of crushing motherhood : a new feminist
 cinema / Olivia Landry.
Description: Urbana : University of Illinois Press, 2025.
 | Includes bibliographical references and index.
Identifiers: LCCN 2025013261 (print) | LCCN
 2025013262 (ebook) | ISBN 9780252046858
 cloth | ISBN 9780252088957 paperback | ISBN
 9780252048395 ebook
Subjects: LCSH: Mothers in motion pictures | Motion
 pictures—History—21st century | Feminist film
 criticism | LCGFT: Film criticism
Classification: LCC PN1995.9.M63 F36 2025 (print)
 | LCC PN1995.9.M63 (ebook) | DDC 791.43/6525—
 dc23/eng/20250325
LC record available at https://lccn.loc.gov/2025013261
LC ebook record available at https://lccn.loc.gov/2025013262

Contents

Preface vii
Acknowledgments xi

Introduction
A New Cinematernity 1

One   Regret 21
Two   Exhaustion 43
Three   Rage 69
Four   Shame 89
Five   Guilt 117
Six   Disgust 139

Conclusion
Warning: Mothering Can Crush! 159

Notes 165
Filmography 181
Bibliography 183
Index 199

Preface

Thematically, this book emerges at an important axis of time and place.

I began working on this book in the former east Berlin neighborhood of Prenzlauer Berg, of all places. Since the early 2000s, Prenzlauer Berg has maintained a reputation as a neighborhood for young, well-to-do, mostly white families. Massive strollers and bicycle trailers bombard the sidewalks. Practically every other corner has a park with a playground, and every other store is either an ice cream parlor or is dedicated to expensive, eco children's clothing and toys. On my part, the location was neither intentional nor strategic, though it did serve to set a certain mood for this study.

It is also July 2022. The 1973 decision *Roe v. Wade* to make access to abortion a civil right in the United States was recently overruled by the US Supreme Court. As a result, many states have severely restricted abortion access for women, even banning abortion completely. What this means, among other things, is that women have limited ability to choose if, when, and how they want to have children. Witnessing this historically regressive event from Berlin, I was also reminded of the challenges of accessing an abortion in Germany. Abortion is illegal in Germany. It is only not punishable within the first twelve weeks of pregnancy and under specific conditions, including receipt of counselling.

I also began researching and writing this book in the aftermath of the COVID-19 pandemic—or better, two years into the COVID-19 pandemic—during which many parents, overwhelmingly mothers, were faced with the sudden additional burden of lockdown, in particular, closed day cares and schools. With few other options, many mothers left their jobs to stay home and attend to their children. The radical gender imbalance of the

FIGURE 00.1. El Bocho's "Lockdown Mum" in Prenzlauer Berg, Berlin, 2022. (Photo by the author)

weight of care work and household responsibilities on the shoulders of women and mothers had forcefully come to the fore.

This is not an anthropological or sociological study of motherhood. But it is irrevocably marked by the context in which it emerges and also by the author I am. I am not a mother. Yet, Eula Biss maintains that "women's lives are defined by motherhood whether or not we have children," and I have to agree.[1] Two years later and leading up to the 2024 federal election in the United States, women's choice to not have children, or even simply to not have biological children, has increasingly come under public scrutiny and criticism.

A note on usage and pronouns: As Sara Ruddick writes at the start of *Maternal Thinking: Toward a Politics of Peace*, "Throughout history and still today women assume disproportionately the responsibilities of caring for children. Therefore, even though mothering work is as suitable to men and nonbinary people as to women, I use feminine grammatical forms when I refer to mothers."[2] This remains the case several decades later; therefore, I, too, use feminine pronouns when I refer to mothers.

Acknowledgments

This book would not have been possible without my sister, Christinia Landry, who first introduced me to the insights of feminist philosophy so many years ago, whose gifted copy of *The Second Sex* to our mother with the inscription, "You really need to read this, Mom," I admittedly stole, and whose personal copy of Orna Donath's *Regretting Motherhood* with insightful notes I was generously bestowed. Christinia also coauthored an article for *New Review of Film and Television Studies* with me on Beauvoir, Deleuze, housework, cinema, and time, which in many ways formed the beginnings of this later project.

Tracing back origins also takes me to Reconsidering Feminism, Film Authorship, and Performance, a wonderful symposium co-organized by Angelica Fenner and Barbara Mennel at the University of Toronto in 2019, during which I presented some precursory material. I am also grateful to Angelica and Barbara for inviting me to contribute to a special issue of *Feminist German Studies*, which allowed me to develop some ideas further. My article on the cinema of Angela Schanelec also informed this book, especially chapter 2.

I am beholden, too, to Erica Carter, Özgür Çiçek, and especially Tamara Moya, who during the European Communication Research and Education Association Film Studies conference in Lisbon in 2022 enthusiastically provided a list of further films about motherhood to consider, several of which made it into this book. I am equally grateful to Patricia White and the Camera Obscura collective for their interest, encouragement, and further recommendations.

For being exceptional interlocutors over the last few years, heartfelt thanks to: Diana Anselmo, Hester Baer, Claudia Breger, Meryem Deniz, Ela

Gezen, Emily Goodling, Mary Hennessey, John Hoffmann, Teresa Kovacs, Priscilla Layne, Maria Roca Lizarazu, Ervin Malakaj, Eszter Polonyi, Brad Prager, Mert Bahadır Reisoğlu Benjamin Lewis Robinson, Sasha Marianna Salzmann, Tanya Shilina-Conte, Katrin Sieg, Lizzie Stewart, and Brangwen Stone. To Alana Dunn as well I owe so much, not only for catching all my typos, bad grammar, and odd phrasing but also for her support and effusive enthusiasm. She truly ushered me through with such warmth and cheer.

I cannot thank Randall Halle enough. He is a tremendous mentor and friend who has always been so supportive. His recommendation to contact University of Illinois Press with this project could not have been more valuable. Working with UIP has been such a pleasure. My editor Danny Nasset is outstanding, and I marvel at his speed, clarity, and discernment. Gary Smith, Megan Donnan, and Mary Lou Kowaleski at UIP have similarly been enormously helpful. I also want to thank the two anonymous readers of the manuscript for their stunningly detailed and thoughtful reports. Their enthusiasm for the project was very encouraging, and the intellectual generosity and care with which they considered the manuscript helped me to see it in a different light. I am grateful, too, to Julian Anselmino, Felizitas Hoffmann, Merle Grimme, Martin Kosok, and Thomas Spitschka at DREIFILM for generously sharing a copy of the film *Regretting Motherhood* and for granting me permission to use an image from the film.

I wrote this book while at my new institutional home, Virginia Commonwealth University, a move that enriched my life and work in so many ways. Among other things, for the first time after so many years, I am able to live with my amazing partner, Ihsan Topaloğlu, without whom I would be completely lost. I thank my colleagues in the School of World Studies, where I began at VCU, and now in Gender, Sexuality, and Women's Studies, where I have since ended up. The collegiality, encouragement, and openness of my colleagues here have been very motivating. And, yes, for you, my dear Ihsan, the most delightful part of my life and now my colleague, too, I am filled with immense gratitude. Thank you so much for everything.

But these acknowledgments would not be complete without a note to my mother, Sally Landry, whose sacrifices I never quite understood and to this day wonder if she regrets. Still, I cannot thank you enough, Mom.

Some material in chapters 1 and 4 appears in "Motherhood That Is *Einfach anders*," *German Studies Review* 48, no. 1 (2025): 67–85. I gratefully acknowledge Johns Hopkins University Press for permission to reuse this material.

Cinema
of Crushing
Motherhood

INTRODUCTION

A New Cinematernity

In Maggie Gyllenhaal's 2021 debut film *The Lost Daughter*, Olivia Colman's maternal figure Leda cautions the nonplussed and heavily pregnant Callie (Dagmara Dominczyk) that "children are a crushing responsibility." The word "crushing," not to mention Colman's almost tragic delivery of the line, patently bears the weight of oppression. Rocks crush; boulders crush. To crush is a violent act; it can destroy. The word does not appear in Elena Ferrante's homonymous 2006 novel upon which the film is based; it is added to the film no doubt for dramatic effect. As we learn, this "crushing responsibility" became too much for Leda, and she left her children. Motherhood can crush. This film and others explored throughout the book render accounts of the crushing weight of motherhood borne out over experiences of regret, exhaustion, rage, shame, guilt, and disgust. But the films do not stop there; they do some crushing of their own. *They crush motherhood*. That is to say, they present mothers who devastate the dominant ideologies of motherhood, what Adrienne Rich famously critiqued as the "institution of motherhood."[1] Frequently at odds with the actual experience of mothering, this institution prescribes how a mother should look, act, and even feel. Through the revelation and expression of negative feelings, the mothers in these films destroy the image of the perfect, self-sacrificial, devoted, and, of course, happy mother. The object of *Cinema of Crushing Motherhood: A New Feminist Cinema* is straightforward: it probes the bad feelings mothers have about motherhood through recent representations in films produced in Australia, Europe, and North America to paint a picture of a new cinematic moment.

In a twofold mode of illustration and performance, description and enactment, crushing motherhood as a concept for film introduces a yielding approach. The violent physicality of the word becomes reinforced through its etymology. To crush, the *Oxford English Dictionary* informs, derives from the old French term *"croissir"* or *"croisir"* meaning to gnash (the teeth), crash, or break.[2] Furthermore, to gnash, the verb's direct cognate, intensifies both the embodied impact of crushing and its affective force—amplifying proximity to maligned feelings. One gnashes one's teeth in rage or pain. In *Paradise Lost*, John Milton briefly but formidably canonizes the affective force of gnashing: "Gnashing for anguish and despite and shame."[3] Thus, crushing, its roots tell us, is an inextricably embodied action and a response to and with negative feelings. Deriving from this etymology, "crushing" offers a trope for the brutal physical force of motherhood and the ugly emotions it can elicit. This fierce coalescence comes alive on the screen through tales of destruction, or at least depletion, and as a collective smashing of motherhood in the films *Madonnen* (Madonnas, directed by Maria Speth, 2007), *Das Fremde in mir* (The stranger in me, directed by Emily Atef, 2008), *We Need to Talk about Kevin* (directed by Lynne Ramsay, 2011), *The Babadook* (directed by Jennifer Kent, 2014), *Mommy* (directed by Xavier Dolan, 2014), *Regretting Motherhood* (directed by Merle Grimme and Felizitas Hoffmann, 2017), *Mater Amatísima: Imaginaries and Discourses on Maternity in Times of Change* (directed by María Ruido, 2017), *Tully* (directed by Jason Reitman, 2018), *Ich war zuhause, aber . . .* (I was at home, but . . . , directed by Angela Schanelec, 2019), *The Lost Daughter* (directed by Maggie Gyllenhaal, 2021), *Cinco Lobitos* (Lullaby, directed by Alauda Ruiz de Azúa, 2022), *Baby Ruby* (directed by Bess Wohl, 2022), *Saint Omer* (directed by Alice Diop, 2022), *Earth Mama* (directed by Savanah Leaf, 2023), and *A Thousand and One* (directed by A. V. Rockwell, 2023) and two series, *The Baby* (created by Lucy Gaymer and Siân Robins-Grace, HBO, 2022) and *Pieces of Her* (created by Charlotte Stoudt, Netflix, 2022).[4] Assembling films about motherhood released between 2007 and 2023, hailing from Australia, Canada, France, Germany, Spain, the United Kingdom, and the United States and diverse in genre, aesthetics, and mode, *Cinema of Crushing Motherhood* offers a broad, if not global, contemporary feminist cinema (most of these films are also written and directed by women) invested in the subjective experience of motherhood—that is, how mothers themselves experience motherhood. As the films reveal, the experience can be agonizing and rife with bad feelings.

Some of the films predate the COVID-19 pandemic; others coincide with it or directly follow. None of the films explicitly engages with or even references the pandemic. It is, nevertheless, impossible to address motherhood in this age without evoking this crisis that so brutally brought the nuclear family to the brink and witnessed the absolute sapping of mothers. Indeed, the pandemic refocused much public attention on mothers. Once again, the world was reminded that women and mothers still perform the greater share of domestic labor and childcare and that this work continues to go unpaid and frequently unnoticed.[5] Isolation and the additional burdens of round-the-clock childcare, homeschooling, and caring for elderly relatives, to say nothing of a health crisis, exacerbated the crushing weight of motherhood. The public health directive "stay home," furthermore, became a condemnation for many, especially those experiencing housing instability, food insecurity, single parenting, or abusive situations.[6]

In the early days of the pandemic, scholar and journalist Andrea Flynn attested to the severe impact on women and mothers: "The coronavirus has laid bare many divisions in our society. And, like any serious crisis does, it has elevated the extent to which structural sexism permeates our lives: impacting the gendered division of labor within the home and also shaping what is possible for women, and particularly mothers, in the public sphere."[7] Women, in particular, grappled with the additional socially enforced responsibility to assume disproportionate domestic work: women's "second shift" became all the more taxing.[8] Many mothers even left the workforce (often by necessity) and settled back into the role of full-time caregiver. If any recent event in history truly crushed mothers and unleashed congeries of bad feelings, then it was the COVID-19 pandemic. This event cannot help but set the tone for a study of recent cinematic representations of motherhood.

Why are films that lay bare such maternal burden and rue novel or shocking? The catch, of course, is that mothers are not allowed to feel bad. Even at its most hellish, motherhood privileges positive affect above all else. Happiness is compulsory. Feeling bad contradicts the normative expectations of happiness and therefore also the edicts of the institution of motherhood. Having feelings of regret, exhaustion, rage, shame, guilt, and disgust, as documented in *Cinema of Crushing Motherhood*, can thus lead to a mother's ostracization as a "bad mother." But what constitutes a bad mother? If anything, this is the most elastic of labels. Certainly, monstrous mothers of horror cinema come to mind. Consider some features, classic and new: Alfred Hitchcock's *Psycho* (1960), Brian De Palma's *Carrie* (1976), David Cronenberg's *The Brood* (1979), Veronika Franz and Severin Fiala's *Ich seh, Ich seh* (Goodnight Mommy, 2014, and its 2022 US remake directed by Matt Sobel), Ari Aster's *Hereditary* (2018), and Jordan Peele's *Us* (2019). These mothers embody violence, sadism, and control. But, as Sarah Arnold indicates, the bad mother may "simply reject her prescribed role within the dominant nuclear family model."[9] Taking a playful approach to the bad mother epithet, Jon Lucas and Scott Moore's 2016 American so-called mom-com *Bad Moms* portrays its central figures as fun-loving mothers with their own desires, but they nevertheless always have their children's best interests in mind.

According to E. Ann Kaplan, if the good mother follows the myth of "all-nurturing and self-abnegating—the 'Angel of the House'" and "[t]otally invested in [her] husband and children," then the bad mother "refuses the self-abnegating role" and "demand[s] her own life."[10] The binary categories of good mother and bad mother serve much less as a heuristic opening than as an assaulting postulation of blame. Solidified under capitalism as a means to control and manipulate women depending on the needs of the workforce, the duality of the good mother and bad mother became theorized hand in glove through psychoanalysis as the split between the angelic and the phallic mother.[11] As Sara Ruddick confirms in *Maternal Thinking*, the ideologies of good and bad mothers cast long shadows "on actual mothers' lives."[12] Cinema has certainly played a role in the perpetuation of these inveterate ideologies.[13]

All of the mothers examined in the present book might invoke the bad mother label either by dint of their negative feelings toward motherhood or their shunning of the absolute self-sacrifice required of the good mother. In some cases, the designation sticks for other reasons, too. Several of these films do contain plots of abandonment, violence, and even filicide. But these maternal figures are a far cry from Kaplan's "evil witch" or Barbara Creed's "monstrous mother."[14] Attuned to both this cinematic history and to the accreting ambit of the figure of the bad mother in European and North American cultures and the attendant assault of blame, the films comprising the cinema of crushing motherhood trouble these ideologies.[15] Their figures struggle under the crushing weight of the maternal role. As a result, they either refuse to hew to the sacrificial demands of good mothering or through no dearth of effort fail to achieve them. Both paths occasion bad feelings. To say the least, the impossible and perfidious myth of the good mother as "cheery suburban matron utterly devoted to her brood" begins to crumble here.[16]

The novelty of these films compared to their possible predecessors in early melodrama, horror, and even recent comedies such as *Bad Moms* and its spin-offs is both their uncompromising subjective position of the mother (*she* looks, *she* speaks, *she* feels) and their rich exploration and affirmation of negative affect. This is a different kind of feel-bad cinema not invested in viewer-oriented, disturbing experiences but, rather, in the inexorable ugly feelings conjured by the experience of motherhood felt by (and heavily mediated through the perspective of) the mother.[17]

Cinema of Crushing Motherhood is a sensorium of affects and its categories of feeling both cathartic and noncathartic and yet inexorably dysphoric in nature—characterized generally by existential uneasiness, unhappiness, and dissatisfaction.

A Brief History of Motherhood on Film

Abounding in representations of motherhood, cinema was in certain ways formed by the archetypes of the "good mother" and the "bad mother." Lucy Fischer begins her pathbreaking study *Cinematernity: Film, Motherhood, Genre* (1996) with examples from Eadweard Muybridge's protocinematic *Animal Locomotion* (1887) and the plates subtitled the "Good Mother" and the "Bad Mother."[18] Consider these once more (figures 0.1 and 0.2).

Figure 0.1 features a seated woman whom a child approaches and offers a small bouquet of flowers. The woman enthusiastically receives the flowers and then affectionately kisses the child. Figure 0.2 provides a 360-degree pan of a woman who repeatedly spanks a child slung over her bent knee. Both affection versus discipline and joy versus rage become the two poles of maternal representation in these contrasting plates. With late nineteenth-century protocinematic chronophotography, the tropes of the "Good Mother" and the "Bad Mother" became cemented in cinema avant la lettre. As noted above, these tropes subsequently developed as constituent ingredients of the cinematic genres of melodrama and horror. We observe them from King Vidor's *Stella Dallas* (1937) all the way to Alfred Hitchcock's *Psycho* (1960) and beyond. A panoply of studies engages with this important history from within a distinctively psychoanalytic frame: Kaplan's *Motherhood and Representation: The Mother in Popular Culture and Melodrama* (1992), numerous articles on melodrama by Linda Williams, Annette Brauerhoch's *Die gute und die böse Mutter: Kino zwischen Melodrama und Horror* (The good and bad mother: Cinema between melodrama and horror) (1996), Fischer's aforementioned *Cinematernity*, and Sarah Arnold's *Maternal Horror Film: Melodrama and Motherhood* (2013).[19] Kept afloat by melodrama and horror cinema, only slowly have these threadbare roles of the mother as good or bad finally begun to fray.

"Cinefeminism," feminist film with origins in the women's movement of the 1970s, challenged these detrimental designations of "good" and "bad" in order to address the hitherto silent struggle of mothers and the wearisome weight of child-rearing and housework, labor without recompense and without security. Much feminist cinema of the 1960s and 1970s focused on the mother from the perspective of the daughter, who

FIGURE 0.1. The "Good Mother." Eadweard Muybridge, *Animal Locomotion* (1887). (University of Southern California Digital Library / Philadelphia Museum of Art)

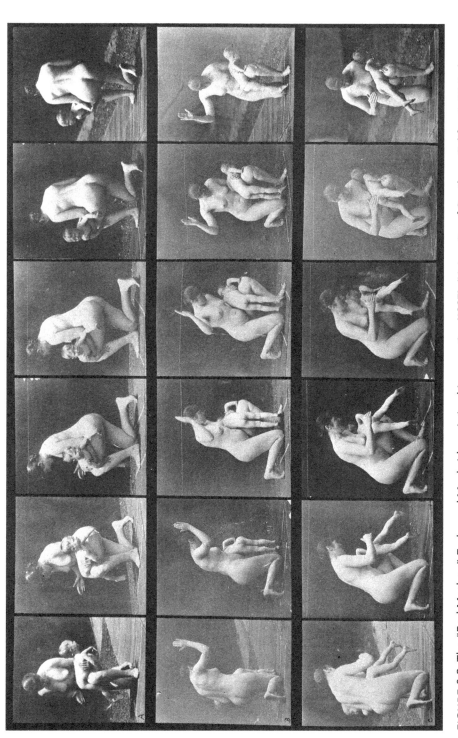

FIGURE 0.2. The "Bad Mother." Eadweard Muybridge, *Animal Locomotion* (1887). (University of Southern California Digital Library / Philadelphia Museum of Art)

struggled with the vast generational gap and perceived her mother as an agent of patriarchal order. Some important exceptions prevail, however.[20] Films such as Chantal Akerman's realist drama *Jeanne Dielman, 23 quai du Commerce, 1080 Bruxelles* (1975) and Helga Reidemeister's documentary *Von wegen Schicksal* (Is this fate? 1979) present distinctive yet striking examples of films invested in visualizing the toll of motherhood and domestic labor on women. A host of other films of this period likewise called attention to the strain of balancing motherhood with work outside the home, particularly, political work. In this respect, several films stemming from New German Cinema of the 1970s are notable: Alexander Kluge's *Gelegenheitsarbeit einer Sklavin* (Part-time work of a domestic slave, 1973), Helke Sander's *Die allseitig reduzierte Persönlichkeit—Redupers* (The all-round reduced personality—redupers, 1978), and the Austrian outlier, Valie Export's *Unsichtbare Gegner* (Invisible adversaries, 1976). But though these films finally made mothering and housework visible onscreen as a source of frustration, exhaustion, and struggle for many women, they often neglected to explore the affective lives of women who harbor adverse feelings toward motherhood itself. By the same token, the rich archive of scholarship that tracks the histories and developments of global feminist cinema movements, especially since the 1970s, pays only passing attention to the situation of the mother. Consider Julia Knight's *Women and the New German Cinema* (1992), B. Ruby Rich's *Chick Flicks: Theories and Memories of the Feminist Film Movement* (1998), Christine Gledhill and Julia Knight's *Doing Women's Film History: Reframing Cinemas, Past and Future* (2015), and Patricia White's *Women's Cinema, World Cinema: Projecting Contemporary Feminisms* (2015). Perhaps, as Lisa Baraitser contends, "'The mother' after all is the impossible subject, par excellence"?[21]

What if we begin to imagine a new cinematernity? If Fischer's book and coinage give breath to the study of what she describes as "the mother's status as a figure in fiction, experimental, and documentary film" until the early 1990s, what happens in the films that come after?[22] A look at the present demands that we also recalibrate our starting point. Rather than with Muybridge's plates, what if we begin with actual moving images of motherhood and the examples put forth in Irene Lusztig's *The Motherhood Archives* (2013)? An archival essay film composed of found footage hailing from educational and medical training films about childbirth and motherhood dating from 1919 to the present, it complicates the categorical representations dispensed by Muybridge's plates.[23] Against the whirring sound of a film projector, a voice-over narrator opens the film with the following observation: "In archives, libraries, hospitals, and community centers, there is a history of motherhood in celluloid fragments." Amid these celluloid fragments, Lusztig pieces together a history of motherhood centered erstwhile on education and control. She reflects on how pregnant women's bodies have become sites of knowledge and surveillance.[24] In these moving images, the mother or mother-to-be learns about motherhood. This education through early film, the voice-over narration tells us, even sought to dictate our very feelings about motherhood: "The archive unspools to the edge of the twenty-first century. We are still learning lessons about what we should want and feel as we become mothers."

Emerging from what Kate Eichhorn identifies as the broad archival turn in feminism and feminist filmmaking, Lusztig's film repurposes the footage that historically hinged on and shored up the perception of maternal ignorance and docility.[25] But by sifting through and recycling archival material something happens: "Archival retrieval and remediation set in motion processes of engagement, interruption, and even contestation."[26] Seizing the images, shuffling, and reorganizing them into her own history, Lusztig's remediation evolves into a feminist project. Hester Baer similarly discusses the value of remediation for feminist filmmaking "as an explicit engagement with and transformation of aesthetic and theoretical precursor texts in order to draw attention to the history, materiality, and representational practices of media."[27] For Laura Mulvey, this is a radical process of archival distortion, what she calls "gleaning" or "détournement."[28] As Domietta Torlasco expounds, such a strategy advances a "reinscription rather than neutral recording," insofar as the images "not only expand but also confront, disturb, and ultimately reconstitute the memory of cinema we have inherited."[29] Beyond the images, the soundtrack reinscribes as well. A mix of original sound, jarring atonal music, and a narrative voice (the filmmaker herself) punctuates this footage with critical and often poetic reflection. Finally, Lusztig supplements the found footage with three documentary interviews with mothers who share their own personal experiences, impressions, and feelings about pregnancy and childbirth—some positive, some negative. These episodes of self-narration provide critical counterpoints to the stories the archive tells *about* women and motherhood, almost exclusively from the perspective of male doctors and scientists. As a source of historical representation of motherhood, *The Motherhood Archives* documents the audiovisual influences that have shaped the discourse, not dissimilar to Muybridge's motion photography of Good and Bad Mothers. Mothers must be trained about how to be good mothers, because they are assumed to be ignorant, if not bad and failing.[30] However, Lusztig's film intervenes and contests such injurious representations from the past, and at this site (and in the spirit) of contest a new critical cinema about motherhood manifests itself.

A Tale of Two Discourses

Coinciding with and in certain ways shaping new cinematic explorations of motherhood, we also witness the unfolding of two discourses. The year is 2015. It marks the publication of J. J. Gleeson and K. D. Griffiths's family-abolitionist article "Kinderkommunismus: A Feminist Analysis of the 21st-Century Family and a Communist Proposal for Its Abolition" and Orna Donath's "Regretting Motherhood: A Sociopolitical Analysis." Unfolding in the United States, the first relaunches and expands on the 1970s feminist proposal to abolish the family through a return to Marxist political theory. The second, an Israeli study, proposes that some mothers regret having children, and if they could turn back time, they would be no one's mother. Only occasionally brought into conversation with one another (referenced in passing by Sophie Lewis), abolition of the family and regretting motherhood took exceedingly different paths.[31] Yet, their emergence registers with a general discontent of the familial structure, which continues to support the housewife-based (capitalist) model and has, to notable extent, only heightened under neoliberalism. Is it not the injunction of neoliberal postfeminism to nurture positive feelings and affirmative mothering?[32] Consider postfeminism's redomestication of women through the salvaging of the figure of the Good Mother under the guise of new-momism or, even more recently, 1950s-inspired "tradwife" subculture: "Feminism won; you can have it all; of course you want children; mothers are better at raising children than fathers; of course your children come first; of course you come last; today's children need constant attention, cultivation, and adoration."[33] This trend of intensive, stay-at-home, "perfect" mothering, which understands child-rearing as a solitary, individual practice, has only served to further burden and isolate mothers, now wholly responsible for the well-being and flourishing of their children. Mothers are exhausted; mothers are frustrated; mothers have had enough! We might say that regretting motherhood is the affective counterpart of the abolition of the family.

Gleeson and Griffiths's article responded to the conversative lament in the United States about the breakdown of the family allegedly through, among other things, the nationwide legalization of same-sex marriage. The authors remind the reader that the Left was historically founded on the abandonment of the institution of the family, regarded then and now as a pillar of capitalist society and the accumulation of private property.[34] In *The Communist Manifesto*, Karl Marx and Friedrich Engels radically called for the abolition of the family and its replacement through social education. "Abolition of the family!" they rallied. "On what foundation is the present family, the bourgeois family, based? On capital, on private gain."[35] But if Marx and Engels assumed the vanishing of the family as a matter of course through the vanishing of capital, then Gleeson and Griffiths turn this around and propose that by dismantling the housewife-based model of the family, and especially maternal obligation, we also begin to dismantle capitalism. They conclude their essay thus: "Put simply: capitalism cannot survive without the family; revolutionary communism cannot survive with it."[36] Although, as Sophie Lewis surmises, it might be easier even now to imagine the end of capitalism than the end of the family.[37] A number of thinkers followed Gleeson and Griffiths's line of thought—and flight. At the turn of the last decade, an explosion of books on the topic of family abolition followed. US-based authors, such as Tiffany Lethabo King, Sophie Lewis, M. E. O'Brien, Dorothy Roberts, and Kathi Weeks, expanded on the many trajectories and possibilities of family abolition. They not only hark back to Marx but also to 1970s feminist writing and activism through a critical review of radical feminist Shulamith Firestone's work. Abolition of the family was not only the most infamous communist proposal; it was "the most infamous feminist proposal," too.[38]

Donath's article, likewise, first appeared in the US context, specifically in the feminist journal *Signs*, but it did not gain much traction in US academic circles. Instead, it went viral on social and mainstream media in Europe, especially in Germany and Spain. A much more personal study of individual mothers who confess to feelings of regret, Donath focuses on the phenomenon of regretting as a psychological position rather than a political, historical, or material one. Interviewees for her project hailed from different class and educational backgrounds within the Jewish Israeli community. Her theoretical framework returned to the insights of Janet Landman and her paradigm-shifting approach to regret in *Regret: The Persistence of the Possible* (1993). Contra popular perceptions of regret as a futile and painful emotion that causes us to dwell in the past and renders us powerless to change, Landman declares that regret can provide an aperture to unexpected possibilities and revelations of reason, what she terms "felt-reason or reasoned-emotion."[39] Donath's study struck a chord with mainstream audiences and developed into a popular discourse, rather than an academic one, with the swift response and publication of a slew of books targeted at general audiences, including Donath's own book-length study, as well those of Germany-based authors Esther Göbel, Christina Mundlos, and Sarah Fischer. The discourse of regretting motherhood explicitly recasts the already well-established discourse of maternal ambivalence. If ambivalence still teeters on mixed feelings, both positive and negative, toward mothering, regret says no. It inveterately covets the forbidden path of nonmotherhood.[40] Distinct from the discourse of family abolition, regretting motherhood exploded in the mid-2010s and then almost as quickly fizzled out. Yet, it left many critical traces, not least a gash in the social fabric; the emotional lives of mothers could be ignored no longer. Perhaps more important for this study, it left us with cinematic documents. We witness the direct crossover between discourse and cinema through regret. A debate-turned-movement of maternal feelings captured in real-time through documentary film provides a starting point in the first chapter.

Between abolition and regret, the model of crushing motherhood for film pays witness to the negative emotions that family and motherhood conjure in the many women, who feel isolated, abandoned, and oppressed in their role often as sole caretakers. It does not explicitly call for the end of motherhood or the revolutionization of kinship, but it certainly crushes the veneer of pure joy and bliss that champions the ideal of the housewife-family model. In light of this confluence, perhaps Diana Karklin's proposal to "undo motherhood" most fittingly aligns with my own project. In the photo-essay collection *Undo Motherhood* (2022), she presents seven individual booklets, each dedicated to a different negative feeling in its documentation of the story of a mother. These include acceptance, anger, exhaustion, fear, guilt, isolation, and resignation. The unnamed mothers are driven to anonymity because of social pressure and stigma. Karklin reports: "The women in this project love their children and are excellent mothers when judged according to society's standards, and yet they hate the oppressive mother role that robbed them of their own existence and suffer through it in silence, feeling it to be the worst mistake they have made."[41] The influence of regret is evident, but Karklin takes her project further. She gives space to other feelings that contribute to maternal unhappiness and probes them through text as well as image. If nothing else, *Undo Motherhood* offers a template for *Cinema of Crushing Motherhood* in form and aesthetic that complements the discourses of abolition and regret. Finally, my own choice to focus on mothers rather than parents, or family, more generally, derives from the films themselves. They present a steady onslaught of representations of struggling mothers.

Crushing Motherhood: A New Cinematic Model of Feminist Subjectivity

I am struck by how many of the films gathered here are debut features and that thirteen of the sixteen films I explore are directed by women. Suffice it to say, the experience of motherhood tenders a rich subject matter for new filmmaking endeavors. Negative maternal feelings, furthermore, provide unchartered terrain for unimaginable narrative and aesthetic exploration. Many filmmakers have remarked on the absence, or at least paucity, of difficult narratives about motherhood on screen. Such accounts have remained safely tucked away, out of sight and out of mind. Among these filmmakers, Lusztig declares her own film as a break with this tradition of repression.[42] Few filmmakers explicitly cite the discourses of the abolition of the family or regretting motherhood as influences for their work, but all recognize the urgency for films committed to the subjective experience of the mother. With the exploration of subjective experience, a more nuanced picture of motherhood takes shape—the highs as well as the lows. In their renunciation of the fantasy and utopia so deeply entangled in motherhood plots, these films collectively intervene and subvert the inundating images of the maternal ideal of the spirited, joyful, and docile mother.

Eager to draw out these maternal performances, I find myself returning to the insights of Simone de Beauvoir, not simply because she was the first philosopher to analyze the woes of the housewife and mother but for her ability to grasp and write so poignantly about the lived experience of these situations, so often tied to one another. Unlike any other thinker, Beauvoir understood the ontological state of a housewife's exhaustion through the drudgery of mechanical labor that never ends. In its wake, an existence bereft of greater meaning, creativity, and transcendence wanly takes form. So, too, did she perceive the unrelenting guilt of the mother who struggles with the ethical obligation to relinquish her freedom, to say nothing of her entire being, for her child. Beauvoir took maternal unhappiness and alienation seriously. At a time when no other thinker dared, she sundered the fable of unequivocal maternal fulfillment. Although much recent scholarship is wont to depart from Beauvoir, not least for her gender essentialism, she still offers us much. For this reason, *The Second Sex* weaves in and out of this book, complemented, of course, by variegated philosophical and theoretical provinces of thought.

My rubric of affect and structuring an analysis of the films around negative feelings comes from the films themselves. Both in their performances and effects, the affective intensities of these films exhilarate. By feeling out these films, so to speak, we deepen our understanding of their accounts of motherhood and sometimes come to very unexpected conclusions. I trace each featured affect through its individual historical, philosophical, and theoretical trajectory, engaging each step of the way in conversation with different thinkers and discourses. Affect studies offers a rich dialogue, in particular, the divergent writings of Eve Kosofsky Sedgwick, Sianne Ngai, Sara Ahmed, and Eugenie Brinkema. Still, no one model fits all. With each chapter and exploration of a particular feeling, I begin anew. Each affect unfolds through its own history, its own capacious archive of thought. For all the scholarship on affect, however, there is scant writing on the affective lives of mothers within the field. Such dearth precipitates a turn toward motherhood studies and a historical return to Adrienne Rich, and for similar reasons I find myself in the company of Beauvoir. Granted, though, the discourse of maternal ambivalence, which Rich gave breath to over half a century ago, has for many run its course, her embrace and honest rendering of the feeling maternal subject pulling through under the crush of raw-edged nerves continue to stun and penetrate.

To Rich we also owe our understanding of the diametrically opposed poles of motherhood: the real experience versus the institution, that is, the reality of motherhood and the external expectations and pressures of the same. Motherhood as an institution subjects mothers to surveillance, control, and censorship. Mothers are instructed how to act and even how and what to feel, often in gross neglect of their actual experiences and emotional responses. In Rich's formulation, "two meanings of motherhood, one superimposed on the other: the *potential relationship* of any woman to her powers of reproduction and to children; and the *institution*, which aims at ensuring that that potential—and all women—shall remain under male control."[43] Subsequent thinkers have revisited this distinction and offered new rhetorical strategies. Disinclined to relinquish the role of the "mother" wholesale, Andrea O'Reilly calls for "mothering against motherhood."[44] Renegotiating the terms of mothering and motherhood, Black feminist thinkers have pushed this distinction further. In their edited volume *Revolutionary Mothering*, Alexis Pauline Gumbs, China Martens, and Mai'a Williams propose that *mothering* is affirmative and revolutionary, whereas *motherhood* not only represents an institution of control but also an identity and status historically denied to Black mothers.[45] The history of Black motherhood in the US context and elsewhere is often one of oppression, loss, and dispossession, Saidiya Hartman states with such excoriating lucidity.[46] Slavery destroyed motherhood. In the afterlives of slavery, Black motherhood continues to be denied. As Christina Sharpe echoes, *partus sequitur ventrem* endures.[47] Indeed, a study of motherhood, any study of motherhood, presses the question not only of different individual experiences but also different collective histories. Patricia Hill Collins recognizes the importance of always thinking about motherhood through the lenses of class and especially race: "Motherhood occurs in specific historical situations framed by interlocking structures of race, class, and gender. . . . Racial domination and economic exploitation profoundly shape the mothering context, not only for racial ethnic women in the United States, but for all women."[48] Cinema tracks these differences. Alongside recent cinematic tales of maternal regret, exhaustion, rage, shame, guilt, and disgust, others about tragedy and resistance continue to appear. We might consider Chinonye Chukwu's biographical drama *Till* (2022), about the atrocious, historical murder of fourteen-year-old Emmet Till by a mob of white supremacists in Mississippi and his mother's intrepid will to bring attention to the horrors of racialized violence—"to let the world see" her son's mutilated body. Another recent film, Paula Eiselt and Tonya Lewis Lee's timely documentary *Aftershock* (2022), explores reproductive injustice, obstetric violence, and the distressingly high rate of postpartum mortality among Black mothers in the United States. Certainly, diverging cinematic pursuits of motherhood continue to coexist. Individual films may even contain blended narratives of mothers fighting for their children and experiencing the crush and negative feelings in their roles as mothers.

Many of the films in this book focus on white, middle-class mothers but not all of them. Notwithstanding its inward leaning toward subjective experience and personal politics, the cinema of crushing motherhood does not exclusively map white maternal negative feelings.[49] Affected in very different ways, the lives of all women and mothers are all touched by these structures of power, and no study on motherhood can ignore them. Without dismissing or superseding the distinct histories, the devastating presence of anti-Black racism, and the powerful public role of mothers in the era of Black Lives Matter (BLM) in the United States and elsewhere, I analyze films about Black mothers and white mothers within the rubric of crushing motherhood. Jennifer C. Nash's work presents critical insight at this juncture. She carefully cautions against the categorical distinction between maternal narratives solely based on race. In her review of *Revolutionary Mothering*, "The Political Life of Black Motherhood," she confesses, "As a black feminist scholar, I remain both seduced by and skeptical of the representation of black motherhood as radical and revolutionary, as spiritual and transformative." Can we not, she continues, also imagine "accounts of [Black] motherhood that find mothering profoundly unradical, perhaps even tedious, exhausting, or upsetting?"[50] Turning to recent films about motherhood, we find an answer to Nash's provocative question. Different mothers, often confronted with very different, even incommensurable, challenges, still find themselves exhausted, overwhelmed, and broken down by the pressures of mothering. No edict that motherhood is supposed to be affirmative, joyful, and, yes, even radical can change that. This is the cinema of crushing motherhood.

Some Notes on the Chapters

Along with Diana Karklin's contemporary photo-essay collection *Undo Motherhood*, *Cinema of Crushing Motherhood* also humbly aspires to the ambitions of Sara Ahmed's *Cultural Politics of Emotion* (2004) and especially Sianne Ngai's *Ugly Feelings* (2005), two groundbreaking monographs on affect theory now two decades old. Similar to those monographs in structure, this book presents a series of studies on the philosophy and aesthetics of feelings, specifically negative ones. Each chapter engages with an affect in a sweep of its philosophical, feminist, and film theoretical history. All six chapters in this book mobilize a unique affective frame to investigate recent examples of motherhood in cinema. Examining fourteen films and two series in total, the chapters mostly partake of new examples. The only overlap arises with Jennifer Kent's *The Babadook* and Maggie Gyllenhaal's *The Lost Daughter*, two films I take up in two different chapters, respectively. Not only do these two films explore more than one bad feeling in striking ways, both present remarkable examples of new cinematic treatments of the maternal experience as challenging and burdensome. They are to some extent models of the cinema of crushing motherhood.

The theme of motherhood cuts across all of the chapters, of course. The films compellingly connect through this and other minor elements of plot and aesthetics. Building our knowledge and expanding our thinking about contemporary representations of motherhood, these chapters constitute a whole, but their arc is not linear and does not evolve nor develop through a singular line of thought or according to chronological sequence. The reader could pick up this book at the beginning, middle, or end. Similar to Karklin's *Undo Motherhood*, *Cinema of Crushing Motherhood* is a collection, not necessarily a collective voice, of mothers and affects.

This book begins with the emotion that has in part reshaped the discourse of motherhood of late: regret. Chapter 1 introduces the reader more fully to the regretting motherhood debate that garnered significant attention in the national contexts of Germany and Spain. I survey these national trajectories through two nonfiction films, Merle Grimme and Felizitas Hoffmann's *Regretting Motherhood* (Germany, 2017) and María Ruido's *Mater Amatísima: Imaginaries and Discourses on Maternity in Times of Change* (Spain, 2017). Before delving into the films, this chapter pursues a philosophical and ethical history of regret. Like all negative emotions, regret has a fraught history. Feminist thinkers Elizabeth Spelman and Sara Ahmed exercise caution. For them, regret can obstruct action and perhaps even serve as a renunciation of responsibility. But Janet Landman and Brian Price are more optimistic. They discuss the epistemological and political value of regret through its evocation of thought over ready-made knowledge. Regret, they opine, invites change and is therefore transformative. Maternal regret, according to Orna Donath, follows the latter. In their direct response to regretting motherhood, the films that fill out this chapter—the first, a short documentary of interviews with mothers and the second an experimental compilation film—explore maternal regret, inter alia, as a critical reminder of the feminist argument that the personal is political and that even the private experiences of mothers are part of a broader plot of political engagement.

Subsequent chapters explore feelings contributing to maternal regret and the capacious archive of fiction films that comprise the cinema of crushing motherhood. Chapter 2 takes on that omnipresent feeling shared by many mothers: exhaustion. Though not an affect or an emotion per se, exhaustion does become an existential state in films such as Kent's *The Babadook* (Australia, 2014), Jason Reitman's *Tully* (United States, 2018), A. V. Rockwell's *A Thousand and One* (United States, 2023), and Angela Schanelec's *Ich war zuhause, aber . . .* (I was at home, but . . . , Germany, 2019). Through the insights of Beauvoir's immanent situation of the housewife and mother, condemned to quotidian existence of domestic drudgery and Sisyphean repetition, and Gilles Deleuze's postwar time-image inhabited by tired bodies in a state of suspension, exhaustion in maternal cinema assumes ontological dimensions. In the films, exhaustion first manifests in the haggard faces and bodies of the maternal figures, but it does not always simply settle there. Conditioned by exhaustion, the worlds the films open up are precarious and even prone to violence: attempted filicide, a near-fatal car crash.

Treating that far less savory feeling, rage, chapter 3 galvanizes things. Despite the rich history of righteous anger from ancient philosophy to feminist theory and thought—namely, from Aristotle to Audre Lorde, Marilyn Frye, and Sara Ahmed—maternal rage remains a taboo topic. Now half a century old, Rich's radical plaint that the coexistence of love and anger for one's child is, for so many, inconceivable still resonates. Mothers are simply not given to rage. As a matter of course, maternal rage has long been pathologized and, in turn, attributed to the monstrous in cinema. It is a staple of the horror genre. But what of the mother who experiences rage for good reason? A mother pushed to her limit? Chapter 3 traces rage through the perspective of the mother. More-recent films and series have begun to explore maternal rage that justifiably develops as a result of exhaustion, frustration, and injustice. *The Babadook* makes a return in this chapter as a horror film of a different sort—from the position of the mother. Even when rage explodes to the point of violence in this film and in Lucy Gaymer and Siân Robins-Grace's horror-comedy HBO series *The Baby* (United Kingdom, 2022), we find reprieve in its arrival. These mothers are not creating horror; they are responding to it. But rage does not always lead to violence. I pair these two horror stories with a more subtle example of maternal rage on the screen, Caroline Stoudt's Netflix thriller series *Pieces of Her* (United States, 2022), directed by Minkie Spiro. Here, rage culminates instead in the form of a feminist snap.[51]

Chapters 4 and 5 connect broadly through the phenomenon of mother blaming. The first examines shame; the second, guilt. But blame serves merely as an impetus to probe these feelings, which, as each chapter respectively reveals, also differ in significant ways. In both philosophy and affect theory, shame boasts a critical status inextricably linked to bodily presence and exposure—an unyielding being-seen-by-the-Other. Chapter 4 takes the reader from Emmanuel Levinas, Maurice Merleau-Ponty, and Jean-Paul Sartre to Silvan Tomkins and Sedgwick on a winding trail of shameful feelings betrayed under the alien gaze of another. Four distinct dramas track the role of shame in motherhood: Maria Speth's *Madonnen* (Madonnas, Germany, 2007), Savanah Leaf's *Earth Mama* (United States, 2023), Gyllenhaal's *The Lost Daughter* (United States, 2021), and Alice Diop's *Saint Omer* (France, 2022). All of these films locate shame in the mothers' experiences of perceived failure because they cannot live up to the impossible standards of the good mother. These stories of shame conclude in acts of abandonment of their children—to their own mothers, to adoptive families, to their husbands, or even to the sea. One of the most visually rendered affects, cinematic shame often plays out in vivid performances of thwarted gazes, restive bodily gestures, and hesitant camera frames.

If shame awakens a sense of exposure for wrongdoing (perceived or otherwise) in chapter 4, then chapter 5 plunges into the depths of ontological and ethical responsibility and emerges with guilt. Following a philosophical trajectory of care and *Schuld* (indebtedness) from Friedrich Nietzsche and Martin Heidegger to Emmanuel Levinas and Simone de Beauvoir, this chapter examines the mother's absolute obligation to support the well-being and flourishing of her child, her being-for-the-Other. Guilt in this chapter's films—Alauda Ruiz de Azúa's *Cinco Lobitos* (Lullaby, Spain, 2022), Lynne Ramsay's *We Need to Talk about Kevin* (United Kingdom, 2011), and Xavier Dolan's *Mommy* (Canada, 2014)—arises through an internalized notion of failure and bad mothering. The mothers in these films struggle with the imperative of motherhood to sacrifice themselves fully to the labor of care; they hesitate to relinquish their own freedom, projects, and desires. Burdened with the inescapable sense that they are shirking their maternal duties, feelings of guilt transpire. Guilt may linger simply as a feeling of inadequacy and resentment. It may also hewer with all its weight as the experience of children's unhappiness and even deviance, which the mothers perceive as a reinforcement of their guilt.

The final chapter of this book turns to that most miasmatic of affects: disgust. Another variation of the Bad Mother, the "disgusting mother" likewise haunts maternal horror and terrifies in her abject nature. But what of the *disgusted mother*? Chapter 6 examines a series of films that take into account the mother's perspective and subjectivity with regard to disgust. Emily Atef's *Das Fremde in mir* (The stranger in me, Germany, 2008), Bess Wohl's *Baby Ruby* (United States, 2022), and Gyllenhaal's *The Lost Daughter* (United States, 2021) present mothers who repel at the sight of their babies, at their postpartum bodies with their oozing fluids and sagging flesh, or in retrospect at the near-traumatic reminders of these objects years later. A study of disgust takes the reader through a brief history of philosophical aesthetics. If early aesthetic theory treated disgust with snobbish disdain, from the nineteenth century onward it wiggled its scatological way to a central position in the discourse. The chapter briefly traces this trajectory, landing finally with both Aurel Kolnai's phenomenological *Sosein* (so-being) of disgust and Julia Kristeva's corporeal abjection. It is impossible to consider maternal disgust without engaging Kristeva, whose theory of abjection takes as its main object the maternal body. But her approach requires an inversion, which, broadly conceived, speaks for the entirety of *Cinema of Crushing Motherhood*: instead of "I feel like vomiting the mother," in these films, the mother feels like vomiting motherhood.[52]

A concluding chapter summarizes the arguments of the book and how the films assembled here challenge the demands of happiness placed on mothers. It once again makes the case for a focused study of contemporary film and reiterates how the cinema of crushing motherhood has moved from the narrow parameters of genre cinema, such as horror and melodrama, to embrace many types of film. Beyond turning and surveying the achievements of the book, this chapter also further reflects on the gendered focus of the study in connection to the 2024 US Surgeon General advisory that parenting tout court has become a mental health crisis. What would an advisory about the hazards of *mothering* look and sound like? I invite you to turn the page.

CHAPTER ONE

Regret

Roughly midway through Ari Aster's psychological thriller *Hereditary* (2018), the mother, Annie (played by Toni Collette), confesses to her son that she did not want him. "I never wanted to be your mother," she blurts out. "I was scared. I didn't feel like a mother.... I tried to stop it. I tried to have a miscarriage, however I could. I did everything they told me not to do, but it didn't work." As a result of this confession, her teenage son bursts into flames in his bed. Her maternal regret quite literally obliterates his existence. In a subsequent scene, Annie awakens with a start: it was just a nightmare. Beyond this scene, *Hereditary* does not explore maternal regret in great depth. If anything, Collette's Annie, mother of two, struggles more as a daughter to a recently deceased tyrannical mother. But this outburst of regret as nightmarish confession provides some important food for thought. Immediately after divulging that she never wanted to be her son's mother, Annie covers her mouth, as the shock and shame of this proclamation washes over her. This revelation appears to surprise even her. On the one hand, *Hereditary* presents maternal regret as pathological, insofar as Annie becomes increasingly disturbed and eventually monstrous. On the other hand, this is one of the few scenes in the film in which Annie appears to speak truthfully and meaningfully from a position of subjectivity. The film's expression of regret bears cinematic precursors, most famously Ingmar Bergman's 1966 classic, *Persona*. In this psychological drama, it is not the mother, Elisabet (Liv Ullmann), who expresses her regret about having her preadolescent son, but her nurse, Alma (Bibi Andersson), who confronts her with this truth about herself. This denouement is a shocking revelation that is told twice near the close of the film. Riddled with guilt, unable to reconcile her regret, Elisabet has stopped speaking. At a pivotal moment in the film, she discovers in her bedside book the photograph of a Jewish boy in the Warsaw ghetto, hands held high, as he is marched out of the ghetto by force of extreme violence. We recognize the infamous archival photograph captured after the quashing of the Warsaw ghetto uprising as a symbol of the Holocaust. Does the mother recognize her unwanted son, whose photo she previously tore up, in this boy persecuted by the Nazis? The invocation nevertheless terrifies. Separated by half a century, the acknowledgment of maternal regret in these two films continues to shock. I bring forth these films and their alarming instances of maternal regret as an entry point into the topic and as a hint at its troubled terrain.

Cinema of Crushing Motherhood takes regret as a point of departure because precisely this phenomenon and its recent discourse spurred my initial thinking about maternal subjectivity and the persisting taboos against negative feelings. Regret has a capacious sensorium; it can be motivated by myriad negative feelings. Still, as the opening chapter of this book, I hope that a discussion of regret and its contemporary discursive relevance will position this broader project within an important historical trajectory. This manifests as a shift from ambivalence to regret.

As early as the mid-twentieth century, Simone de Beauvoir articulated the ambivalence of mothers about motherhood in her feminist opus *The Second Sex* (1949). Beauvoir is the first thinker to break with taboos and assert the formidable weight of the responsibility of motherhood as an ethical rivetedness to another being, whose flourishing is often completely in the mother's hands. She also recognized the experience of alienation that can come with motherhood. Mothers frequently feel alienated from their pregnant and postpartum bodies as well as from their former lives. Beauvoir boldly rejected the conception that mothers are naturally and authentically given to devotion and self-sacrifice for their children and that motherhood alone fulfills a woman. "Many are the mothers who are unhappy, bitter, and unsatisfied," she unapologetically wrote. For her, maternity, rather, unfolds as "a strange compromise of narcissism, altruism, dream, sincerity, bad faith, devotion, and cynicism."[1] To say that Beauvoir maintained an altogether negative attitude toward motherhood would be false. Her attitude toward motherhood, as feminist thinkers and scholars have also later observed, is one of ambivalence borne not of indifference but of a rush of mixed and diverging feelings.

Adrienne Rich writes most powerfully and compellingly about maternal ambivalence. In *Of Woman Born*, she propounds the inescapable sense of ambivalence. "It is the suffering of ambivalence," she confesses in her opening paragraph, cited from a personal journal entry, "the murderous alternation between bitter resentment and raw-edged nerves, and blissful gratification and tenderness." The mixed feelings of maternity, the "anger and tenderness," Rich herself experiences as the mother of three sons, fly in the face of assumptions about motherhood as unconditionally gratifying and selfless. The institution of motherhood insists on the incompatibility of love and anger. Impelled by the ambivalence that did not square with expectations of motherhood, Rich investigates the deep fracture between the real experience of bearing and caring for children and the institution of motherhood. "Institutionalized motherhood," she writes, "demands of women maternal 'instinct' rather than intelligence, selflessness rather than self-realization, relation to others rather than creation of self."[2] The pursuit of this "sacred" paradigm of motherhood, developed over centuries, has proven detrimental to the individual mother, who not only endures the quotidian struggle of mothering but also finds herself constantly measured against near-impossible standards. For both Beauvoir and Rich, ambivalence signals the conflict and struggle that plays out in the experience of motherhood that, contrary to common credo, is not all positive and joyful for women.

Ensuing thinkers and scholars have followed in Beauvoir's and Rich's footsteps. Rozsika Parker describes maternal ambivalence most straightforwardly as a feeling of being "torn in two," which, she adds, is "shared variously by all mothers in which loving and hating feelings for their children exist side by side."[3] Barbara Almond describes ambivalence likewise as "a combination of the loving and hating feelings we experience toward those important to us."[4] Finally, Sarah LaChance Adams follows up with a similar sentiment: "Most simply, maternal ambivalence can be described as the simultaneous and contradictory emotional responses of mothers toward their children—love and hate, anger and tenderness, pity and cruelty, satisfaction and rage."[5] Despite ubiquity and the interest it has engendered among scholars, however, as Almond notes, maternal ambivalence "remains highly unacceptable in our culture."[6] But ambivalence, despite more popular notions, does not actually lean more forcefully toward negativity. Lauren Berlant reminds us that ambivalence's etymology is "strongly mixed, drawn in many directions, positively and negatively charged."[7] Only in some measure negatively charged, then, when we speak of maternal ambivalence there is always a "yes, but"; "I am exhausted, but . . . "; "My children enrage me, but . . . " The negative is always qualified, rebutted even, and bent toward something positive in the same breath.

Often entangled with but ultimately distinct from ambivalence, regret forsakes the positively tilted qualifier "but." It professes an unshakeable sense that one made the wrong decision. For the mother, regret means wishing to undo motherhood. Unlike ambivalence, which still maintains that motherhood ultimately holds (some) advantage, regret relinquishes all possibility. In her radical study *Regretting Motherhood*, Orna Donath argues that "we need to rethink the axiom that motherhood is necessarily experienced as worthwhile by all mothers everywhere."[8] Not just more decidedly against motherhood than ambivalence, asserting regret is of an accord with asserting one's subjectivity as a woman beyond her status of mother, who has desires and a sense of self and is in charge of her destiny.[9] Picking up where ambivalence leaves off, regret spurns the institution of motherhood. It continues to lay bare the deception that being a mother is the be-all and end-all—a source of endless personal fulfillment, pleasure, and joy for all women. Taking things one step further, in its reflection on "roads not taken," regret "embodies contemplation on systems of power, on systems that institutionalize which roads are forbidden from being taken," such as the road of nonmotherhood.[10] Regret opens up a space for women to question why they became mothers in the first place and if they could go back to that point in time would they have decided differently. Regret unmakes and remakes the self.

In 2017, in the wake of what became a major debate about regretting motherhood, especially in Europe, two experimental nonfiction films appeared: *Regretting Motherhood*, a short documentary film by Merle Grimme and Felizitas Hoffmann, and *Mater Amatísima: Imaginaries and Discourses on Maternity in Times of Change*, a compilation film directed by María Ruido. In different ways, both films directly engage the topic of regretting motherhood and Donath's study. The latter even contains footage of Donath giving a lecture about her book in Spain. Unlike the fiction films invoked in the opening paragraph of this chapter, these nonfiction films directly pursue the complexities of maternal regret and its taint of ineffability. They also emerge contemporaneously as part of a paradigm shift. For the first time in history, a serious discussion about regretting motherhood has opened up. An exploration of these films and their creative engagement with maternal regret expands the possibilities of this discourse. But before such an excursion into the audiovisual, a survey of the divergent vectors of regret offers a valuable guide.

Donath's study on regretting motherhood takes a sociological approach. It comprises summaries of interviews conducted with twenty-three Israeli mothers of different ages and socioeconomic backgrounds. The regret of becoming a mother unites them all. If they could undo their motherhood, they would. For them the disadvantages of motherhood outweigh the advantages.[11] First published as an academic article in the feminist journal *Signs* in 2015, Donath's exploration of regretting motherhood immediately struck a nerve, in particular, in Germany, where her ideas were republished as part of an article, "Sie wollen ihr Leben zurück" (They want their lives back), in the major daily *Süddeutsche Zeitung* by freelance journalist Esther Göbel. It triggered a heated debate on social media that also found its way back to major newspapers and news channels under the English-language hashtag #regrettingmotherhood. According to Valerie Heffernan and Katherine Stone, Donath's study unleashed a widespread debate in Germany because it stirred local "sensitivities about the cultural construction of motherhood . . . and its effect on the lived experience of women."[12] In her article about Donath's work, Göbel highlights the cultural and historical construct of the romanticized mother image in Germany as a specter of National Socialism, when women had no other role than to bear children for the Führer.[13] It is noteworthy that the German construct of the Aryan mother maintains an extended history that stretches back even earlier than the twentieth century. German women and mothers have long served the image of culture-bearers of whiteness. Beginning in the late nineteenth century, Germany's era of colonialism also witnessed the glorification of the white German mother in her apparent capacity to safeguard national interests and eugenic ambitions against the perceived threat of cultural and racial Otherness.[14]

If the romanticized image of the mother, what Rich similarly critiques as the "sacred calling" of women, emerged as a creation of the Industrial Revolution and the rise of the domestic sphere, then in Germany, in particular, this creation long served as a biopolitical edict for the white family and population, which peaked in the era of National Socialism.[15] Heffernan and Stone concur that "the sense that motherhood was subject to ideological distortion during the Third Reich has undoubtedly contributed to an atmosphere of critique regarding discourses about women's roles as mothers."[16] However, they also observe responses to the regretting-motherhood debate that link it to the more recent history of the division of Germany and the radically distinct approaches to motherhood in the German Democratic Republic versus the Federal Republic of Germany, which clashed in the fallout of unification in 1990.[17] In sum, the genealogy of Germany's relationship to the mother myth is anything but straightforward.

Due to the overwhelming response to Donath's work in Germany, her full study was first published in book form in German, rather than English (or Hebrew, for that matter), under the title *#regretting motherhood: Wenn Mütter bereuen* (When mothers regret) in 2016 with the publisher Knaus, an entire year before the English-language edition appeared. Although largely unchanged from the German to the English version, the former does contain a paragraph specifically addressing the debate in Germany and its unique permutations:

> The lively debate in Germany on the subject of remorse has mainly related to the concept of "perfect mother" versus "*Rabenmutter*" [raven mother] and shows that, in addition to regret itself, we are dealing with a wide range of emotions eagerly waiting to be expressed. It makes it clear that something is still missing, something that is on the tip of the tongue, waiting to be spoken and heard. Then there would be no doubt that the subject of regretting motherhood is a deeply ingrained taboo.[18]

The concept of the *Rabenmutter*, literally translated as "raven mother," is unique to German, with a long history of usage. It typically denotes a bad mother who is perceived as abandoning or neglecting her children in order to pursue a career or other projects. Germany's authoritative dictionary *Duden* defines *Rabenmutter* as a *lieblose, hartherzige Mutter, die ihre Kinder vernachlässigt* (loveless, hard-hearted mother, who neglects her children).[19] The word derives from the old folk belief that the raven hardly cares for its young and throws them out when it no longer wishes to feed them. A derogatory term, *Rabenmutter* is intended to shame mothers who cannot measure up against impossible standards and is of a piece with the label Bad Mother in the English-speaking context, understood broadly by Molly Ladd-Taylor and Lauri Umansky as an extremely elastic term deployed with the ultimate intent of blame.[20]

A mother who regrets having children might be quickly labeled a Rabenmutter or worse. As is so often the case, however, at the heart of this affront lies a misunderstanding that hinges on both antifeminism and racism. Mothers of color are frequently burdened with additional challenges of providing for their children financially and have no choice but to also work outside the home. Elisabeth Wellershaus troubles and reappropriates the term. In her account, young ravens indeed leave the nest early, but this is, as she indicates, "not because their mothers heartlessly evict them." Instead, mother ravens, Wellershaus reveals, "continue to keep a watchful eye on their offspring even after they have already left the nest. They protect the fledglings, but at the same time give them space to try things out and explore their environment."[21] Yet, the "nation-mother idiom" of Rabenmutter, as Wellershaus calls it, erroneously persists and foretells, among other things, Germany's attentiveness to the regretting-motherhood debate.

Shortly before Donath's longer study appeared in German, two works were published about regretting motherhood: Göbel's extended study to her *Süddeutsche Zeitung* article, *Die falsche Wahl: Wenn Frauen ihre Entscheidung für Kinder bereuen* (The wrong choice: When women regret their decision to have children) (2016), and Christina Mundlos's *Wenn Mutter sein nicht glücklich macht. Das Phänomen Regretting Motherhood* (When being a mother doesn't make you happy: The phenomenon of regretting motherhood) (2015). The former begins with a summary of the #regrettingmotherhood debate in Germany and an analysis of Donath's work. Göbel follows with her own series of interviews with mothers in Germany, France, Israel, and Switzerland to demonstrate the international (certainly, European) breadth of this phenomenon of regret among mothers.[22] The latter presents a study similar to Donath's but exclusively in the German context. Mundlos begins with an exploration of maternal regret and then delves into the stories of eighteen mothers. Distinct from Donath's and Göbel's texts, Mundlos's book concludes in the design of a self-help book with advice and tips for mothers, fathers, expecting mothers, and child-free women to navigate the phenomenon of regret. Other works quickly followed, including the more personal account of maternal regret by Sarah Fischer, *Die Mutterglück-Lüge: Regretting Motherhood—Warum ich lieber Vater geworden wäre* (The maternal happiness lie: Regretting motherhood—why I would prefer to be a father) (2016).

Part of the tempestuous riposte to these studies and what it reveals lies in our troubled relationship with regret itself. Regret, we have been given to believe (at least in the realm of popular culture), is a useless emotion. "Don't cry over spilled milk," we so often hear. Like so many negative emotions also explored in this book, regret, so the perception goes, holds us back, causes only suffering and pain. It leads to our dwelling in the past, in the face of which we are powerless to change. Janet Landman paints an evocative picture of popular attitudes toward regret as "a stringy-haired, boneless woman stuck in the dead arms of the past . . . half-sitting, half-lying in the shadows of a musty room empty of everything but cobwebs and ghosts—forever staring with glazed eyes out a window, forever straining to hear ancient footfalls, which, were they to appear, would be muffled by the drone of her mutterings about what might have been."[23] To regret is to be condemned to the past and therefore unable to register the events of the present. But Landman employs this vivid description as a means of moving beyond it. In her groundbreaking study *Regret: The Persistence of the Possible* (1993), Landman explores the possibilities of regret and its epistemological value. Regret tells us something is wrong. It "can also constitute a path leading onward and upward. [It] is better viewed as a form of practical reason appropriately informed by emotion."[24] Landman calls this "an experience of felt-reason or reasoned-emotion."[25] More recently, Brian Price has explored the political value of regret in his study *A Theory of Regret* (2017). In his analysis, regret is not merely informative but also transformative.[26] As Price sees it, regret invokes thinking rather than knowing and, therefore, the present and future rather than the past. Regret is "a way of becoming responsive to things that may not be of concern to me—at least not yet, nor in memory."[27] Not all recent approaches to regret have viewed the emotion with such promise, however. Critical race feminists Elizabeth Spelman and Sara Ahmed argue that regret does not do enough and can even get in the way of action. According to these thinkers, statements of regret are empty speech acts without an assumption of responsibility.[28] In Ahmed's words, "Regret becomes an alternative for responsibility and for reparation; it functions as a sign of an injury, without naming a subject that can be called upon to bear witness, to pay back an unpayable debt, or to compensate for what cannot be compensated."[29] Regret not only lacks responsibility, it distracts from it; it is an empty substitution.

The phenomenon of regretting motherhood takes a slightly different approach. Although Donath makes reference to the characterization of regret as "felt-reason or reasoned emotion" and, particularly in her earlier article, to Landman's book, overall she appears less interested in theorizing regret than in the sociological reality of its existence for some mothers as well as its individual terms.[30] The questions raised by other studies on regret are largely absent here. What are the possibilities of regretting motherhood? Is such an act informative or transformative? Or is regret perhaps just a substitution for responsibility? Near the end of her study, Donath does offer the following food for thought: "[W]hereas in legal arenas expressing regret is perceived as assuming responsibility for one's actions, when it comes to child-rearing and motherhood, regret is perceived as mothers' *renunciation* of responsibility. And while in court, regret might be considered evidence of a person's sanity and moral standing, expressing regret in the sphere of motherhood is perceived as evidence of immorality and the absence of sanity."[31] Despite the informative and transformative possibilities of regret for individual mothers, social perception and stigma continue to weigh heavily on any expression of the emotion.

Donath's study shows that despite its prevalence, regret among mothers is a very personal attitude for which there are no explicit or political grounds. Embarking on motherhood, unlike committing a crime or causing another pain or grief, is not an act that typically elicits regret, in the sense that someone has done something wrong. Rather, regretting motherhood seems to indicate the loss of time and experience for oneself, the way one might regret not having traveled enough or enjoyed the good things in life. A mother might say: "I regret having children because being a mother was a job that gave me no joy and kept me from the things I really wanted to do as a woman, as a person." Although mothers who regret may not be able to directly learn from this emotion insofar as they may change their actions, it does afford them reflexivity, self-recognition, and self-acceptance in a society otherwise hostile to them and their experiences. Donath succinctly describes the act of regretting as *"a self-identification of women themselves."*[32] By expressing regret, women learn more about themselves. By way of this reflexivity, they also begin the process of unmaking and remaking themselves.

From within this groundswell of discursive regret, I return to the two films in focus in this chapter. In different ways and from within different national contexts, the two nonfiction films *Regretting Motherhood* and *Mater Amatísima*, a documentary and a compilation film, respectively, explore the topic of maternal regret. Through creative means, they directly contribute to this debate as audiovisual studies of their own. Not dissimilar to Donath's study, through personal interviews, on the one hand, and reassemblage of historical film material, on the other, these films offer further counternarratives and alternative histories of motherhood.

Documenting a Movement

Feminist documentary arose as part of the women's movement in the 1970s. As Julia Lesage states in her pioneering article, "Many of the first Feminist documentaries used a simple format to present to audiences (presumably composed primarily of women) a picture of the ordinary details of women's lives, their thoughts—told directly by the protagonists to the camera—and their frustrated but sometimes successful attempts to enter and deal with the public world of work and power."[33] This early practice of self-narration for the camera and its demand that a new space be opened up for women on women's terms resonates even years later with the short documentary *Regretting Motherhood*, which also presents a simple format of self-narration and is a mere eighteen minutes in length. Directed by two Munich-based filmmakers, Grimme and Hoffmann, as part of a student project for the University of Television and Film Munich, the aim of this film was to provide mothers a place to speak about their regret and what it means for them.[34] Even beyond its telltale title, *Regretting Motherhood* positions itself plumb at the center of the German debate on the topic. "As in many countries, motherhood in Germany is still something sacred. This makes it almost impossible for women to question the status quo, to openly and honestly talk about what it means to be a mother. In 2015 Germany launched a debate on 'Regretting Motherhood.' This is the first documentary film, that gives women the chance to talk about their feelings and experiences freely and anonymously."[35]

A broader sweep of feminist documentaries stretching back to a period preceding the regretting-motherhood debate but also about mothers who regret does catch a handful of others. Consider, for instance, Clio Barnard's *The Arbor* (United Kingdom, 2010) and Sarah Polley's *Stories We Tell* (Canada, 2012). Both explore the maternal subject through a range of home videos, cinema verité, reenactments, and (in the case of the former) verbatim theater, beyond the one-dimensional shadow figure of sacrifice and nurture. These mothers are complex. As Sue Thornham indicates, they claim autonomy and a voice beyond their roles as mothers.[36] Particularly in *The Arbor*, the maternal figure, the young playwright and self-destructive Andrea Dunbar, struggles to balance writing, drinking, and childcare. She openly expresses regret about having her first child, Lorraine, whom she conceived at an early age with a Pakistani man. She wishes she had had an abortion, she allegedly declares one night in a drunken stupor. It is difficult to know if Andrea's regret stems from her own trauma of the abusive relationship that resulted in Lorraine's conception or from her own racism. The confession and the neglect traumatize the young Lorraine, who is the only witness to this declaration, and torment her into adult life. Compelling as counterpoints, *The Arbor* and *Stories We Tell* ultimately present reconstructions of the mother, who in both cases has died, through the perspective of her children, and particularly a daughter, and not in direct engagement with the mother herself. They follow on the heels of earlier experimental feminist documentary about motherhood such as Michelle Citron's *Daughter Rite* (1978), a film B. Ruby Rich and Linda Williams analyze as an important turning point in documentary representation of mothers and daughters in its break with "patriarchal definitions of womanhood that the mother implicitly foists upon the daughter." Here, the daughter is traumatized, angry, and crushed with the matrophobic fear of becoming her mother: "I hate my mother and, in hating her, hate myself."[37] Similar words echo in *The Arbor*. Lorraine herself becomes a drug addict, loses two of her children to foster care, and then causes the death of the third through gross neglect. She has strong words for her mother, too: "Every day I feel hurt, pain, anger, hate." Moving away from this tradition of daughters confronting their mothers, important in its own right, the film *Regretting Motherhood* is all about the mother from her own perspective—her doubts, fears, desires, and regrets.

Similar to those in Donath's book, the women interviewed in Grimme and Hoffmann's film remain anonymous. This anonymity in image and identity affords privacy and eschews the risk of exploitation potentially entangled in the position of embodying what Patricia White calls the "'visible evidence' of their situation."[38] It furthermore challenges the problematic of identification and, with it, the false and easy notion of truth that burden feminist documentary. Only in the opening interview does the camera show the first interviewee as she responds to questions and prompts by a voice off-screen. An elegantly dressed woman of eighty-eight years and mother of two (according to the identificatory caption) sits comfortably in an armchair, presumably in her own living room. This brief opening interview introduces the topic as a question to the interviewee. A voice off-screen says: "I don't know if you've heard, but for about a year now there has been a debate or discussion in Germany called 'regretting motherhood.'"[39] The interviewee requests clarification: are these women who regret having children or regret not having children? Without simply stating one or the other, the voice off-screen carefully formulates the response: "They're women who say that they love their children, but they don't like the job of being a mother, or they don't like being a mother, and they regret becoming a mother." The interviewee's response is insouciant, almost cavalier; she is not surprised by the topic. She summarizes her attitude toward the subject with her final statement: "I hardly know any ladies (*Damen*) with whom I would speak about such things, because it's uninteresting." There is a cut to black. The opening credits appear, and, with them, the noises of the beach resound: seagulls cawing and children yelling.

    The opening scene serves as a kind of prologue. It establishes both the presence of a movement and the continuity of the problem of expression and communication about feelings of regret. This elderly mother (possibly also grandmother) does not speak about such matters with other women because, as she claims, it is "uninteresting." This discernment of the topic of regretting motherhood as "uninteresting" and the interviewee's use of the word "*Damen*" (ladies), rather than "*Frauen*" (women), appear to frame the film and its interviews with judgment that verges on censorship. "Proper ladies do not talk about regretting motherhood," this opening interview seems to suggest. It sets up successive interviews as unique opportunities for mothers who otherwise have no other outlets to share their stories of regret. But it also anticipates, even prescribes, their request for anonymity. Throughout this eighteen-minute video, we hear three different anonymous mothers speak. The first two simply respond to the question posed by voices off-screen, understood as the filmmakers themselves, about why they would like to remain anonymous. Both fear judgment, condemnation, and even attacks because by admitting that they regret motherhood, they dismantle the sacred image of the mother as

FIGURE 1.1. Ablaze in *Regretting Motherhood*. Directed by Merle Grimme and Felizitas Hoffmann, 2017.

always good and self-sacrificing. The second also expresses concern about hurting her daughter with such a revelation of regret. The lingering black screen of anonymity reminds the viewer of this stigmatized attitude. Only as the second mother finishes speaking does the black screen transition to a series of thematic images: first, a puddle displaced by running children and then a children's bicycle with training wheels ablaze (fig. 1.1).

Without prompting, this time, the voice of a thirty-nine-year-old mother of two daughters begins her narration against the bike on fire. The initial participatory quality of the film, the label Bill Nichols assigns documentary whose interactions, rather than observation, guide the viewer through the development of a historical account, gives way to the autobiographical—not to mention the confessional.[40] This mother's voice becomes the sole voice we hear until the end of the film. Shaped by feminist work on autobiography, identity, and memory, feminist documentary traditionally takes the form of historiography.[41] This mother shares her experience and, by doing so, tells a different story about motherhood, a kind of counternarrative. She begins with her own self-probing questions in a manner that asserts her as author of her narrative: "Would things be better if I didn't have kids? What would my life be like now? And wouldn't I be happier than I am now? Of course, I don't know. But I do have those thoughts."[42] With clear pangs of regret, even guilt about feeling regret—"these are horrible feelings"—she narrates her situation as a mother and the struggles she faces.

Accompanying the voice-over, a subdued diegetic soundtrack provides minor background noise. As the camera zooms in to capture the burning bicycle in close-up, the crackling of fire can be heard in slightly lower volume. The visual and auditory proximity of the fire creates an intensity that verges on the synesthetic. The sensation of unbearable heat arises. It becomes difficult to dismiss the imagery and its double symbolism: at once, a burning bicycle presents a destructive attack on an object associated with children and evokes the metaphoric "burning" issue of regretting motherhood, still very much hot to the touch. The scene changes and the camera pulls away. Again pictured at a distance, the fire has stopped; the bicycle frame, still intact, now smolders. Subsequent images are all of natural landscapes: a billow of clouds, a mountain range, a forest, the seaside. The camera moves languidly over these nondescript, misty images of nature. Ceasing to grab our attention, the visual track eventually surrenders to the background, secondary to the voice and the embedded subtitles in English. The images serve to create a contemplative, clarifying, and calming atmosphere, which indirectly shapes our reception of the voice and what it says.

Over these images, the sound of the voice continues in a mode of confessional self-narration, punctuated by nonverbal speech: hesitant pauses, minor stutters, and sighs. Authenticity and emotion rather than authority—traditionally associated with the voice-over in documentary—suffuse the voice. Lasting nearly twelve minutes, this particular drawn-out narration is a troubled monologue that juxtaposes a string of self-imposed questions, doubts, anecdotes, and contemplations about the burdens of motherhood, about the lack of freedom, the exhaustion, the sense of inadequacy, and the perpetual performance to conceal the same. In a dramatic conclusion to the narration, the image sharply cuts to black with these words: "I love my children, but I have to say: my children are not my greatest joy in life. They're just . . . not."

The circumstances of the voice in documentary are almost as old as the documentary mode itself. The voice serves as both a defining formal feature and a central metaphor.[43] The role of *Regretting Motherhood* in providing a medium through which mothers can speak out about maternal regret adheres to a longer and broader history in documentary film studies. Speaking out in documentary, Pooja Rangan reminds us, "is commonly understood as a liberatory act of giving expression to an interior idea, thought, opinion, or wish that inaugurates the subject's entrance into the political sphere and, indeed, into humanity."[44] These mothers seize the opportunity to come to voice as women who struggle and do not find unequivocal happiness in their roles as mothers, something the dictates of society forbid them to openly discuss. Like speaking out, the act of "coming to voice," even if just a figure of speech, holds similar political value in its "achievement of agency."[45] The anonymity of these voices, however, emphasizes the representational challenges of such a documentary. Regretting motherhood presents itself as a topic about which people still feel too uncomfortable to speak in public. If, on the one hand, anonymity provides privacy and a certain degree of freedom to these women, on the other hand, the political agency of coming to voice becomes troubled, even truncated, in their refusal of self-identification. Still, this reflexive, first-person voice-over—that is, the voice that speaks for itself—maintains what Rangan discusses as a "transgressive convention" insofar as it at least indirectly "grapples with who has the right to speak in documentary."[46] In a similar way, these mothers grapple with their right to speak; thus, the history of a film mode echoes the complexity of its subject. Anonymity also serves a slightly different, perhaps unintentional, purpose. Each mother speaks for herself, but, at the same time, she could also be any mother. Through the evocation of early feminist documentary borne of a movement—namely, the women's liberation movement of the 1970s, when the personal was embraced as the political—one voice becomes a plethora of voices, a part of a collective.

Through its pursuit of individual narratives of maternal regret, *Regretting Motherhood* gets at the political through the personal. This strategy resonates with early feminist documentary. But just as feminist documentary ranged from the simple interview format to the highly experimental, so, too, might we discuss the range in style between *Regretting Motherhood* and *Mater Amatísima* brought together in this chapter as short, nonfiction films about regretting motherhood and contemporaneously released in 2017 in response to the public discussions of Donath's book in their respective countries: Germany and Spain.

Compiling a (Different) History

Before its publication in English, Donath's book *Regretting Motherhood* also appeared in Spanish in 2016 under the more descriptive title *Madres arrepentidas: una mirada radical a la maternidad y sus falacias sociales* (Regretting mothers: A radical look at motherhood and its social fallacies) with Reservoir Books. Spanish visual artist and filmmaker María Ruido made her film *Mater Amatísima* in response to Donath's book and the public debate it unleashed. As Heffernan and Stone indicate, although the resonance of the regretting-motherhood debate in Spain did not reach the heights it did in Germany, similar social and political anxieties in the two national contexts contributed to the furor, including contemporary low birth rates and the residual influence of fascism's cult of motherhood.[47] The hashtag #madresarrependitas quickly spread. In sharp contrast to the German context, however, the contributions to this debate in Spain were largely positive. Interest in the topic accrued through recognition of its importance rather than in provocation or outrage.[48] The disparate responses to Donath's study might also account for the varying approaches of the films in this chapter. Distinct from the more conventional format of the participatory documentary we note in *Regretting Motherhood*, *Mater Amatísima* contains elements of the compilation film in its remediation of found footage or previously shot material from home videos and television to narrative and experimental films as well as archival recordings of court proceedings. Esther Pérez Nieto compellingly reads *Mater Amatísima* as an essay film, but its vast reassemblage of existing film material and its explicitly feminist politics align it better with the history and qualities of the compilation film.[49] Notoriously resistant to categorical distinction, as Catherine Russell concludes, the compilation film falls somewhere between the documentary and the experimental film.[50]

Jay Leyda's pioneering study, *Films Beget Films: A Study of the Compilation Film* (1964), locates the origins of the compilation film in the newsreel and as shaped by practices of co-opting, rearranging, and combining. According to Leyda, compilation film emerged as a consequence of film itself, borne of the commercial drive to re-create different film products anew.[51] Despite his criticism of its lack of original artistic value, Leyda, nonetheless, sees great potential in the compilation film. Taking up examples of compilation films from the first half of the twentieth century that engage with and re-present historical events in different ways, Leyda theorizes this mode as a vehicle for ideas and the (re)telling of history. Nichols similarly sums up the compilation film "as a way to understand history in a new way, not a technique for the perpetuation of more of the same."[52] The fragmentary nature of the compilation film as a reassemblage of images and clips from different sources and therefore its formal refusal to provide a strictly linear narrative attest to this. Originating as a form of newsreel, compilation film has without doubt served different ideational purposes since its inception. Its quality of fragmentation and collage has, nevertheless, made compilation film particularly appealing to feminist filmmakers, who often strive to deconstruct linear time and reorder history to create alternative narratives. Borrowing from the title and theme of Agnès Varda's documentary film *Les glaneurs et la glaneuse* (The gleaners and I, 2000), Laura Mulvey discusses feminist compilation filmmaking as a type of "gleaning," a practice traditionally pursued by women. In her words: "The advantage of the term is that it gives a cultural lineage to the process of collecting, accumulating, sifting through, and recycling pre-existing materials. Gleaning offers a trope for women's cultural marginality and the informal anecdotal nature of their traditional cultural practices."[53] According to Mulvey, this process of sifting through, recycling, and distorting becomes a form of "détournement"—literally, rerouting and hijacking—in its critique of the past and presentation of an important example of "women making history."[54] I note similarities between Ruido's compilation film and Irene Lusztig's 2013 essay film *The Motherhood Archives*, where I begin this study. Both engage in the important labor of what Corinn Columpar and So Mayer characterize as a broad feminist project of "historical recovery and retrieval" in the archive.[55] The films pursue an aesthetics of interruption shaped by mothers' fragmented experiences of time and being.

Presenting an alternative narrative and critiquing history, Ruido's film explores different representations of troubled motherhood that fly in the face of what she refers to as "the fetishizing and normalizing character that is given to motherhood in patriarchy."[56] This begins with the film's title, *Mater Amatísima*, from the Latin meaning "beloved mother," and its potential reminder of the Spanish 1980 thriller by the same name about the intense relationship between a mother and her son, who has autism. Ruido's film provides a very different story. As a prelude to the film, the stylized image of a bird and nest appears. The evocation of the Rabenmutter is evident. Ruido offers an opening nod to the transnational relevance of the topic of regretting motherhood and the influence of German politics and rhetoric. The film then begins abruptly with home footage shot on Super 8 and culled from a private family archive. First, we see a sunset, then various familial scenes on a beach appear. In the closing credits, Ruido identifies these as her own. The footage opens with its own noisy mechanical soundtrack: the loud clacking noise of the Super 8 camera reel. Then piano music eclipses the noise of the machine, and two voices emerge. Against hazy, green-tinted images of apparent familial carefreeness on the beach with people playing volleyball and paddleball, the voices of Alexander Kluge and Sophie Rois, Austrian actress and longtime member of the ensemble at the Berlin Volksbühne, discuss the family, Marxism, and finally, the figure Medea. This soundtrack derives from the third part of Kluge's behemoth documentary film *Nachrichten aus der ideologischen Antike—Marx/Eisenstein/Das Kapital* (News from ideological antiquity—Marx/Eisenstein/*The Capital*, 2008), in which Kluge pursues a series of interviews in discussion about Sergei Eisenstein's plan to film Marx's *Das Kapital*, which never came to fruition. There appears to be a disconnect between the harmonious images of a family's summer vacation and the philosophical ideas that permeate Kluge and Rois's discussion about the unsuitability of the nuclear family for socialism. Before the home movies cut, Rois makes the provocative claim, "*Familie produziert Mord und Todschlag*" (Family produces murder and homicide). Her provocation arises in response to the predicament that, unlike all other relationships, those between parents and children are inescapable—except in death. An even more radical take on Marx and Engels's call for the abolition of the family in *The Communist Manifesto* as the institutional preservation of capital and private property, this film unapologetically declares the family as a site of terror and violence, particularly, for children and women. As a space of private coercion, control, and violence, "[t]he family hides in its own terrors," M. E. O'Brien boldly affirms.[57]

Extracted from the image track of *Nachrichten aus der ideologischen Antike*, Rois then appears in an embedded frame and launches into a brief discussion about the tragic Greek figure Medea, the symbol for filicide. As Euripides's classic play relates, Medea sacrifices her own family and homeland to support Jason in his pursuit of the golden fleece, only to later be abandoned by him so that he may marry Creusa, the daughter of the king of Corinth, and take away Jason and Medea's two sons. Aggrieved and enraged, Medea seeks the ultimate revenge against Jason by murdering their sons. But Rois refuses any kind of threadbare reading of Medea as a figure who simply kills her children out of revenge against an unfaithful lover. For her, Medea's actions reflect her denied subjectivity as a woman:

> She does not represent humanity. She represents the problem. . . . She has a feminine problem. As you say, she has the problem of an unfaithful lover. But for me she doesn't have the problem of an unfaithful lover; rather, she has the problem that she is no longer a complete human. And we see that she is one. She does not accept that. She demands her right as a human being.[58]

Rois's comment indirectly draws our attention back to Medea's tragic plaint in Euripides's play that, as a woman, she has been deprived of subjectivity and freedom over her body: "We women are unluckiest of all Creatures alive and capable of thinking: First we must pay a fortune for a husband, And thereby get a master of our bodies—That second evil, greater than the first, Piling an insult onto injury."[59]

Rois's observation that Medea demands her humanity and subjectivity becomes a point of departure for an exploration of Medea as a regretful maternal figure. Ruido also states in an interview about her film, "Medea is interesting not only for opening the wounds of mother-child relationships but also because her character shows a woman that defies her destiny in the world."[60] The sequence cuts to the murder scene from Pier Paolo Pasolini's 1969 film *Medea*, in which the eponymous figure first lovingly bathes and then stabs each of her sons with a dagger, a cinematic portrayal to which Ruido's film will also return in the final sequence with a slightly updated version—namely, Lars von Trier's 1988 film *Medea*, made for television. In the filicide sequence of Trier's film, Medea brings her sons out to an open field and hangs them one by one from the branch of a tree. There are many cinematic portrayals of Medea. What makes these two so powerful and disturbing is their failure to morally judge and therefore demonize Medea and, as Astrid Deuber-Mankowsky puts it, their refusal "to project Medea back into the realm of prehistory or into the circle of hysterical, irrational, and mad women and perverts."[61]

Preceding Rois, Pasolini himself similarly interprets the myth of Medea as intrinsically transcendental, even revolutionary. He illumines his Medea figure and her motivations: "What makes Medea kill is not born from a spasm of vengeance or hate or passion. Rather, her crazed and criminal actions assume the significance of a flight from a world that is not hers and in which she can no longer live. For Medea and her race, death is not an end, but only a prelude to rebirth in another world. So her faith spurs her on to killing her children so that they may return in regeneration."[62] Returning to the 1969 film, I agree that Medea's act of filicide does not turn on jealousy or fear of abandonment by Jason. But rather than a flight, the final scene of the film, a confrontation between Medea (Maria Callas) and Jason (Giuseppe Gentile), appeals to a slightly different reading. In this scene, Medea asserts her subjectivity and her power. A shot-reverse-shot sequence captures her from a low angle (clearly positioned above Jason). She talks down to Jason, who by contrast appears small and powerless. The scene differs from a previous one in which Medea is captured from a high angle, and Jason appears to tower over her. If earlier she seems to acquiesce, offering her blessing for his forthcoming marriage, in this final scene she instead even denies him a final farewell of his sons and a burial. As fire rages around her, Pasolini's Medea asserts her power to both create and destroy everything.

In her analysis of Ruido's film, with its unambiguous evocation of the Medea figure, Pérez Nieto considers the many layers of this figure and the treatment of its myth from antiquity onward: "Medea is often seen as the embodiment of the denial of motherhood, yet she is a much more complex character."[63] Indeed, as most scholars would contend, Medea is a figure that defies simple description.[64] Bookended by these complex adaptations of Medea, the contemporary case of filicide in Spain emerges as a significant part of Ruido's film. Overall, her exploration of regretting motherhood plunges into darker perspectives in its choice to emphasize the conclusions of horror drawn by some critics that regretting motherhood invites violence through the so-called Medea syndrome.

In 2013, a young girl, Asunta Fang Yong Basterra Porto, was found dead in Galicia, Spain. Two years later, after a high-profile court case, her adoptive parents, Rosario Porto and Alfonso Basterra, were convicted of her murder and sentenced to eighteen years in prison. Certainly, not the first case of parents killing their children, it did not exactly fit into the usual pattern of filicide. Asunta was adopted, already thirteen years old at the time, and apparently a model child. The Basterra-Porto family was financially well off, and the mother came from a prominent family in Galicia. The court case and media attention fixated on the mother, Rosario Porto, who was, as in so many cases of filicide, as Pérez Nieto notes, "doubly criminalized." Not only did Porto commit murder but she also threatened the sacred image of the mother as sacrificial caretaker.[65] The father apparently garnered far less attention during the case. Ruido reuses excerpts from official trial recordings, in particular, the footage of Porto's interrogation. In two lengthy sequences, we witness Porto in a high-angle long shot, seated centrally and in proximity to members of the public looking and listening on. In a series of questions put forward by an off-screen judge, she very emotionally denies any knowledge of or participation in the murder.[66] In her statements, Porto portrays herself as a loving mother, dedicated to her daughter's well-being and education. If the remediation of this sequence of court proceedings stands to provoke sympathy for the mother, as Pérez Nieto indicates, it is in my reading because it reveals the enormous public pressure Porto faces to maintain a facade of the loving maternal figure.[67] Despite overwhelming evidence against them, both parents maintained their innocence in the crime. It seems to suggest that to confess to the murder of one's own child is somehow worse than committing it.

Yet, *Mater Amatísima* more broadly explores troubled portrayals of motherhood, mostly in film. Thrice Ruido returns to scenes from Laura Mulvey and Peter Wollen's celebrated 1977 avant-garde feminist film, *Riddles of the Sphinx*. A direct product of the women's movement, the film was one of the first to openly identify with the point of view of the mother, as Lucy Fischer points out.[68] Ruido takes three early scenes from the film that are set in the domestic space and shot in continuous circular pans. Disorientation, vertigo, and claustrophobia shape *Riddles of the Sphinx* in its striking refusal of continuity editing and straightforward cinematography. Accompanying the pans, the original soundtrack of disorienting electronic music composed on synthesizers itself loops. In one of these scenes,

Ruido adds a voice recording of Mulvey herself, who provides voice-over commentary to the film. Mulvey draws our attention to the entrapment of the domestic space captured in these circular pans, representative of a comforting nest, on the one hand, and a space of imprisonment for mother and child, on the other. Nancy Chodorow and Susan Contratto discuss the circular pattern more generally as a sign of maternal isolation: "Mother and child are seen as both physically and psychologically apart from the world, existing within a magic (or cursed) circle. . . . The woman's home is her castle, in which she is isolated and all-powerful in motherhood."[69] Overall, the aesthetics of these pans and their domestic mise-en-scène recall the maternal melodrama. Indeed, as Mulvey also indicates, Douglas Sirk's melodramas served as an important reference for *Riddles of the Sphinx*. Ruido follows that line of thought and brings in a brief scene from Sirk's 1959 *Imitation of Life*, a highly emotional exchange between mother and daughter in the daughter's bright-pink bedroom, when Susie confronts her mother, Lora, about being neglectful and always putting her career first. We do not hear Susie's sobs and screams because Ruido replaces the original soundtrack with unexpected, up-tempo modulated electronic beats. The appropriation of this footage and its repurposing here subverts its original purport. An overly dramatic scene between mother and daughter is presented ad absurdum. Adding excess to an already excessive scene does not criticize Sirk's film so much as it pushes the melodramatic mother-daughter relation further into allegory.

The differences between *Regretting Motherhood* and *Mater Amatísima* could not be starker both in terms of aesthetics and approach to the theme of regret. Radical in its approach, *Mater Amatísima* does not explicitly take up the topic of regret. Beyond the film's placement of footage of Donath discussing her book to an audience in Spain, the film treats the regretting-motherhood debate as an occasion to return to recent and historical representations and events in which regret both manifests itself and is perceived in very different ways. Ruido neither suggests that filicide is a consequence of regret nor that the Medea myth is the corollary of regretting motherhood. If anything, her provocation presents a reflection on the social fact that women who openly declare their regret about motherhood have been identified not only as bad mothers but of a piece with mothers who murder their children. And a murderous mother is a monstrous mother, as far as many are concerned.[70] Hence, the self-preserving demand for anonymity.

However, regret as an emotion can open up new ways of thinking about and understanding the past. As Donath asserts, "It allows us to acknowledge the retrospective gaze as essential, especially if one takes into account that the demand *not to look back* may serve as an instrument for social control."[71] If the taboo of regret serves as an instrument for social control, then *Mater Amatísima* reminds us of the doubly subversive function of "regretting motherhood." Is not the body, especially the maternal body, *the* territory of social control? In voice-over, Ruido states: "The body is one of the fundamental territories of social control. States urge us to reproduce, from children to the family model itself. They control our fecundity and its products, but at the same time, they leave us alone with our children, closed in the domestic space while parenting is framed as something strictly intimate."[72] To regret motherhood therefore means to recognize and at the same time reject social control over one's body and one's life. It opens up the possibility to refute what Ruido calls the "fetishizing and normalizing character that is given to motherhood in patriarchy" and motivates women to ask: "Do we truly choose to be mothers? Why is care, of fundamental vital labor, presupposed as an especially appropriate task for women?"[73] These are questions I return to throughout the chapters of this book. As the backlash to the regretting-motherhood debate has shown, when women begin to openly question their assigned roles within patriarchy, state and social order begin to waiver. Here we witness a crucial overlap of two movements: regretting motherhood and family abolition.

Echoing the women's liberation movement of the 1970s and its infamous call for family abolition or at least revolution, the debate of regretting motherhood also sets the stage for an earnest discussion about motherhood in patriarchy and its ever-fetishizing and normalizing character. Exploring the topic together with its political and social history and consequences, *Regretting Motherhood* and *Mater Amatísima* directly participate in a movement through sound and image. An unfolding toward this broader study on motherhood and perceived negative emotions, this first chapter on regret begins with an emotion that has become widely politicized of late as a movement toward rethinking the institution of motherhood. Certainly, not the first occasion in history motherhood has garnered worldwide attention as a topic of political and social import, its contemporary influence has shaped this study.[74] Distinct from the extensively discussed and analyzed phenomenon of maternal ambivalence, regretting motherhood presents a new way of understanding motherhood in today's world that does not simply make room for mixed feelings but also manifests mothers' desires to not be mothers or to undo their status as mothers. From this more radical stance of regret, subsequent chapters move us through other emotions felt by mothers that rarely elicit deeper exploration because they do not fit into dominant representations of mothers as inherently sacrificial and fulfilled by their role.

Unique from other films examined in this book, however, *Regretting Motherhood* and *Mater Amatísima* are the only nonfiction examples. I do not make any arguments for the relevance of one mode of film over the other as more or less representative of the topic of crushing motherhood. The two films in this chapter do not, furthermore, serve as formal or aesthetic models to be followed. Indeed, a number of the films I take up predate these two films and the regretting-motherhood debate. But as direct responses to this contemporary debate, these films are, nonetheless, crucial to any study of film and motherhood today. This book begins with regret as the fulcrum of a new discourse on motherhood that crushes. The next chapter examines several recent fiction films and their treatment of exhaustion both as a physical and an existential state. Inextricably linked to regret as well as many other maternal feelings explored in this book, exhaustion does not always command attention as a specific quality of maternal discourse or cinema, for that matter, but—no stranger to cinema more broadly—exhaustion brings us further in understanding the cinema of crushing motherhood.

CHAPTER TWO

Exhaustion

"What is it like to stay alongside a child?" Lisa Baraitser asks. "What is it like to be exposed to incessant crying, incessant demands, incessant questioning, incessant interruption?"[1] For one, it is truly and utterly exhausting. Both Baraitser and EL Putnam discuss interruption as characteristic of the maternal experience. What I derive from these discussions is a distorted, fragmented, and intensified experience of time that plays out in repetition, waiting, and enduring that gradually depletes the mother. Exhaustion is a commonly cited motivation for maternal ambivalence, even regret and abolition. The labor of child-rearing is taxing. With the COVID-19 pandemic, the challenge of this role became all the more manifest. Stories of exhausted mothers abound in recent years. In the wake of the pandemic, these stories have resonated with increased measure.

Jennifer Kent's *The Babadook* (2014) and Jason Reitman's *Tully* (2018) are two films released in the last decade that—in different ways and via distinct genres—explore the detriment of exhaustion experienced by mothers. A horror film and a comedy-drama, respectively, these films bring attention to the extreme states of lived motherhood in which absolute exhaustion can lead to delusion and violence. I consider these films in conversation with the maternal exhaustion presented in A. V. Rockwell's drama *A Thousand and One*, about a mother slowly worn down by the sacrificial pursuit of home, family, and stability. Finally, I turn to Angela Schanelec's *Ich war zuhause, aber . . .* (I was at home, but . . . , 2019), about a widowed mother whose young son runs away and returns, an event that leaves an irreparable rift in this mother's life that leaves her restive. Less genre-oriented than the other three films, Schanelec's film pursues exhaustion with greater nuance and limited emphatic violence, but the effects are still present. All of the films addressed in this book render visible maternal exhaustion to lesser or greater extent; however, the films in this chapter are in thrall to a deleterious sapping that shapes their tales of motherhood. Exhaustion becomes existential in its defining of the maternal experience.

Mothers are not supposed to be exhausted, nor should they display their exhaustion to the world. Engaging with both feminist philosophy and film theory, this chapter draws out what Adrienne Rich has identified as the incongruity between the experience of motherhood and the representation of motherhood that lies at the crux of these films. Designed by patriarchy, the representation of motherhood upholds an institution of social expectations, which, as Rich maintains, permits "only certain views, certain expectations" both of and for mothers. These include, above all, unquestionable selflessness and sacrifice delivered with conviction, energy, and even joy.[2] Second-wave feminism sought to undo patriarchy's hold on motherhood by advancing women's experiences and perspectives. Although Simone de Beauvoir did not write extensively on the experience of motherhood, she taught us much about the feminine situation determined by woman's role as housewife and mother within patriarchy. As Beauvoir elucidates, the existential weight of exhaustion bears heavily on this situation.

In *The Second Sex*, Beauvoir discusses the lived experience of domestic labor and its drudgery. This labor exhausts not by mere dint of its difficulty and physical strain but much more on account of its nature of repetition, its lack of productivity, and its dearth of invention. According to Beauvoir, "[The woman] must ensure the monotonous repetition of life in its contingence and facticity: it is natural for her to repeat herself, to begin again, without ever inventing, to feel that time seems to be going around in circles without going anywhere; she is busy without ever *doing* anything." Beauvoir calls this existence the feminine world of immanence. It is one of futility, repetition, and superficial sovereignty to which the housewife and mother are doomed. The nothingness that is housework epitomizes the complete absence of possibility and transformation; it epitomizes the void of creativity and autonomy. Housewives are expected to exercise patience, passivity, and obedience. "Daily cooking teaches her patience and passivity," Beauvoir writes. "[O]ne must obey the fire, water, 'wait for the sugar to melt,' the dough to rise, and also the clothes to dry, the fruit to ripen." The reduction of daily existence to a repetitive-compulsive routine of housework and care work described by Beauvoir produces only exhaustion. Beauvoir conceptualizes the experience of exhaustion as a result of Sisyphean labor. The housewife and the mother are caught in an unremitting cycle of work that is only immanent and never leads to transcendence beyond mere biological existence. Not only does maternity not confer transcendence by proxy unburdened by dependency but this exhaustion also does not accompany a sense of accomplishment or completion but merely the knowledge of boundless labor.[3]

Exhaustion produced by repetition and lack of transformative action has a cinematic history as well. In what might seem like an unlikely pairing, Gilles Deleuze's study of cinema proves illuminating to the context of Beauvoir's existential exhaustion.[4] In *Cinema 2*, Deleuze develops his theory of time-image cinema, which personifies the radical shift in postwar cinema to images replete with "tiredness and waiting."[5] The characters of time-image cinema are simply witnesses of passing time: they observe; they wait; they achieve nothing. In this cinema, time is no longer simply the chronological measure of the cinematic image; instead, it serves as its very condition. Time itself becomes embodied in the image, and the image proffers nothing but duration.[6] Formally speaking, the linearity of continuity editing that observed time's passing through action and movement, as well as cause and effect, in prewar European and Hollywood cinema yields to a lack of continuity in the postwar period. Wrenched from a linear succession of time through discontinuity editing, the cinematic image becomes temporally displaced, no longer affixed in a concatenation of activity and progression. As a matter of course, the bodies on-screen cease to be agents of action and bear the mere function of marking time.[7] They are exhausted from doing nothing.[8]

The gendered nature of some of Deleuze's more significant examples of time-image cinema are notable.[9] Consider, for instance, his revealing description of the young, pregnant maid Maria (Maria-Pia Casilio), in the famous kitchen scene from Vittorio De Sica's *Umberto D.* (1952). Inspired by André Bazin, Deleuze methodically recounts this scene in the opening pages of *Cinema 2*: "The young maid going into the kitchen in the morning, making a series of mechanical, weary gestures, cleaning a bit, driving the ants away from a water fountain, picking up the coffee grinder, stretching out her foot to close the door with her toe. And her eyes meet her pregnant woman's belly, and it is as though all the misery in the world were going to be born."[10] According to Bazin, the scene brings into relief how detached observation becomes the sole means of experiencing the world.[11] Along similar lines, Deleuze calls Maria's tired movements and gestures the "pure optical situation" of the time-image of postwar European cinema, to which she has no response or action. Telic action, or what Deleuze calls "traditional sensory-motor situations," recedes, and here the fatigue of domestic laboring without end or achievement takes over.[12] We might say that the fate of the mother (to be) assumes cinematic form.

Though Deleuze is not particularly interested in the embodied, lived (and certainly not situated) experience of Maria as maid and expectant mother, as his description reduces her body to an object in the kitchen like any other, we may still draw a comparison between Beauvoir's existential situation of the housewife and Deleuze's cinematic-ontological situation of the housewife, and the mother, for cinema.[13] Elena Gorfinkel conceptually initiates this possibility. Although she does not invoke Beauvoir nor feminist philosophy directly, her return to the Deleuzian time-image as a means to analyze women protagonists from more-contemporary films, specifically Jean-Pierre Dardenne and Luc Dardenne's *Rosetta* (1999) and Kelly Reichardt's *Wendy and Lucy* (2008), as representational of what she calls the "embodied durée" draws an implicit connection between Beauvoir and Deleuze. She illustrates this condition of endurance in the following way: these "characters are suspended, even while frenetically mobile, in states of fatigue and waiting."[14] Suspension, repetition, waiting: these states shape the experience of exhaustion for the housewife and mother, too. Bringing Beauvoir back into the mix, the world of immanence of the woman complements Deleuze's ontology of time as exhaustion. For both, immanence as a state of perpetual becoming that never settles in subjectivity nor achieves the creative forces that constitute a life of transcendence and transformation conditions existence—ontologically speaking, a being-for-itself.[15] Beauvoir understands woman's failure to attain full subjective status as tightly bound up in her cyclical, nonlinear temporality. "[T]ime has no dimension of novelty for her," she observes. "[I]t is not a creative spring; because she is doomed to repetition, does not see in the future anything but duplication of the past."[16] As a quality of cinema, Deleuze perceives exhausted life and its attenuation of action as a consequence of a break of the sensory-motor link entangled in a historical moment and a development of conditions and operations. For Deleuze, becoming is not so much condemnation as a "potentialization."[17] These trenches of becoming may be distinct; yet, the bodily signs of time are similar in their assaulting contours.

Exhaustion as the sign of time does, however, mark change, even if this change is not transformative. It leaves its trace on the body. Change is evidenced by the dark circles framing the eyes, the wearied facial expressions and gestures, and even the swelling of the pregnant belly. "[T]ime's sole becoming," Beauvoir writes, "is a slow degradation: it eats at furniture and clothes just as it disfigures the face."[18] The cinema of the body, time-image cinema relies on gestures, attitudes, and postures.[19] Gorfinkel reminds us that Deleuze's cinema project produces an aesthetic of exhaustion.[20] This is also part of the aesthetic of the films explored in this chapter. The maternal body visibly abrades with the ravages of time. Certainly distinct from the cinema of Deleuze's time-image in many ways, in the cinema of (crushing) motherhood, the body also rarely drifts or slides into the sleep that brings with it a promise of rejuvenation. Such acquiescing to lassitude, to gravity itself, is a freedom the mother can seldom afford.

Engaging with a longer tradition of exhaustion in feminist philosophy and cinema, this chapter explores how exhaustion manifests itself in these contemporary representations of motherhood on-screen through repetition, degradation, and disfiguration, both narratively and formally. Not exactly following the anti-genre styles of postwar neorealism exemplified by Deleuze in his study of time-image cinema, exhaustion in the cinema of motherhood cannot help but remind us of cinematic time and its formal relationship to space and action. In a diverse assemblage of films, *The Babadook*, *Tully*, *A Thousand and One*, and *Ich war zuhause, aber . . .*, exhaustion becomes a figuration of struggle, sometimes in an explicitly Manichean sense, as Beauvoir has it, and sometimes in a more obscure way. It is the monster you cannot help but let in, the fantasy world that crashes, or simply the gnawing depletion that slowly breaks you down to a point of defeat and, as it happens, indifference.

Don't Let Exhaustion In!

The Babadook opens with stultified sleep in the throes of an oedipal-tinged nightmare. We later discover that this is the traumatic reliving of the tragic car crash that resulted in Amelia's (Essie Davis) late husband's death on the occasion of their son's birth. The sequence begins with a close-up image of Amelia as she attempts to control her breathing. She looks disheveled—haggard, even. A tousle of unbrushed hair frames her tired face: dark circles, puffiness, wrinkled brow. She presents a striking Beauvoirian image of a mother worn and wearied by time. In slow motion, a spray of water droplets or glass shards strafes her face sidelong, and then there is darkness. From out of this darkness, Amelia's body tumbles backward. The camera remains on her face as she is heaved in and out of the shadows. She does not scream. The slowed-down, reverberating, mechanical hum of the crash fills the soundtrack. Then, from far off, a faint echo of a voice intervenes with the call, "Mum!" This voice, now in repetition—"Mum! Mummy!"—wrests Amelia further, this time from her nightmarish sleep as she falls again into bed and awakens with a final jolt. Even brief intervals of sleep offer no reprieve to Amelia's exhaustion. Not only does her recurring dream about her husband's death trouble her slumber but also any attempt at rest—troubled or not—is interrupted by her son, Samuel

(Noah Wiseman). Her resting and waking hours alike are riddled with disturbances. From this opening scene forward, the child's own sleep and nightmares take precedence over those of the mother.[21] Rife with interruption, the film's opening scene highlights the maternal subject as one, according to Baraitser, who is "subjected to relentless interruption" and "whom interruption enunciates."[22] The mother comes into being through the experience of interruption in *The Babadook*.

Though much as has been written on Australian filmmaker Kent's debut film, the topic of exhaustion as a distinct phenomenon of maternal experience remains unexplored.[23] Is *The Babadook* not in essence a tale of a mother's losing battle with exhaustion? A film about a widowed, working mother with a highly active and imaginative school-age son in an unnamed city in Australia, it immediately connotes struggle, sacrifice, and, yes, even horror—the defining genre of this film. There are two horror stories at play here: the first about an overburdened mother and the second about an intruder in the inceptive form of a mysterious red pop-up book of the story of the monster called the babadook. Or perhaps these two horror stories are one and the same? In the mode of what Sarah Arnold has characterized as the maternal horror canon since the 1960s, the mother does ultimately become the monster.[24] But distinct from its precursors as well as its predecessors, *Psycho* (1960), *Carrie* (1976), *The Brood* (1979), *Ich seh, Ich seh* (Goodnight Mommy, 2014), *Hereditary* (2018), *Us* (2019), and others replete with bad mothers made monstrous, *The Babadook* focuses on the mother not as simply a representational figure but as an embodied person who suffers deeply under the psychic and physical strain of motherhood.[25] Although the film follows through with more-recognizable horror elements of haunting and monsters, the initial scene of disrupted rest settles over this story of Amelia. The film is, in Caitlin Still's words, "striking in its maternal subjectivity."[26] Unlike many maternal horror films, *The Babadook* portrays the perspective of the distressed mother and not the terrified child. It refuses to "take the form of the cinematic manual for bad parenting," Aviva Briefel holds; instead, what unfolds is the horror of parenting itself.[27] In an interview with the *London Guardian* upon the release of her film, Kent confirms this: "Apart from *We Need to Talk about Kevin*, I can't easily think of other examples [that address the subject] and it's the great unspoken thing. We're all, as women, educated and conditioned to think that motherhood is an easy thing that just happens. But it's not always the case. I wanted to show a real woman who was drowning in that environment."[28]

Amelia does drown in an eddy of exhaustion propelled by withheld sleep and the endless repetition of care work. The interruption of sleep that quite literally sets the film in motion is followed by an unspoken ritual of "checking for monsters": under the bed, in the closet, all the usual places. This is not only presented as a ritual because it calls to mind such standard parental procedure but because it is both performed so mechanically, half in sleep, and is repeated in the film. Qian Zhang similarly notes the central role of repetition in *The Babadook*, in particular, the repetition of parenting and housework Amelia performs. Drawing parallels with early feminist cinema, Zhang compares *The Babadook* to Chantal Akerman's *Jeanne Dielman, 23 quai du Commerce, 1080 Bruxelles* (1975).[29] A prescient portrayal caught in loop for nearly four hours of the drudgery of a mother's unremitting domestic laboring, *Jeanne Dielman*'s serial repetition congeals the experience of exhaustion through a cycle of monotony and labor bereft of progress and achievement. Serial repetition continues in *The Babadook*, borne out, in particular, by the bedtime ritual always culminating in a story, read through and then frequently repeated at the behest of the child. That the ostensible object of horror—the babadook—first appears in the form of a children's book speaks volumes about the potential cruelty of ritualized care work. Repetition does occasionally usher in sleep for Samuel and often in the mother's bed. But Amelia is not afforded the same luxury. She tosses and turns, removes Samuel's clinging limbs from her body, and edges as far away as possible. An overhead shot reveals a mise-en-scène of maternal exhaustion (a crushing tableau): mother, neither cuddling nor resting, and son in the parental bed; instead, the mother's supine body is tautly curled with her back to the child and at a distance—the sequence that opens the film and repeats itself. More than just provisioning context, it exposes the horrors of the monster that is motherhood itself.

The actress who plays Amelia, Essie Davis, is probably best known for her role as the "lady detective" in the costume serial *Miss Fisher's Murder Mysteries* (2012–15), in which she plays a wealthy and sex-positive aristocrat who works mostly pro bono as a private detective. She always looks perfect and knows exactly what to do in any situation. Upon first watch, I hardly recognized Davis in her role as the harried mother and seniors' home caretaker in *The Babadook*. The sheer exhaustion of her character is a bodily performance of great magnitude. Her mop of ever-tousled, wavy blonde hair that appears perpetually washed-out, the deep lines and furrows etched into her brow, the cavernous circles around her eyes that can hardly stay open: she bears the signs of time. True to the film's focus on Amelia and her experience, the camera frequently catches her in close-up. Magnifying remnants of the Deleuzian time-image, the camera lingers on her tired face as if it were the real drama of the film. No other character, and certainly not Samuel, receives this attention. When, early on in the film, her elderly neighbor Grace endearingly remarks on Amelia's tiredness, Amelia responds half-jokingly: "Nothing five years of sleep wouldn't fix." But no extended bout of rest comes. Instead, Amelia spirals. Endlessly disrupted sleep leads to insomnia in the brief intervals of quiet following long stretches of ritual in preparation for Samuel's sleep. Amelia begins sitting up through the night watching television, snacking on junk food, and futilely massaging her aching molar, another sign of her neglected well-being.

With exhaustion, the edicts of "good mothering" fly out the window. Desperate, Amelia pleads for sedatives for Samuel, prescribed with perceptible reluctance by his pediatrician. She takes Samuel out of school, unable to attend to and square with the principal's calls for discipline and special help. As things go from bad to worse, she also begins feeding Samuel bowls of ice cream in lieu of dinner. For Amanda Howell and Lucy Baker, Amelia's exhaustion stems from her unremitting yet futile attempts to persevere with the impossible standards of motherhood—her struggles to be the "archetypal Good Mother."[30] Indeed, the harder she tries, the worse things become. Self-sacrifice and devotion run her ragged. The two times she attempts to attend to her own needs through masturbation and skipping work for a solitary trip to the shopping mall, she is interrupted, even indirectly punished, by her needy son and her disapproving sister. Always called back to her maternal role, to the home, Amelia finds no reprieve. Even if we may derive creative possibility from it, interruption, Baraitser and Putnam maintain, still gives rise to physical and psychological tolls on the mother.[31] So, Amelia lets exhaustion in, and it takes over in all of its delusion, terror, and violence that nearly lead to filicide.

The Babadook recalls the 2001 high-profile case of American Andrea Yates, who murdered all five of her children by drowning them in the bathtub. Kent's insertion of a bathtub scene, in which Amelia forces Samuel to sit immersed in water, fully clothed, is telling. One late night, Amelia watches a news report on television about a mother who killed her son. She imagines herself as the murderous mother, peering out the window of the house (the scene of the crime) with a mocking smile. In the wake of the actual murders, *Newsweek* ran both a long piece on postpartum depression and Anna Quindlen's renowned article "Playing God on No Sleep," in which she discusses maternal love as "fraught with fear and fatigue and inevitable resentment."[32] She clarifies, "Every mother I've asked about the Yates case has the same reaction. She's appalled; she's aghast. And then she gets this look. And the look says that at some forbidden level she understands. And the look says that there are two very different kinds of horror here. There is the unimaginable idea of the killings. And then there is the entirely imaginable idea of going quietly bonkers in the house with five kids under the age of 7."[33] These two kinds of horror articulated by Quindlen are very much alive in *The Babadook*. Exhaustion becomes the dangerous provenance of other (more active) maternal feelings. The subsequent chapter returns to this film with attention to rage. Although *The Babadook* does not take things as far as the Yates case, it certainly comes close.

Exhaustion Crushes, and Then It Crashes

Jason Reitman's 2018 film *Tully* also begins with a bedtime ritual. A very pregnant Marlo (Charlize Theron) enters her son's bedroom and then begins to stroke his limbs and back with a soft-bristle brush. We learn later that the son, Jonah (Asher Miles Fallica), suffers from anxiety. The parents could not afford to continue to send him to therapy, so they adopted this do-it-yourself method from YouTube. Distinct from *The Babadook*, this opening scene appears warm, tender, and affectionate. It emanates all of the qualities we have come to expect from maternal care. Supporting this affect, the warm light radiating from the window casts a gauzy atmosphere over this tender scene of mother and son. Marlo turns on music to accompany the ritual of brushing. Dreamy harmonies of the Velvet Underground's tune "Ride into the Sun" fill the soundtrack. Cinematographically, the scene consists of shallow-focus close-ups that tightly wrap it further in touch and intimacy that reach near synesthesia. The visual and aural give way to a reciprocal sense of touch, here of being softly brushed.[34]

A rude awakening follows this paragon scene of maternal tenderness as Marlo struggles to prepare her two unruly children for school the next day amid shrieking and stomping. The chaos ensues when mother and children arrive late to school and are unable to find a parking spot. Jonah kicks Marlo's seat from behind and howls; his sister, Sarah (Lia Frankland), in turn, loudly decries his wails with her own. Without raising her voice at first, Marlo meekly attempts to calm them, then responds in volume and minor profanity, but this, too, remains futile. Although it is just morning, she appears exhausted; her thin, platinum-blonde hair is disheveled, her face is pallid, and her clear eyes are watery. Finally, as the shrieks and kicks from the back seat carry on, she bows her head, and a low-pitched crescendo of noise pierces the soundtrack. Marlo's stress is briefly made audible.

These two distinct sequences in succession set up this film and its portrayal. As much as *Tully* is a film about exhaustion, it is also a film about illusion. Motherhood is presented here as at once outwardly idyllic and crushingly exhausting, again echoing the duality of what Rich refers to as motherhood as institution and motherhood as experience. Motherhood is often viewed from the outside as sacred, instinctual, fulfilling, and, above all, selfless, but the actual experience of motherhood is, among other things, frustrating, angering, self-effacing, and, yes, extremely exhausting.[35] *Tully* is a film about a woman due to give birth to her third child even though she already struggles to care for her two school-age children. Her husband works long hours outside the home and shares almost no role in parenting. With the birth of the third child, Marlo's exhaustion mounts. In addition to her previous duties caring for Jonah and Sarah, not to mention her own job as a bookkeeper, now she is also swept up in what seems like an endless cycle of nursing, cleaning, and changing a new baby. Suddenly, though, there is shift. A "night nanny" by the name of Tully (Mackenzie Davis) begins to watch over the baby. Miraculously, Marlo appears able to sleep again, take walks, bake, enjoy time with her family, and have sex with her husband. Tully not only tends to the baby, she also cooks, cleans, and helps Marlo reinvigorate her life and relationship with her husband. But a near-fatal car accident close to the end of the film reveals that Tully was simply a figment of Marlo's imagination, conjured to help her cope with the crushingly exhausting responsibility of motherhood. Marlo herself performed all these things in a pursuit of the fantasy of perfect motherhood, of being a good mother. Pursuing and maintaining this fantasy nearly kill her.

Just as Amelia struggles under the judging eyes of the world, including those of her sister, her neighbor, and Samuel's school principal and teacher, Marlo does the same. These portrayals resonate with Donath's description: "[I]t is not considered sufficient for a woman to simply mother: mothers are also expected to follow strict and universal rules dictating *how* they should mother. . . . When mothers do not perform according to the moral standards prescribed by this model—whether because they cannot or because they refuse to—they might quickly find themselves labeled as 'bad mothers,' outlaws who are morally and emotionally impaired."[36] Marlo is repeatedly told how she should mother. The school principal's overly friendly and casual tone only thinly veils her admonishment of Marlo and her maternal approach with Jonah, whose "quirkiness" and lack of emotional development are purportedly disruptive. Rich's early observations still hold: "[The mother] is held accountable for her children's health, the clothes they wear, their behavior at school, their intelligence and general development."[37] Marlo must attend not one but three meetings with the school principal about her son, whom she eventually places in another school.

Judgment of the mother and the maternal body is pervasive. While still pregnant, Marlo is even called out by a stranger in a café for ordering decaffeinated coffee because it contains trace amounts of caffeine, which could damage the unborn child. Finally, Marlo's wealthy brother and especially her sister-in-law delight in offering unsolicited advice on parenting. Again and again, the film almost agonizingly affirms, in Donath's words, "Motherhood is not a private enterprise. It is endlessly and exhaustively public."[38] Constantly scrutinized by society, mothers are, above all else, made to feel guilty about what they do or don't do, something chapter 5 explores further. Christina Mundlos discusses this problem in particular among mothers themselves, what she calls *Mütterterror* (terror of mothers): "But often mothers do not feel guilty because they are dissatisfied with their performance, rather because they are made to feel as though they had done something the wrong way by others. . . . Mothers terrorize each other with judgments and know-it-all-comments."[39]

Tully vividly demonstrates how Marlo becomes increasingly exhausted, angry, and isolated following the birth of her third child. First, ambivalence and even contempt shape her hospital stay. She does not coo over her baby and even appears to ignore it. In a hostile verbal onslaught, she lets loose on a nurse who insists that she needs to urinate and closely observes her as she painfully attempts to squeeze out a few drops. Upon returning home, a lengthy montage of scenes suspends Marlo in what appears to be a never-ending cycle of late nights of comforting, feeding, diaper changing, and breast pumping. Against the soundtrack of Rufus Wainwright's lightly melancholic, repetitive ballad "Tiergarten," baby cries and mother rises, on repeat. *London Guardian* writer Peter Bradshaw offers a vivid description: the "'baby feed' montage that reproduces the leaden and yet pitilessly quick and unrelenting rhythms of getting up over and over again in the night to feed the baby, dealing with the used nappies, collapsing back into bed."[40] Suspended in this cycle of care labor, Marlo "wallows in immanence," busy and exhausted in the maintenance of a life other than her own.[41]

Marlo's uninvolved husband only passes through on his way to or from work and rather patronizingly kisses either baby or mother on the forehead. His contribution ends there because, as he only half-jokingly states earlier in the film, "I don't got boobs." This comment echoes what Mary Ann Doane calls "the biological fact of motherhood." In her words: "The biological fact of motherhood is utilized to reduce all argumentation to the level of the 'obvious,' to all statements (e.g., 'Men cannot have babies') which, in their sheer irrefutability, block or preclude all analysis. There 'obviousnesses' then lend credibility to another level, a different

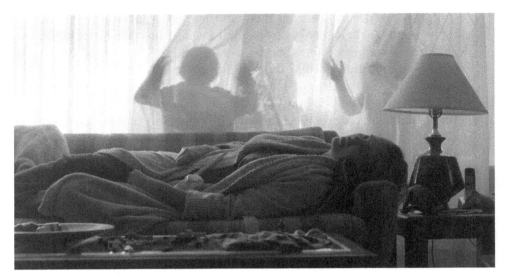

FIGURE 2.1. The chaos of the exhausted mother in *Tully*. Directed by Jason Reitman, 2018.

order of interpretation of sexual difference which assigns fixed positions to mother, father, child—positions authorized by the weight of a primal configuration."[42] Meanwhile, Marlo is drowning in this assigned position. She somnolently shuffles around the house or slumps down stiffly on the couch amid the clutter of children's toys, laundry, and increasing stains of vomit and spills in various states of solidification. Flopped on the couch in one remarkable shot, Marlo appears to have simply collapsed out of exhaustion. Positioned centrally in a heavy housecoat, Marlo's prostrate body almost blends into the furniture in this shot. Her body is not at rest; it has crashed with scant notice of location or comfort. She appears oblivious to the antics of her two children playing behind the curtains. But the audio baby monitor tucked slapdash into her arm signals the need for around-the-clock attentiveness (fig. 2.1). Exhaustion's thrall to violence does not stand up to the horror narrative of *The Babadook*. It works in subtler ways. It is Marlo's grueling pursuit of this unachievable fantasy of perfect motherhood that nearly kills her. Lauren Berlant does not write about the cruel optimism of motherhood, but *Tully* certainly exhibits the dangers of attaching oneself to a problematic object—not the child but perfect motherhood.[43] "The maternal role," Marianne Hirsch explains, "was figured in ways that are ultimately debilitating to women—equally so to those women who could afford to try to live up to the social ideal of maternity and to those who because of economic necessity could not."[44]

Hailed as a film about extreme postpartum depression, *Tully* struck me as a tale about exhaustion as a result of society's impossible demands on mothers to be perfect while providing meager assistance in the achievement of such perfection. For a brief time, Marlo succeeds in fulfilling these demands; she becomes the perfect mother and wife through the hallucination of the young and energetic night nanny, Tully, who, it turns out, is a fantasy projection of Marlo's younger self. But a fateful night out in New York City to reexperience her predomestic, carefree, and queer life ends with Marlo driving the family SUV off a bridge and nearly drowning. In the hospital where Marlo is recovering, the doctor reveals to Marlo's out-of-touch husband that she seems to be suffering from acute exhaustion and sleep deprivation. In a flashback, we then see Marlo performing all of tasks we were led to believe that Tully was performing: staying up all night with the baby, cleaning, baking, and even having sexual role-play with her husband. She completely sacrifices her sleep and well-being in an attempt to be the perfect mother. "Wasn't I great?" she desperately asks her husband as she lies weak and visibly battered from the crash in a hospital bed. In *Tully*, perfect motherhood very clearly comes at a cost.

What is on full display in this film is Marlo's (or more exactly: Charlize Theron's) body. The mother's body marks time; the mother's body itself tells a tale, as Deleuze would have it. This tale resonates with what Elizabeth Spelman has identified as "somatophobia," the fear of and the discomfort of the body.[45] In her reading of Spelman, Hirsch discusses somatophobia in the context of the maternal body: "Nothing entangles women more firmly in their bodies than pregnancy, birth, lactation, miscarriage, or the inability to conceive."[46] For the first twenty minutes of the film, Marlo is a swelling belly. The camera first captures her midriff; she literally enters the frame in the opening scene belly first. Her spherical protrusion determines her way of being in the diegetic world of the film, her interaction with objects and with people. After pregnancy, she is body with baby, attached at the breast or the hip. Still shaped (or misshapen) by the physical strains of pregnancy and birth, Marlo's breasts and stomach remain swollen and leaking. At the dinner table one evening, Marlo, too tired to care, strips down to her bra after her son accidently splatters his milk on her. This sudden exposure elicits her daughter's reproving remark: "Mom, what happened to your body?" Part of the hype about the film was Theron's significant weight gain to play Marlo. More than just a touch of realism to the role of a struggling mother of three, the exceptional heaviness of Theron's body makes her exhaustion visible. After the accident and Marlo's return home, there is a recurrence of the nightly ritual of stroking her son with a brush. This time she lumbers into his bedroom not with a weighed-down abdomen but with a support cane and post-accident injuries. The telling return of this opening scene at the close of the film apparently serves narrative development. The son, Jonah, reveals that he does not see the point of the brushing but enjoys the intimacy with her. It is difficult to ignore the continuity of Marlo's physical state, her persistent lack of mobility, and her struggle, however. The overall exhaustion between these two scenes and the permeating sense of repetition and suspension settle over this story of motherhood.

A Devastating Transformation

Just released from Rikers Island Women's Prison, Inez is back on the streets of Brooklyn, full of energy, embracing her freedom, and determined to make a mark. A hairstylist by trade, she hustles clients in cars and on sidewalks, does hair on doorsteps, and moves with an energy and self-confidence that match her tough but always stylish exterior, played by actress and singer Teyana Taylor. So begins American filmmaker A. V. Rockwell's debut drama, *A Thousand and One*, alive with images of Inez on the go, captured in a suggestive early sequence from a low angle, in which she appears to tower over the city. Then Inez reencounters her preadolescent son, Terry, who is now living in foster care, and her life takes another turn. The once fiery and energetic Inez gives up her dreams of becoming a hairstylist and gives herself over to motherhood. Eluding the authorities, she removes Terry from foster care and from that moment on strives to create a loving and stable home. But this aspiration also steadily wears her down. The family manse, the titular object "1001," becomes another kind of prison for Inez.

In order to finance the apartment in Harlem for her and Terry, she must give up hairstyling and assume the joyless job of cleaning a nursing home in Brooklyn. The film no longer shows her out in the world, on the streets, meeting with friends, styling hair. We also don't even see her at work; her diegetic life exists almost solely within the confines of the private home. By contrast, her son and her boyfriend-then-husband, the kind but unfaithful Lucky, come and go as they please, and their stories take us to different settings in the city. Lucky represents the man, Beauvoir describes, who "wants a home but also to remain free to escape from it; he settles down, but he often remains a vagabond in his heart; [. . .] repetition bores him; he seeks novelty, risk, resistance to overcome, camaraderie, friendships that wrest him from the solitude of the couple."[47] Inez does not have the same freedom. In one scene, following a fight, Lucky prepares to leave again, and Inez cries out: "I wonder what would happen if I leave, too?"

Her question, more rhetorical than anything, hangs with a heaviness in the stifling domestic air. Lucky briefly stops in his tracks. The full weight of the question only becomes clear later on, however: if she left, there would be no home. So, she stays. The unequivocal melodramatic oppression of this scene and this tale of motherhood and home looms. Certainly, the home as prison is one of the primary tropes of melodrama.[48]

Still, nothing can be maintained forever. To say nothing of Inez's loss of freedom, the cyclical nature of housework and the double burden of caring and cleaning for both family and others as her work outside the home not dissimilar to Amelia in *The Babadook*, "what feminist scholars called the double shift," steadily wear her down—"a slow degradation" over the course of the film.[49] Exhaustion sets in, and her body and movement signal its eroding force. Inez gradually abandons her makeup, her styled hair, and her form-fitting wardrobe, so intrinsic to her look and performance earlier in the film. She begins to don loose-fitting sweats and a bandana on her head. Her face becomes drawn. Even her voice resonates more softly than before, assuming a ragged edge. "She undergoes a breathtaking physical transformation, her sacrifice and devotion to Terry visible in a face that grows increasingly drained," a critic for the *Washington Post* writes.[50] Ironically, or tragically, the home that both imprisons Inez and becomes her absolute raison d'être likewise begins to fall apart. Crushed under the pressures of the nuclear family, mother and home symbolically become one and suffer the same fate. Beauvoir reminds us that existential exhaustion gnaws at both body and home, "eat[ing] at furniture and clothes just as it disfigures the face."[51]

But what of external factors and racial politics? Must we not also take into account the fact that Inez is not only a working-class, mostly single mother not dissimilar to Amelia in *The Babadook* but also a Black woman in New York City at a time of a draconian gentrification sweep in the late 1990s and early 2000s? Yes, certainly. To be a struggling and exhausted white mother is not the same as being a struggling and exhausted Black mother. It is a manifest truth that, as Patricia Hill Collins observes, "[f]or women of color, the subjective experience of mothering/motherhood is inextricably linked to the sociocultural concern of racial ethnic communities—one does not exist without the other."[52] Inez's struggles with incarceration, foster care, poverty, and the overall lack of state support bespeak this difference. Her battles extend well beyond the private household. Unlike *The Babadook* and *Tully*, *A Thousand and One* does not represent motherhood primarily as a private hell.

In this later film, motherhood is as much onerous as it is life affirming. Inez sacrifices everything so that Terry can grow up in a home with a stable family, instead of in foster care, and he does thrive as a result. *A Thousand and One* echoes the rich discourse of Black feminist thought invested in the power of Black motherhood from Audre Lorde, Angela Davis, Alice Walker, Patricia Hill Collins, and bell hooks to more contemporary scholars such as Dorothy Roberts, Jennifer Nash, and Alexis Pauline Gumbs. In Nash's words, "black feminist theory has become squarely invested in reimagining and amplifying the potential, power, and possibility of black motherhood."[53] But Rockwell's film makes space for other emotions, too. It insists on documenting the burden of motherhood apart from the threat of systemic racism and state violence. It responds to Nash's inquiry, cited in the book's introduction: "[I]s there a space for maternal unhappiness in the black feminist theoretical maternal archive, space for accounts of motherhood that find mothering profoundly unradical, perhaps even tedious, exhausting, or upsetting?"[54] Nash herself encounters a dearth of representations and explorations in the Black feminist theoretical archive that do not pursue motherhood, or at least mothering, as reparatively radical and worldmaking. Only Walker's testimonies of struggle being a mother and a writer perhaps come closest to describing maternal labor as exhausting and tedious. In 1976, the same year that Rich's *Of Woman Born* was first published, Walker's essay "A Writer Because of, Not in Spite of, Her Children" also appeared. In this brief, personal exploration, Walker candidly acknowledges the frustrations of motherhood, in particular, balancing motherhood and writing: "'I wrote nothing for a year,' I offered, 'that didn't sound as though a baby were screaming right through the middle of it.' . . . What kind of woman would think the 'background noises' of five children 'sweet'?"[55] On the whole, though, these voices are rare.

Cinema presents further possibilities. *A Thousand and One* comprises many layers. Inez's story is irrevocably different from that of Amelia's or Marlo's, but she, too, becomes crushed under the weight and exhaustion of motherhood. The film maps her exhaustion with stunning visibility. On a rare occasion, Lucky meets Inez on her way home from work in one striking scene. Together they walk along through the gray flush of the early morning. He tells her she should be proud of herself because "she made it." Inez looks on suspiciously without responding, her face drawn and washed out (fig. 2.2). Sleep deprived, she has just returned from the nightshift. "You don't seem happy," he reproaches. He is incapable of fully comprehending the life-altering extent of her sacrifice for motherhood and her resulting existential exhaustion.

Then suddenly everything falls apart. First, in a heinously underhanded effort to drive Inez and her son from their rented apartment, the new landlord sends a maintenance crew into their home, ostensibly to make

FIGURE 2.2. A glaring look of total and utter exhaustion in *A Thousand and One*. Directed by A. V. Rockwell, 2023.

some simple repairs, and they damage the stove and shower to a point of disuse. When a pipe also bursts in the ceiling, flooding parts of the apartment and leaving a gaping maw, the collapse of the family home comes full force. There is no denying the film's minor narrative about the violent onslaught of urban gentrification and the devastating effects it has on working-class Black residents, especially, in areas such as Harlem, Brooklyn, and Queens. For Inez, though, the apartment becomes her own looking glass. We observe this struggling mother, broken down by work, a lack of freedom, and sleep deprivation, who—of a piece with her home—begins to acquiesce under the steady abrasion of her body over the years. As tragic as the loss of their home is, displacement ultimately trembles with a sense of liberation for Inez. Overall, the precarity of the family, so desperately shored up for years, reaches crisis. Lucky, who has been ill in hospital, dies from lung cancer. Finally, Terry discovers that Inez is not actually his biological mother but the woman who found him when he was abandoned as a child.

The revelation that Inez saved Terry from what Dorothy Roberts aptly calls the "benevolent terror" of foster care all those years ago—not out of maternal obligation but in the name of kinship of another kind, with nothing to offer but energy and heart and the dreams that slowly deflate—jolts the entire film.[56] Yet, Saidiya Hartman documents the significant history of different kinds of kinships beyond biology within Black communities in cities like New York: "[U]nwed mothers rais[ed] children; same-sex households; households with female breadwinners; families composed of siblings, aunts, and children; households blending kin and strangers; serial marriages." Further, "[f]lexible and elastic kinship were not a 'plantation holdover,'" Hartman insists, "but a resource of black survival, a practice that documented the generosity and mutuality of the poor."[57] Inez is a survivor. Bereft of property and family at the end and now a fugitive from the law because of her abduction of Terry so many years ago, Inez perseveres. What narratively strikes the viewer as a tragic ending in its tearful separation of mother and son takes a different turn. Terry, now nearly eighteen, presumably goes to live with a longtime family friend. Inez is on her own again. The groovy R&B tune with its constant beat and dreamy harmonies that opens the film, in which we see Inez on the streets, self-confident and determined, returns. Her hair is shorter now and braided but for the first time styled and free of the bandana. She also dons the jean jacket she wore at the beginning of the film. In the closing shot, the camera captures Inez in a close-up. Still tearful, she sits in a taxi. Then a small smile creeps across her face when the driver asks, "OK, Miss, where to?" Inez has cast off the sacrificial bonds of motherhood and the crushing responsibility that had for so long shaped her life and steadily sapped her strength. Now she is on her own; and despite all the uncertainty, she can pick her destination.

Bodily Slumps

Distinct from the genre-driven, more mainstream films discussed in this chapter, the films of Angela Schanelec are often highly inscrutable, yet they, too, weigh heavily with exhaustion. The pronouncement that *"Es ist eine Müdigkeit hier"* (There is a tiredness here) from Schanelec's 2007 *Nachmittag* (Afternoon) could broadly describe the atmosphere of much of Schanelec's cinema as conditioned by weariness. Schanelec does not portray exhaustion as a maternal situation alone, but the figure of the mother does play a prominent role in many of her films.[58] In one of her more current releases, *Ich war zuhause, aber* . . . (I was at home, but . . . , 2019), maternal exhaustion prevails. As perplexing as Schanelec's films can be, one could summarize this film as follows: a woman has recently lost her partner and is left to raise two children on her own. Her story opens in the wake of the disappearance and return of her adolescent son, who had briefly run away from home. In many ways, this is a film about trauma and mourning that takes shape in the destabilizing aftermath of tragedy. The mother, Astrid (Maren Eggert), struggles as she attempts to balance single parenting, her position at a university, and a new boyfriend all while attending to lingering grief.

Astrid is constantly on the go. She first appears in a long shot as she dashes across the basketball court of her son's school from the point of view of the school director positioned at a window. A second shot captures her clambering up the stairs. She then falls to her knees in front of her prodigal son. Throughout the sequence, her labored breathing dramatically fills the soundtrack. Given the hitherto absence of speech in the film, already seven minutes in, the amplified sound of breath in this scene is striking in its potential as placeholder for verbal expression. Indeed, the woman's body, the maternal body by extension, is often linked to silence or nonverbal expression, long a trope of melodrama. But perhaps more distinctly, breath here accentuates the body, for the breathless body reminds us of its physicality and vulnerability. Audible respiration in cinema calls forth myriad interpretations. In her study of breath in cinema, Davina Quinlivan confirms that even in its invisible or barely visible presence, breath is always a dimension of the material body.[59] More specifically, the breathing body amplifies the body either in a state of discomfort or pleasure.[60] It follows that diegetic heavy breathing is elemental to both horror and porn films in different ways. As Jean-Thomas Tremblay indicates, Linda Williams's identification of "body genres," with their bodily excesses, resonates with an exploration of breath in cinema.[61] Heavy breathing signals the exertion of the body at its limits of pain and pleasure.

Neither horror nor porn, there are hints of that other body genre, melodrama. *Ich war zuhause, aber* . . . introduces its main character through her labored breath and consequently also draws attention to her body—here the breathless maternal body. What Luce Irigaray conceives of as a gift of both life and autonomy, the breath of the mother's body (originally shared with the fetus) in this scene of reunion becomes instead a site of struggle.[62] In its overwhelming—even uncomfortable—audibility, Astrid's breathing body shapes her character from the start as winded and tired out. This body exhibits at once relief and exhaustion. It is as though Astrid has mustered all of her energy to run to her returned son, who remains calmly seated in the school director's office. When she arrives, she collapses to her knees before him. Astrid's collapse is off-screen. Hardly ceremonial, Astrid's genuflection settles into a bodily slump in what appears to be a surrender to exhaustion. The film presents a series of bodily slumps. These are not unlike Deleuze's "sliding of postures," characterized, for instance, as "a body leant against a wall, which lets itself go and falls to a sitting position on the ground."[63] Perhaps more than any of the films examined in this chapter, Schanelec's film models the bodily attitudes of the cinema of inaction articulated by Deleuze. Gorfinkel also calls these postures in which bodies acquiesce to gravity "histrionic."[64] Though emptied of ceremonial meaning and distinct from Marlo's collapse on the couch, Astrid's slumps do maintain an air of the theatrical and are certainly symbolic.

Amid the rhythms of her hectic daily life, Astrid frequently slumps down in drawn out pauses. Not bouts of respite or moments of rest in which the body unwinds, these instances of physical recline appear to suspend Astrid in strangely composed cinematic tableaux.[65] Schanelec's early work in the theater and general penchant for long takes present many opportunities for tableaux to emerge. But the tableaux also bear narrative, or at least thematic, continuities in this film about a woman who is both mother and art historian. Critics describe Astrid's personal trauma and crisis as of an artistic nature: she begins to question her perception of everything, including art.[66] Narrative meets form; life imitates art. As Ágnes Pethö comments, the tableau signals cinema's intermediality and its connection to painting, photography, and theatrical mise-en-scène.[67]

Much has been written on the topic of the cinematic tableau. David Bordwell ardently championed the tableau's important narrative significance and depth with its often highly theatrical staging, especially in early cinema.[68] Eugenie Brinkema, by contrast, more recently describes the tableau as "a radical flattening of space, a collapse of the cinematic into the theatrical and a foreclosure of spatial and representational depths that may lead elsewhere."[69] In Schanelec's films, the tableaux present odd pauses, and their compositions often appear out of place; however, they do invite a reading that moves beyond a bracketed and flattened out moment in time extracted from narrative relevance. Brigitte Peucker's more flexible understanding of the tableau in its different iterations proposes that, in certain cases "the tableau reduces narrative to a spectacle supported by the body." In the same vein, she continues, "tableau scenes also render the body as text."[70] Not simply void of narrative, the tableau forces us to read the narrative of the film differently—that is, through the spectacle of the body and the ragged body, in particular.

The most striking of the tableaux in *Ich war zuhause, aber* . . . comes in the final twenty-five minutes of the film during an extended sequence of mother and daughter at a public indoor swimming pool. The setting is hardly extraordinary for Schanelec's films, which frequently include scenes from public recreation centers. Following a swim, the setting changes to the locker room, where mother and daughter prepare their things to dress. They are silent. Then Astrid walks off-screen and verbally, though barely

FIGURE 2.3. Mother as iconographic Pietà in *Ich war zuhause, aber . . .* Directed by Angela Schanelec, 2019.

audibly, beckons to her daughter, Flo, with a whisper: "Come here." Flo appears to hesitate but then follows. In a second shot in the locker room, Astrid, seated on a bench, slumps against the wall. She loosely cradles Flo, who sits sideways on her lap, barely covered by a towel and with one arm slung over Astrid's shoulder. A curtain of damp hair covers her face. With her own head slightly tilted to the right, Astrid's gaze is cast downward in an almost sorrowful expression. The two towel-covered bodies are positioned centrally, but the camera maintains its distance from this intimate scene, giving the image depth, the impression of being hidden. Flanked by a row of lockers and ensconced in dimness, the two remain completely still for the duration of the shot, a total of fifteen seconds. The beckoning of the mother suggests a ritualistic practice. Perhaps, the embrace follows the application of some cream? We don't see that. As I have also indicated in previous work, the composition of the bodies within this shot evokes Michelangelo's Pietà sculpture of Mary holding on her lap the body of Christ after his crucifixion (fig. 2.3).[71] One of the most popular Christian iconography and images, the Pietà represents the themes of maternal sorrow, loss, and grief, not to mention pious devotion.[72] The mimesis of the sculpture in this tableau further puts the maternal body on display as it "enacts [Christian] myth" in this scene.[73]

Tucked away into the depths of a dark and empty locker room, the setting of this tableau of Christian iconography, of a remarkable sacrificial embrace, is unexpected, to say the least. The tableau surprises further because Astrid is otherwise notably unaffectionate, neglectful, and even irritable toward her children, especially her daughter, whom she frequently leaves home alone (though she cannot be older than ten) and whom she reprimands in one scene for using the stove unsupervised. On the one hand, to propose that the tableau is divorced from or contradicts the narrative of the film would be false. On the other hand, a direct reading of the tableau as representative of Astrid's tarrying grief—suspended in a moment of "still and heavy pain"—oversimplifies its role in the film.[74] Let us try something else. The theme of the grieving mother brought forth in this tableau through the composition of bodies has an aesthetic precursor. In an earlier scene in Berlin's Bode Museum, a museum that houses principally Byzantine sculpture, the camera lingers on the bust of Our Lady of Sorrows (Mater Dolorosa), attributed to Pedro Roldán in the late seventeenth century. In this place of representation, we see another woman, Claudia (Lilith Stangenberg), gazing at the bust. In the film's minor, secondary narrative, Claudia and her boyfriend, Lars (Franz Rogowski), experience relationship troubles when he begins pressuring her about having children despite her desire for freedom. The link between these two narratives appears ambiguous, but the topic of motherhood, especially troubled motherhood, connects them thematically, if nothing else. Circling its vitrine container, Claudia carefully studies the dramatically lachrymose face of the Mother Mary on display. Then she performs her own tableau: positioned in front of the bust, she appears to mimic it. Astrid is also at the museum. The scene provides the only clear overlap in space and time between the two narratives. She herself pauses before a work of art. However, without a reverse shot it is unclear what has caught her gaze. Defying the rules of continuity editing—given the sequence of shots from Claudia in front of the bust to Astrid's intent stare—we may draw an association between the two. The aesthetics of motherhood and the pathos of grief and sorrow in this film form a compelling nexus. But the film's image of motherhood is not simply virtuous and aesthetic; in other words, it does not only participate in what E. Ann Kaplan calls "the maternal sacrificial paradigm," the mother who "subordinates her desires and needs to those of her husband and children" and "maintains the saintly, nurturing, all-forgiving position."[75]

The film's direct reference to the *Stabat Mater* (the suffering Mother Mary) also invites a reading with Julia Kristeva and her important essay by the same name, in which she incisively critiques this image of motherhood as an "idealized misapprehension."[76] Similar to the institution of motherhood, this representation does not reckon with women's actual experiences of motherhood. *Ich war zuhause, aber* ... dramatically asks Kristeva's still pertinent question: "[W]hat is it about this representation that fails to take account of what a woman might say or want of the Maternal, so that when today women make their voices heard, the issues of conception and maternity are a major focus of discontent?"[77] Posed in the 1980s, Kristeva's question arises here again because little has changed with regard to our perceptions of motherhood and the expectations placed on women. Kaplan confirms in the early 1990s that Kristeva's question had remained unanswered. But in her influential study on motherhood, Kaplan, too, leaves it open and focuses on popular representations of motherhood rather than mothers' experiences.[78]

Writing around the same time as Kristeva and similarly evoking the Stabat Mater, Rich corresponds with a very personal narration again of the cleft between representation and experience as a mother: "I realize that I was effectively alienated from my real body and my real spirit by the institution—not the fact—of motherhood. This institution allowed me only certain views, certain expectations, whether embodied in the booklet in my obstetrician's waiting room, the novels I had read, my mother-in-law's approval, my memories of my own mother, the Sistine Madonna or she of the Michelangelo *Pietà*, the floating notion that a woman pregnant is a woman calm in her fulfillment or, simply, a woman waiting."[79] No one tells you how "exhilarating, bewildering, and exhausting" it can be, she adds.[80] That the film brings forth these floating notions of motherhood as wholly virtuous and even aesthetically beautiful is not a reinforcement of the institution of motherhood but, I argue, a dismantling. Schanelec creates her own Pietà vivant that reflects a truer reality of motherhood. If the tableau of mother and daughter caught in an embrace in a dark, dank locker room puts the body on display, then this is not a portrayal of the serene and virtuous Mary, covered in cloth and veil, but the real maternal body, slumped uncomfortably on a bench and wrapped in a towel. This is the body mothers are not supposed to show. This is the body of exhaustion.

In the final scene of the film, time has passed; it is now summer. Astrid slumps, this time more deliberately, with shoes discarded, on a large rock jutting out into a flowing river. She is in nature. The camera rests on Astrid's supine body in a long take. She does not move, but the water rushes around her. Does Astrid finally "drop from exhaustion" in a summation of all her slumps, as Jean-Luc Nancy might put it in his study of sleep, *Tombe de sommeil* (literally translated as drop from exhaustion)?[81] Indeed, this is the first time we see Astrid prostrate with eyes closed. At first glance, this concluding scene renders Astrid's path to rejuvenation an overcoming of accreting exhaustion, a giving over to sleep at exhaustion's other end. At odds with *The Babadook* and *Tully*, there is no near-death experience that dramatically ushers in the possible catharsis at the close of *A Thousand and One* or *Ich war zuhause, aber . . .* , but tragedy besieges both. Utterly distinct, the loss of everything leaves Inez in *A Thousand and One* both bereft and liberated in the film's climatic ending. For Astrid in *Ich war zuhause, aber . . .* , time is already in the aftermath of tragedy: the aftermath of Astrid's partner's death and of her son's disappearance and reappearance. Exhaustion also does not unravel into an apogee of violence as it does in *The Babadook* and *Tully*; instead, it just steadily abrades the body in these later films: Inez slowly withers, and Astrid slumps down under the plinths of motherhood.

Exhaustion assumes distinct forms in the four films central to this chapter. From the monster to the dangerous or at least depleting fantasy, to the formal register of the bodily slump that opposes idealized representations of motherhood, maternal exhaustion in this chapter serves as more than just an antecedent to sleep, to evoke Nancy.[82] Exhaustion as a result of toil and repetition is a state of being that comes with its own peril; a state so integral to the experience of many mothers, yet exhaustion is rarely explored, much less valuated as a real concern. As I have discussed throughout the chapter, drawing mostly on second-wave feminist writings but also on more-contemporary studies concerning motherhood, including Black motherhood, exhaustion does not have a place in representations of motherhood or its institution, neither old nor new. Mothers are expected to express the joy of sacrifice but never the backbreaking weariness it forges. Exhaustion signals a glitch in the institution of motherhood; therefore, it must be suppressed or fantasized away. All four films do what films about mothers so seldom do: they offer portrayals of motherhood that resonate with the experience *of mothers* in all of their lethargy. These films show the sleepless nights, the abeyance of daily repetition, and the desperate attempts to persevere, to press oneself into the service of the never-ending and isolating labor of motherhood.

Despite their distinctions in genre, each film pursues exhaustion vividly through the body. The body of the mother is put on full display: Amelia's drawn face in close-ups; Marlo's heavily pregnant, then post-accident injured body; Inez's depleted body; and finally, Astrid's slumped body. The exhaustion of motherhood becomes a performance of bodily struggle and, to some degree, defeat. It defies the idealization and even the strength so often attached to the body of the mother. Different images emerge through these films, which unapologetically portray the experiences of the mother rather than the projection of motherhood produced by patriarchy. Exhaustion weighs on many if not all of the films examined in the chapters to follow; it forms as an almost elemental state of motherhood. It is gnawingly present. As we shall see, maternal exhaustion can also generate other states of being. Moving from exhaustion to rage in the next chapter, energy begins to surge in violent outbursts and irritated snaps. This transition comes directly in the film *The Babadook*, for instance, which demonstrates the possible trajectory of hellish weariness to writhing anger.

CHAPTER THREE

Rage

"Mother-love is supposed to be continuous, unconditional. Love and anger cannot coexist. Female anger threatens the institution of motherhood," we have often been told.[1] No one has spoken of maternal rage with such eloquence and conviction as Adrienne Rich, and in doing so she also laid bare one of the many falsehoods of motherhood; that is, that mothers do not experience anger. Since Rich's pathbreaking work, ample literature in the English language has emerged that explores and takes seriously maternal rage. Many of these studies have appeared in just the last half a decade. Authors such as Minna Dubin, Darcy Lockman, and Sara Petersen have dared to once again raise this taboo topic.

Distinct from other emotions explored in this book, maternal rage draws direct influence from feminist discourse. Re-emboldened by contemporary political movements, including #MeToo, anti-Trumpism, and Black Lives Matter, feminist rage continues to carry tremendous weight. The renewed focus on and mobilization of rage present a response to the persisting antifeminism and racism in today's world as well as an embrace of the power and creativity of this emotion.[2] Recent work on feminist rage turns to an alternative genealogy that recognizes and legitimizes it as an acceptable and necessary response to social injustice, rather than as a wholly negative affect capable of conjuring violence, and a threat to friends, family, and the society at large.[3] This alternative genealogy advances from ancient philosophy through to Black feminist theory.[4] It begins with Aristotle, who, even in his tempered approach, viewed anger as reasonable passion. He maintained, "There is praise for someone who gets angry at the right things and with the right people, as well as in the right way, at the right time, and for the right length of time."[5] Righteous rage leads all the way to the late twentieth century and to the wisdom of Audre Lorde and bell hooks, who found clarity, strength, and liberation in the emotion. In sum, as Sue J. Kim remarks, "Feminist theorists have long argued for the validity of anger not only politically but also epistemologically."[6]

Despite this rich influence and its resulting steady breaking of the silence, maternal rage—especially against one's own children—remains outside of the realm of reason and ineffable for many. Over forty years later, Rich's plaint about the perception of motherhood still resonates: love and anger cannot conceivably coincide. Minna Dubin echoes Rich in a recent article for the *New York Times*, appropriately titled "The Rage Mothers Don't Talk About," in which she writes: "Mother rage is not 'appropriate.' Mothers are supposed to be martyr-like in our patience. We are not supposed to want to hit our kids or tear out their hair. We hide these urges, because we are afraid to be labeled 'bad moms.' We feel the need to qualify our frustration with 'I love my child to the moon and back, but . . . ' As if mother rage equals a lack of love. As if rage has never shared a border with love."[7] Maternal rage remains that experience whose name we cannot speak. The exploration of this emotion, however, "makes it possible to confront both the cultural construction of motherhood—the angry abandoning or abandoned mother has reached the status of a cultural icon—*and* maternal responses to that construction," Marianne Hirsch reveals.[8] Contemporary film sets forth such a possibility for confrontation.

Interpreting film broadly as also serial productions on streaming platforms, this chapter explores the portrayal of maternal anger in Jennifer Kent's *The Babadook* (2014), Lucy Gaymer and Siân Robins-Grace's HBO series *The Baby* (2022), and finally Charlotte Stoudt's Netflix series *Pieces of Her* (2022). The first two, released nearly a decade apart, get at a mother's rage through the horror genre. The fright and violence of horror are not always components of maternal anger, but they certainly serve the expression and performance of this emotion in cinema emphatically. Maternal rage is nothing new to horror film; maternal horror films are rife with anger. The mothers in horror classics such as *Psycho*, *Carrie*, and *The Brood* serve as paragons of maternal anger, except their anger is pathological because it is not given clear cause; in other words, it is often bent on revenge and violence without due reason. Presented as monstrous villains, enraged mothers in horror cinema have something wrong with them. Their display of anger stigmatizes both themselves and the emotion. In David Cronenberg's *The Brood* (1979), maternal anger becomes directly embodied in the mother's diabolical, dwarf-like offspring. These creatures do their mother's bidding—attacking and killing the people with whom she (both consciously and unconsciously) becomes enraged. Barbara Creed discusses the film as a portrayal of the illegitimacy of maternal anger, which manifests as a congenital disease passed from mother to child.[9] Taken to an extreme in horror cinema, the stigma of anger has deep roots. Furthermore, the trope of the angry mother in horror cinema is without doubt deeply antifeminist.

Among recent endeavors to recuperate anger as a useful political category, contemporary affect theory has critiqued both the stigma of anger and the stigmatization of the person who expresses it. Sara Ahmed writes extensively on anger as the emotion frequently dismissed or stigmatized by others, especially when expressed by a woman of color. A performance of anger frequently leads to the judgment that there is something wrong with the person and not that something could be wrong with the situation, society, and so forth.[10] Precisely the hostility toward anger, especially anger as expressed by women, has hampered closer examinations. This directly extends to feminist film theory as well. According to Tania Modleski, "Feminist film theory has yet to explore and work through this anger, which for women continues to be, as it has been historically, the most unacceptable of all emotions."[11] Two decades after Modleski, Kathleen McHugh reminds us of this sustained absence and points to just a small handful of films that explore feminist anger. Among earlier films, we might consider Marlene Goris's *De stilte rond Christine M.* (A question of silence, 1982) and Lizzie Gordon's *Born in Flames* (1983); more recently, films such as Alice Lowe's *Prevenge* (2016), Rungano Nyoni's *I Am Not a Witch* (2017), Gina Kim's *Bloodless* (2017), and Jennifer Kent's *The Nightingale* (2018) capture our attention.[12]

An exception in which women's anger plays a significant and generally legitimate role is in tales of revenge; indeed, most of the films listed above are just that. Within the field of horror studies, we encounter the "rape-revenge" genre. Coined by Carol Clover, this genre encompasses films such as *I Spit on Your Grave* (Meir Zarchi, 1977), in which the enraged woman protagonist is raped and then seeks revenge against her rapist. At the same time, Clover reveals that there is much more at stake in this film (and others like it) than can be summarized in this basic premise. What becomes relevant to the present study is the effect of rage in such films and its capacity to elicit sympathy rather than sheer disgust or terror. Rape-revenge films represent one of the few genres in which women's anger is perceived as a reasonable and understandable emotional response; however, as Clover analyzes it, this sympathy is often fraught. The film does not invite the audience to identify and sympathize with a woman seeking revenge against patriarchy; instead, many of older rape-revenge films develop into reprisal tales against othered masculinities.[13] Revenge narratives involving mothers contrast from those explored by Clover, but they likewise achieve legitimacy and sympathy. Tales of a mother avenging wrongs committed against her children inundate cinema, past and present. All sorts of violent acts become permissible under the guise of protection of and even the vengeance for a wrong committed against one's children. As Sarah Arnold clarifies, in these films "[the mother's] goal is not self-preservation but the preservation of her children. Indeed, she may die to achieve this goal."[14]

In some films, women do avenge both the violence visited upon their families and themselves. Consider Kent's more recent feature *The Nightingale* about an Irish woman prisoner in Australia in the early nineteenth century, when the country was a British penal colony. In the aftermath of unspeakable violence committed against her and her family, she seeks revenge against the British colonizers. In another example, Alice Lowe's comedy-slasher *Prevenge* subversively plays with horror's tendency to link women and mothers by presenting a heavily pregnant serial killer whose gruesome murder spree to avenge her dead partner, apparently at the behest of her unborn baby, is also rife with humor. However, Arnold warns against placing women and mothers in horror cinema under the same mantle. The prescriptiveness of women's roles in horror speaks in support of Arnold. In the case of the films under scrutiny in this chapter, the fact that these women are perceived solely as mothers—and not as individuals or women—proves significant in the generation of their rage.

The Babadook and *The Baby* do not present examples of revenge cinema, at least not in the sense explored by Clover or Arnold. If anything, they draw on the tropes of the monstrous or phallic mother in their loathing behavior toward their offspring (Barbara Creed and E. Ann Kaplan, respectively).[15] But distinct from their predecessors of horror cinema, these films do not pathologize maternal rage. Instead, rage unfurls as an inevitable effect of motherhood. These films break taboos by showing, rather than concealing, the events and occasions of frustration and even violence that can usher in a mother's rage. Staying true to their horror genre, the films follow a trajectory of rage that often materializes in cruelty. No doubt, rage in cinema often plays out in action-packed violence. However, maternal rage certainly does not always lead to violence. As a counterpoint, I include the series *Pieces of Her*. A drama about a young woman trying to discover the truth about her mother's mysterious past and a mother seeking to escape from the same and protect them both, this series explores maternal anger as a sliding scale of ambivalence. Maternal anger can manifest in different ways and for different reasons, but frequently it arises as a consequence of the albatross of motherhood: the labor, the exhaustion, the isolation, and the frustration.

In the context of this chapter, maternal anger is both experiential and political; it reflects embodied experience and the injustice of gender hierarchy. Cleaving open the wells of maternal anger, Rich confesses, "I remember going back to bed starkly awake, brittle with anger, knowing that my broken sleep would make the next day a hell, that there would be more nightmares, more need for consolation, because out of my weariness I would rage at those children for no reason they could understand."[16] For Rich, anger is that inexorable emotion that arises as a result of the daily tasks and challenges of motherhood. Anger has long stood at odds with the image of the caring, serene mother, all too ready to sacrifice time, sleep, and energy for her children. Promulgated by the institution of motherhood, this image of the mother bade anger's suppression. Rich fearlessly paid heed to maternal anger at a time when no one spoke openly about it. But to more fully understand anger as a tool to be wielded against patriarchy and the institution of motherhood—that is, beyond the experiential and into the political—contemporary affect theory becomes instructive.

Sara Ahmed, in particular, takes experiential anger and expands on its possibilities within the sphere of the political. Ahmed aligns feminism and anger as strategies of against-ness and responses to injustice. "[F]eminism," she contends, "is shaped by what it is against, just as women's bodies and lives may be shaped by histories of violence that bring them to feminist consciousness."[17] Anger takes a similar shape. One must, however, take care not to consign anger—and feminism, for that matter—to reaction alone, as that affect that gets stuck on an object, for that, too, can call on the pathological.[18] Ahmed understands the against-ness of anger as also a being for something, even if that something lies in the future and has not yet been articulated.[19] Among others, Ahmed returns to Lorde and her important embrace of anger as both response and future in her groundbreaking critique of racism against Black women. In a widely cited passage from her essay "The Uses of Anger," Lorde powerfully lays out the usefulness of anger in the Black feminist struggle: "My response to racism is anger. I have lived with that anger, ignoring it, feeding upon it, learning to use it before it laid my visions to waste, for most of my life. Once I did it in silence, afraid of the weight. My fear of anger taught me nothing. . . . [A]nger expressed and translated into action in the service of our vision and our future is a liberating and strengthening act of clarification."[20] Drawing on Lorde, Ahmed theorizes anger as a political strategy of refusal to participate in the present conditions of inequality and injustice and a beckoning toward a more equal and just future.[21]

The path back to maternal anger, and here mostly white maternal anger, in particular, is not a direct one. Neither Ahmed nor Lorde directly addresses maternal anger, and their approach is firmly anchored within a Black feminist context that maintains the critical intersectionality of sexism and racism. Yet, their feminist strategies of operationalizing anger against injustice of all kinds and toward a future of liberation and clarification become useful more broadly in the rejection of the repressive institution of motherhood and its societal demands on women and mothers. Bringing these thinkers into the conversation permits an important traversal of the experiential and the political.

The anger expressed in *The Babadook* firmly reflects Rich's scrutiny of experiential anger in its unabashed portrayal of a single mother driven to the brink by a highly active and imaginative child. *The Baby*, by contrast, offers a decidedly political tale of unbidden motherhood and one woman's tragic oppression: forced to give birth to and mother a child she does not want with a husband she loathes. Anger culminates in violence as she battles against patriarchy in her pursuit of freedom. Finally, *Pieces of Her* presents a potentially more palatable instance of maternal rage in the form of a snap. Unlike the other two films, here violence (at least of a filicidal nature) remains implicit. I begin with a brief but grounding analysis of *The Babadook* as a known example of nuanced maternal rage on-screen to eventually lead into two more recent ones. In all three cases, experiential anger as well as political anger come to the fore.

Repressed Rage Turns (Nearly) Filicidal

Kent has gained a reputation as an auteur of anger. Considered the successor of Jane Campion, Kent does not shy away from uncomfortable emotions, characters, or scenes that repel the audience.[22] *The Babadook*, much like Kent's second feature, *The Nightingale*, foregrounds strong emotions, especially rage. As much as *The Babadook* portrays maternal exhaustion, investigated in the previous chapter, it also depicts maternal rage. Rich certainly maintains that the two go hand in glove.[23] With the depletion of energy and patience, exhaustion builds; so, too, does rage. The widowed mother, Amelia, struggles with her seven-year-old son, Samuel (Noah Wiseman), who appears to hold total control over their relationship. Not an altogether terrible child, Samuel is, nonetheless, extremely active, highly emotional, and often out of control. Amelia's mounting frustration shows, but at first she suppresses her anger. She appears haunted by what Rich calls "unexamined assumptions" of motherhood: "that a 'natural' mother is a person without further identity, one who can find her chief gratification in being all day with small children, living at a pace tuned to theirs; that the isolation of mothers and children together in the home must be taken for granted; that maternal love is, and should be, quite literally selfless."[24] These unexamined assumptions return in the series *Pieces of Her*, too. In other words, mothers are not supposed to experience nor, by all means, express anger toward their children, for this would assert an identity, desires—moreover, a pace—outside of motherhood.

With clenched jaw, Amelia restrains her rage when, for instance, Samuel breaks a window by firing a homemade weapon in the house, brings the same weapon to school and she is called in, pushes his cousin out of a treehouse, and the list could go on. Her desperate attempt to suppress her rage toward Samuel proves futile as time passes; it simply grows. The mysterious and ominous babadook picture book directly alludes to this in printed word: "The more you deny me, the stronger I get." First, her anger manifests implicitly through the body. Eight minutes into the film, Amelia's body begins to betray her and show signs of repressed rage: her jaw starts to ache. Ostensibly the side effect of a toothache, the aching jaw represents much more. The clench of repressed rage becomes too much to contain and takes on a life of its own. The babadook monster embodies many things, among them Amelia's rage. Plainly festering in her since the beginning of the film and the first rude awakening by her son, Amelia's anger and its embodiment as the babadook, Jessica Balanzategui suggests, have even longer prehistories that emerge with Samuel's birth, which also occasions the death of her husband.[25] Midway through the film, her long-repressed emotion begins to manifest itself in obscene ways after she has unwittingly consumed the black, viscous material of the monster. Transformed, Amelia embraces her rage (fig. 3.1).

FIGURE 3.1. The enraged mother in *The Babadook*. Directed by Jennifer Kent, 2014.

In an attempt to rest after another long and sleepless night, Amelia lashes out at Samuel for the first time. She reproaches him for bothering her and tells him to "go eat shit" if he's hungry. Amelia's anger surfaces. Her hitherto almost pleadingly soft-spoken voice abruptly changes registers. She becomes loud, aggressive, and cruel: she becomes a monstrous mother. Barbara Creed describes the monstrous mother as perverse, possessive, and dominant. The monstrous mother represents for Creed the phallic or castrating mother epitomized by Norman's mother figure in Hitchcock's *Psycho*.[26] Although Amelia does not exhibit these qualities from the start, they begin to show once her anger creeps in. She not only scolds and berates Samuel but she eventually also imprisons him inside, locking the doors and cutting the phone line. During this fateful night shuttered in the house, the babadook fully possesses Amelia, rendering her even more abusive and violent. She breaks the dog's neck and nearly kills Samuel as well. Yet, as much as *The Babadook* avails itself of many of the quintessential tropes of horror and maternal horror, in particular, Amelia is not a typical monstrous mother.

Distinct from the enraged and villainous mothers that populate many horror films, Amelia is sympathetic. When she finally releases her anger more than halfway through the film, we even breathe a sigh of relief. The film spends significant time tracking her troubles and struggles as a mother, unable to sleep or even enjoy a moment to herself. From the first scene in which Amelia is wrenched from sleep by her son, who has had a nightmare, her desperation captures our attention and our pity. Her maternal situation does enrage. The expectations placed on her by society, here in the form of her sister, and by her friends, the school principal, the pediatrician, and social services, assign undue pressure, as her son also grows more and more insufferable in his neediness and unruliness. Amelia is clearly drowning, as Kent herself indicates.[27] As chapter 2 discusses, it is Amelia and not Samuel who is the film's central focus.

Through the use of lingering close-ups, we come to identify with Amelia and her growing anger and frustration, not Samuel or his potentially growing fears. Amanda Howell and Lucy Baker note that Samuel is presented exclusively through the eyes of Amelia "as an increasingly abject, even frightening figure from which she draws away." She becomes his worst nightmare, yet the film "is also clearly driven by her predicament as a woman, committed to and entirely burdened by her role as Samuel's mother."[28] *The Babadook* directly rejects the psychoanalytic perspective of the child toward his mother and his evaluation of her care as either good or bad. As both Nancy Chodorow and E. Ann Kaplan critically observe, psychoanalysis has directed much attention to the mother and her central role in caring for the child, but it has occluded her own experience of motherhood from the picture in favor of that of the child.[29]

At the height of her rage, Amelia confesses her deepest, darkest, most forbidden secret: her desire to harm her child. "Sometimes I just wanna smash your head against a brick wall until your fucking brains pop out," she shrieks. Tess Pyles reminds us in this instant of *The Babadook* of Barbara Almond's experience as a psychotherapist treating mothers. Many of her patients, Almond admits, "express anger at their offspring" and voice similar murderous threats: "I could have killed her!" "I felt like hitting him over the head with a baseball bat!" As Almond further indicates, "they mean it," but "they don't do it."[30] Confessional moments of filicidal desires remain taboo as well. Rich explains, "For centuries no one talked of these feelings."[31] Not much has changed nearly four decades later. Kent herself was concerned about the negative reaction to Amelia's rage from the audience, especially from women and mothers, but to her surprise encountered relief.

> I didn't want to pull away from this very big taboo of parents wanting to kill their children. That's another reason why I chose the horror realm, because you can go to those places in this genre, whereas you can't always go that far in drama. I honestly thought I would get a lot of flack from women and mothers, but what has surprised me is how relieved they are, actually, to see a character who's real. I'm not saying, "Let's go and contemplate killing our kids," but it puts a real complex human being up on the screen. I'm glad that women feel it's a good representation.[32]

Ultimately, Amelia does not murder her son, despite several attempts. Instead, they battle it out. Using his own *Home Alone*–style resourcefulness with homemade weapons and boobytraps, Samuel presents an unexpectedly formidable match for his raging mother. The film plays it safe, both with violence and with maternal rage. It does not let them wane but, instead, redirects them toward the monster. In a turn of events, Amelia eventually employs her rage to protect, rather than harm, her son and to scare off the babadook. "You are nothing. You're nothing!" she screams this time to the babadook. "This is my house! You are trespassing in my house!" Despite the film's tempered conclusion, however, maternal rage does live out spectacularly in this tale of mother and son. Marking a departure, *The Babadook* unapologetically explores and displays maternal emotion in all of its complexity. Against all taboos, it has activated a new cinematic commitment to the expression of maternal rage that is not only nuanced but also empathetic. More examples are rushing in.

Angrily Refusing Motherhood

In Kaplan's celebrated study *Motherhood and Representation: The Mother in Popular Culture and Melodrama*, there is an exceedingly brief description of what she refers to as "Woman-Who-Refuses-to-Mother." At the time of the book's release in the early 1990s, it seems there were few representations of such women in popular culture. The dearth of these representations endures. An eight-episode British horror comedy released on HBO in 2022, *The Baby*, provides an exception to the rule. In nuce, this is a tale about a woman who refuses to mother. Rejected and abandoned, the mother's baby becomes possessed and immortal. For fifty-odd years, the baby vengefully seeks the motherly love first denied him. He malevolently forces himself on women who have willfully chosen not to mother and engineers their deaths when, in due course, their love and care fall short or become exhausted. The premise of *The Baby* gives at first an antifeminist impression: women who refuse motherhood are violently punished. However, the series treats the important experience of women and the demands placed on them to mother, even against their will, and to mother according to the conditions of a patriarchal system. Critics have aptly called this series a post–*Roe v. Wade*, dystopian tale, which is all too real.[33] Even in the United Kingdom, the overturning of *Roe v. Wade* has served as a reminder that reproductive rights cannot be taken for granted. As news reports at the time informed British citizens, the Christian Right that drove the movement to restrict abortion rights in the United States is also active in the United Kingdom.[34] *The Baby* ushers in an era in which women are fighting a losing battle for reproductive justice, and, as a result, many will be forced to mother children against their will. In a series ostensibly about the rage of a baby once abandoned and since then fixed on revenge, maternal rage offers a powerful antipode. This rage arises as a response to the oppressive demands of motherhood, which can entrap and even enslave women.

The main narrative of the series follows Natasha (Michelle de Swarte), a thirty-eight-year-old London-based chef and bachelorette for whom motherhood holds absolutely no allure; as a consequence, she begins feeling isolated from close friends who have become fully absorbed by it. *The Baby* opens with a small gathering of best girlfriends drinking, smoking, and playing cards at Natasha's apartment. The fun abates, however, when Natasha's friend Mags (Shvorne Marks), a new mother, must attend to her crying infant. Much to Natasha's chagrin, all attention turns to the baby and the topic of motherhood. Her other friend, Rita (Isy Suttie), announces that she is three months' pregnant and does not take kindly to Natasha's flippant remark that it is still not too late for an abortion. After a disastrous evening and a falling-out with her two best friends, Natasha decides to get away for a period and rents an old cabin next to the sea. On that fateful first night in the cabin, a baby falls from a seaside cliff and literally lands in Natasha's arms. Try as she might, from that moment on Natasha is unable to free herself from this baby, who, as she slowly discovers, is no ordinary offspring; indeed, he is a serial killer.

The extreme violence the baby wreaks disturbs on many levels, yet what perhaps strikes the viewer most is the abrupt change to Natasha's life, her complete lack of freedom, rest, and individuality. From the moment she becomes saddled with this baby, she is perceived by outsiders as a mother, nothing more. Eventually, a strange, older woman, Mrs. Eaves (Amira Ghazalla), comes into Natasha's life. Mrs. Eaves has spent the last half a century tracking this murderous baby with the ultimate goal of destroying him. Why she has made this her life goal remains unclear at first. Although burdened by her new role and unsure of what to do, Natasha is reluctant to assist Mrs. Eaves with the task of killing the baby. The infanticide of even a possessed baby seems unduly cruel to her. Though dark and gruesome, the first three episodes playfully balance heaviness with humor. Beyond that, Natasha's vexation at the situation and the baby is forcibly tempered by the ever-present threat of violence; she must stay calm because maternal anger can set off the baby, not dissimilar from the murderous dwarf-like children of Cronenberg's *The Brood*. However, the fourth episode, "The Baby," directed by Faraz Shariat, takes an even-darker turn as it jumps back in time to the 1970s to provide the origins of this baby and the history of his birth mother.

Shariat is a German Iranian director whose films frequently explore intersectional experiences of being queer and of color in a predominantly white society. Shariat directs episodes 3, 4, and 5 of *The Baby*. Episode 4 provides an origin story. It tells of Helen (Tanya Reynolds), a young, British woman stuck in an unhappy, traditional marriage in 1970s England. Helen, we quickly learn, is a lesbian and in love with Nour (the younger Mrs. Eaves, played by Seyan Sarvan) and soon runs away with her. But before Helen can sneak off into the night as the two had planned, her husband, Jack (Karl Davis), coerces her into having sex; as fate would have it, she becomes pregnant. As a married woman, Helen has scant freedom; as a mother-to-be, even less. Helen and Nour's love affair and freedom are thus short-lived. Helen is fired from her job at the library, and once her husband discovers she is pregnant, he sends the police to look for her at a women's commune, where she and Nour find a temporary home and relative safety from the outside world. Scenes in this commune, essentially a multiroom house shared by many women, mostly women of color, and in some cases their children, evoke the zeitgeist of the 1970s and the women's movement. Posters advertising readings by Lorde and performances by Nina Simone adorn the walls of the house. It is a commune for different kinds of kinship living and care, much in line with the endeavors toward the abolition of the traditional bourgeois family that upholds the housewife model and along with it oppression, sexual coercion, and even violence. As M. E. O'Brien emphasizes, "*Family abolition is the communization of care.*" Universal and unconditional, this care refuses "the harmful relationships of domination that the family form enables."[35] At first averse to Helen—a white, middle-class, married woman—upon her arrival, the women eventually embrace her and offer protection when the police come looking for her. However, the film also shows the fragility of this utopian world when pitted against the patriarchal outside—the fragility of women's rights and strength of their collectivity. Helen seeks an abortion, legalized within certain parameters under the Abortion Act of 1967 in Britain, only to wake up afterward still pregnant, having been abducted by her husband and his brother, who were apparently informed through a network of male doctors. The scene of Helen's awakening is the stuff of nightmares.

As Helen gradually comes to, the camera lingers on her face in close-up. A blurry reverse shot reveals two figures. Upon seeing her eyes open, one figure speaks to her directly. It is Helen's husband. In a patronizing tone, he attempts to reassure her: "You're safe now, Helen." The cruel irony of his words resonates: removed from short-lived freedom and safety among a community of women, Helen is now imprisoned in the domestic sphere by a husband she finds abominable. An overhead shot presents a Lynchian setting. Through a fish-eye lens we see a small room with red carpet. Ostentatious floral patterns adorn the wallpaper, the heavy curtains, and the bedspread. The bed is flanked with bouquets in a manner reminiscent of a funeral parlor. This allusion is compelling; Helen's fate is sealed. Here she must stay and bear out the pregnancy.

Once the baby is born, Helen refuses to have anything to do with it. It clearly repulses and angers her. To mother this baby has literally meant a complete loss of her liberty, love, and self-will. For as a mother, she is held prisoner through an extreme form of "reproductive coercion." The abusive act of forcing women—directly or indirectly—to give birth, reproductive coercion is linked to intimate partner violence. Defined by Karen Trister Grace and Jocelyn C. Anderson as "behavior that interferes with the autonomous decision-making of a woman, with regard to reproductive health," reproductive coercion is more common than one might think and certainly not a phenomenon of an earlier period.[36] From the coercive sexual act to the hindering of abortion and, finally, compulsory childbirth, Helen's autonomy is completely wrenched from her. The baby symbolizes this deprivation, this abuse. It becomes abject in her eyes. First as a whisper and then in a desperate yowl, "Get him off me!" Helen cries in response to her sister-in-law's insistence that she at least hold the baby. "You're a monster!" the sister-in-law declares, and she scoops the baby up again. A perfect embodiment of what Christina Mundlos calls mother terror, the sister-in-law judges, polices, and reproaches Helen for not only being a bad mother but also for rejecting her supposedly natural role of motherhood.[37]

Captivity, abuse, postpartum depression: Helen is pushed to the brink. Only then does she embrace her monstrousness—that is, her monstrous rage. She hatches her plan to escape. Left alone with her sister-in-law, while her husband and his brother attend the funeral of their father, Helen requests to make a phone call to her sister, who she claims has a birthday. The spiteful sister-in-law insists on dialing the number herself and then dialing back once Helen has finished her conversation. On the other end is Nour. Before the sister-in-law has time to admonish or punish, Helen stabs her in the neck with one of her own knitting needles. Enough is enough. After over a year of entrapment, the terror has to stop. Helen lingers only briefly at the crib of the baby but makes no effort to bring him along. Meeting her husband unexpectedly on the stairs, Helen pushes him down and rushes past. She escapes to the cabin near the sea, to the place to which she and Nour had first run off. There they meet again. The respite is brief. Helen's burden quite literally follows her. That same night the baby inexplicably appears in the cabin. It was all for naught; Helen realizes that she will never be free and drowns herself in the sea. Shrouded in horror, we take it as given that *The Baby* exaggerates and indulges in shock and violence. Yet, nearly every element of this episode seems tragically true to life, even the reappearance of the baby at the end, which symbolizes the ghastly and inescapable weight of motherhood—chosen or not. Lucy Mangan goes as far as classifying the series as a documentary: "In fact—at least to those mums who would not classify ourselves as earth mothers—it is more or less documentary."[38]

Maternal rage manifests in this episode of *The Baby* as the rage against patriarchy, which forcibly mandates how women should live, whom women should love, when women should have children and with whom, and, finally, how women should mother those children. Maternal rage arises from the expectation that women should mother—perceived by many as their ultimate purpose in the world. This is nothing new. Feminist thinkers have long drawn our attention to these issues. In her chapter on

"The Mother" in *The Second Sex*, Beauvoir opens with the following line: "It is through motherhood that woman fully achieves her physiological destiny; that is her 'natural' vocation." She continues: "Indeed, from childhood woman is repeatedly told she is made to bear children, and the praises of motherhood are sung; the disadvantages of her condition—periods, illness, and such—the boredom of household tasks, all this is justified by this marvelous privilege she holds, that of bringing children into the world."[39] Beauvoir's words still hold relevance today, particularly, in light of new and persisting antiabortion laws in the United States and elsewhere. In 1986 Rich writes: "The antiabortion movement trivializes women's impulses toward education, independence, self-determination as self-indulgence. Its deepest unwritten text is not about the right to life, but about women's right to be sexual, to separate sexuality from procreation, to have charge over our procreative capacities."[40] *The Baby* responds to all of this. Despite the ostensibly historical setting of episode 4, the story is by no means anchored in the past; it endures. If anything, it displays the provenance of enduring maternal rage against patriarchy, embodied by Helen's husband, his brother, the doctors, the police, and even the perpetually pregnant sister-in-law (patriarchy's handmaiden). Helen's story is not unique. In a subsequent episode, the basic plot of Helen's story resurfaces as that of Natasha's estranged mother, Barbara (Sinéad Moira Cusack), who we learn also abandoned Natasha and her sister when they were young because she simply could not cope. The burden of motherhood was too great.

In certain ways, *The Baby* and the story of Helen, in particular, presents a reimagined version of Roman Polanski's early horror classic *Rosemary's Baby* (1968) about a young married couple who move into an apartment in Manhattan and have strange encounters with the neighbors. The wife soon becomes pregnant under unsettling circumstances and begins to suspect that her neighbors are part of a satanic cult and have plans for her unborn child. She is gaslighted, treated as though hysterical by her husband, doctors, and outsiders. When she finally gives birth, her suspicions are confirmed: her baby is monstrous. A trajectory of what Lucy Fischer calls "an odious fable of parturition" certainly links the two: coerced conception, nightmarish pregnancy, and monstrous progeny.[41] Fischer also refers to *Rosemary's Baby* as a "skewed 'documentary' of the societal and personal turmoil that has regularly attended female reproduction."[42] The difference lies in Rosemary's and Helen's responses to both their captivity and their monstrous offspring. In *Rosemary's Baby*, the film concludes with Rosemary's relative acceptance of her alien child. Maternal love conquers all. Helen will have none of it. She retaliates and refuses to embrace the baby as her own; she would rather die than mother it. Maternal rage, not maternal love, unfurls as the outcome of this nightmarish tale of parturition. Rage may result in violence, as in the case of Helen, or not, as in the case of Natasha's mother and Natasha herself when she becomes strapped with the responsibility of caring for a baby out of the blue. The baby in this series represents the calamity of motherhood, especially when forced on women. Helen refuses to grin and bear its consequences. She becomes enraged. She fights. But the threat does not disappear; it persists and returns along with the baby. In true horror style, the baby returns in an epilogue to the final episode even after Mrs. Eaves has finally drowned him in an attempted murder-suicide (which she ultimately survives). The series rages against reproductive injustice with the recognition that it has still not disappeared.

From Maternal Ambivalence to Rage

Rage is borne of ambivalence in *Pieces of Her*. In this thriller series based on the best-selling novel of the same name by Karin Slaughter about a single, (purportedly) widowed mother, Laura (Toni Collette), and her adult daughter, Andy (Bella Heathcote), conflict arises after the mother effortlessly confronts and kills a homicidal gunman in a restaurant in their sleepy retirement town of Belle Isle, Georgia. Suddenly, the mother appears to be hiding something from her past, and the daughter is determined to uncover her secrets. Gradually, together with Andy we learn that Laura (in actuality, Jane) became pregnant at a young age and brokered a deal with the FBI to assume a new identity in exchange for information about the ringleader (and her former lover and father of her child) of a radical political group. The group is sought, inter alia, in connection with the murder of Laura's pharmaceutical titan father. The mother-daughter relationship plays a central role in this series and presents a current example of what Marianne Hirsch calls the "mother/daughter plot," an important narrative that reframes traditional familial structures and focuses instead on mothers and daughters, a perspective long neglected and still not that common.[43] Even in this book, the films about mothers and their sons outnumber those about mothers and their daughters.

The premise of the mother's double life provides a compelling means of addressing another side of motherhood so often unheeded and silenced. Maternal anger acts as a means of overcoming silence. When Laura speaks out in anger, she also reveals parts of herself, pieces of her life and past. Coming to voice through anger recalls Marilyn Frye's discussion of feminist anger as a speech act. By speaking out in anger, "you do not just assert or report something about yourself, you also reorient yourself and another person to each other."[44] Ahmed, likewise, takes up Frye's claim and her important reassessment of anger as an address to someone and not just a random act.[45] Thinking about anger as performative, in the sense of J. L. Austin, as a speech act with illocutionary force does come with conditions, however. As Frye indicates, anger does not "'come off' if it does not get uptake."[46] If the addressee (mis)reads the anger as just a burst of personal emotion detached from a social act, then anger as a speech act can fail. Such is frequently the fate of women's expression of anger when voiced outside certain domains deemed feminine.[47] Misread or not, the speech act of anger, nevertheless, becomes an assertion of subjectivity. As Hirsch puts it, "To be angry is to claim a place, to assert a right to expression and to discourse, a right to intelligibility."[48] With this assertion, Hirsch reinterprets Frye's concept of anger as an "instrument of cartography" as more than just "the limits of the intelligibility of our anger" and, instead, claims it as a means "to map the subjectivity of those who are denied it by culture and discourse; in this case, mothers."[49]

In the thriller series *Pieces of Her*, maternal rage works in subtler ways compared to the earlier examples explored in this chapter. Laura gives vent to her anger without violence. Yet, this emotion's affirmation of subjectivity here shores up no less force. From the beginning, Laura displays her frustration with her daughter. Already in her early thirties, Andy has recently moved from New York City back home, where she has taken up shift work as a dispatcher for nonemergency calls at the local police station. Laura wants more for her daughter. She also wants space for herself; after all this time, she wants a life not entirely determined by her role as mother. This becomes especially apparent in the seventh episode during a series of flashbacks from Laura's perspective. She recalls a period several years prior when she was battling breast cancer and had to regularly undergo chemotherapy treatment at the hospital. Andy had come home at that time, too, in order to care for her mother. Through various conflicts and intimations of histories, the series of scenes in the hospital raises the topic of both feminist and maternal anger.

In an initial scene in the hospital, Laura sits in her chemotherapy chair as Andy hovers around her adjusting this and that. Laura becomes irritated: "Andy, go home," she entreats. The daughter resists and instead goes to wait for her mother in the cafeteria. Andy's obduracy lingers as a source of annoyance even after she finally leaves. Laura sets about reading her book, Toni Morrison's *Beloved*. The canonical American novel about a mother haunted by the past and her murder of her eponymous daughter, Beloved, in order to spare her the horrors of enslavement, it is also one of the most complex portrayals of filicide and the mother-daughter relationship in Western literature. The novel's appearance in this series about a mother and daughter is not merely coincidental. Never openly discussed, the visual citation of the novel does not draw a straightforward analogy between Sethe's (the mother in Morrison's novel) story and Laura's story. These two mother-daughter plots are incommensurable. However, the shared themes of maternal ambivalence and even anger between the novel and the series are notable. If the picture pop-up book in *The Babadook* (specifically designed for the film) presents a literary mise en abyme of filicide in that horror film, then here *Beloved* evokes the subject and its historical entanglements without drawing direct connections. In her investigation of "the dark side of motherhood," Almond considers one way of reading the novel as through the tension of what she describes as "the narrow and shifting border between maternal love and protection and maternal possessiveness and unconscious aggression."[50] Such tension arises in the series and plays out in the expression of rage.

On another occasion, again seated in her chemotherapy chair and looking increasingly frail, Laura watches television footage of the women's march on Washington, DC, the day after the inauguration of Donald J. Trump as president in January 2017. A sea of pink pussyhats fills the embedded diegetic screen as Laura looks on. The camera lingers. This embedded image of the largest single-day protest in US history, when women marched in outcry against Trump's antifeminist and overall hateful rhetoric and policies, serves as a reminder of feminist activism and mobilization—even the possibility and legitimacy of women's anger when rights are breached. In a reverse wide shot, Laura slouches in her chair, legs elevated, bundled in blanket and scarf. She, too, dons a wool hat, but it is not pink; it is not a symbol of protest. Instead, it covers her completely bald head—a result of the chemotherapy. A shadow figure of this protesting crowd, she is frail, immobile, seemingly powerless. With lips pursed and eyes squinted, Laura glowers. The patient next to her, Gloria (Genevieve Lemon), begins prattling on about a planned trip to Disney World with her grandchildren. Laura quickly grows irritated and snaps at her: "Oh, for Christ's sake, will you shut up? You're not gonna ride Space Mountain or take selfies with Jiminy Cricket, or see those stupid fireworks, because you're not going to Disney World. You're dying. . . . I'm dying. That's why we're here stuck in these goddamn poison chairs. So just please stop chattering. You're giving me a fucking headache." Witness to her mother's outburst, Andy finally, hesitantly enters the room from her position in the doorway. Gloria grows silent. Andy attempts to remove her mother's food tray, and Laura snaps at her, too: "Leave it!"

Ahmed introduced us to what she calls "the feminist snap." A breaking point and a potential embrace of anger, the snap can present a response and call to action; it "is about how we collectively acquire tendencies that can allow us to break ties that are damaging as well as to invest in new possibilities."[51] The televised women's march gives cause to consider the collective call to action in this scene. Women snapped at residual and rising antifeminism and hate. Ahmed does not automatically link snapping to an outburst of anger, however; the feminist snap could also just be provoked through irritation.[52] According to Sianne Ngai, irritation is that "minor negative affect," that not-quite-anger.[53] Not exactly an affect, irritation develops more as an objectless mood.[54] At the same time, the appearance of Morrison's novel signals more severe machinations of the snap. Variable in its motivation, the feminist snap can, likewise, have minor or major consequences. But Laura's snap here certainly builds to an outburst of anger in the following scene.

Later that same day, mother and daughter exit the hospital. Andy reproaches her mother for her cynicism and for not even trying to fight the cancer. Laura responds apathetically at first: "Can we please just go home." She turns and begins to walk away, but Andy forces her back. "Mom!" she declares. Called out by both this name and the assertion of identity in a kind of interpellation, Laura stops in her tracks, turns, and responds in rage: "Well, maybe I didn't think my life would end up this way." Andy takes this as her mother's dissatisfaction with her as a daughter and the assumption that her mother's only identity is that of mother. Laura rebukes this view of motherhood as women's destiny and "natural vocation," echoing Beauvoir. In Laura's words: "Contrary to what you may think, my life didn't begin the moment you were born. Not everything about me is about you." Rich called this the first "unexamined assumption," to wit: "that a 'natural' mother is a person without further identity."[55] As Sarah LaChance Adams indicates, "mothers need independence from their children—including alone time, a sense of boundaries, and opportunities to flourish outside of mothering activities."[56] In flashbacks, we learn that Laura became pregnant by accident and at a young age. Her lover and the father of her child also turned out to be physically abusive. Indeed, he is the person from whom she erstwhile sought protection. Through anger, Laura releases frustration, but she also asserts a right to expression and a right to subjectivity both with and apart from her identity as a mother.

Throughout the film, Laura demonstrates an ambivalence toward motherhood. Laura loves and protects her daughter, but she also loathes her constant presence, clinginess, and lack of independence. Despite the series's balance of screen time and points of identification between mother and daughter, from beginning to end the mother remains the stronger, wiser, and more sympathetic character who must constantly swoop in and save her daughter, a good-natured but utterly naïve, weak, and unresourceful young woman whose curiosity and trustful nature consistently give rise to trouble. Online critics of the series have remarked on how infuriatingly incompetent the daughter appears to be; that is, I believe, the point. Laura grapples with the unyielding grasp of both a past life and a needful daughter. As an audience, we can identify with Laura's ever-building frustration and finally vexation with Andy.

Pieces of Her investigates the complexity of motherhood and the ambivalence it can engender: the love and the hate, the delight and the rage. It does not tap into the darker side of maternal rage the way *The Babadook* and *The Baby* do, but it does draw on this possibility. Most important, its mother-daughter plot unravels against a broader history of the precarity of women's rights and especially the entanglements of race. In these hospital scenes where maternal anger percolates, signs of history and its politics inundate. From the appearance of Morrison's canonical novel *Beloved* to the live broadcast of the 2017 women's march on Washington, which was a powerful movement but also perceived as a "white women's march," not inclusive enough in its activism and solidarity, the political very much comes to bear on the personal struggles of Laura, inter alia, as a mother.[57] Maternal anger is far-reaching; it must be. Praised for her candid and insightful writing on motherhood, Sara Petersen's confessional embrace of maternal anger emerges from the personal but indicatively extends well beyond her own experiences of motherhood. She relates:

> I feel angry often.... I'm angry that my desire to give the best of myself to my kids fights against my desire to give the best of myself to my work. I'm angry that my husband doesn't feel this same warring of selves.... I'm angry that any woman sobs alone and unsupported as she battles postpartum depression. I'm angry that women are forced to work while still bleeding from childbirth. I'm angry that mothers are being torn from their children at the border. I'm angry that child care is unaffordable for many. I'm angry about the shameful mortality rate of black mothers. I'm angry about our nation's laughable stance on family leave. I'm angry that we're even talking about birth control.[58]

Petersen speaks to and with collective anger. Beyond ambivalence as a psychological or ethical maternal position of "mixed feelings," she embraces anger explicitly as a politics. Such outrage at the gendered and racialized limits of the world comes forth in the series as well, albeit through visual hints as much as verbal expression. In its wide range of citations, *Pieces of Her* pays witness to different manifestations of maternal anger. The historical as well as the political context provided by the placement of Morrison's novel and the nested image of the women's march reinforce Laura's anger in her position as woman and mother. If nothing else, these scenes evoke Julia Lesage's injunction that "we must understand the different structures behind different women's rage," for "[i]f we do not understand the unique social conditions shaping our sisters' rage, we must run the risk of divisiveness, of fragmenting our potential solidarity."[59] To propose that *Pieces of Her* earnestly addresses the divisiveness of social conditions would accord far too generous a hand to the series, whose gestures do not entirely deflate at closer examination but also do not fully develop into political lessons. Overall, however, we come to grasp Laura's expression of anger as at the very least suggestively self-conscious, political, and even collective, not simply as individual, remarkable, or monstrously grotesque.

Distinctive in their manifestations and compelled by diverse genre expectations, the films considered in this chapter come together in their performance of maternal rage. Influenced by feminist anger and its political possibilities, embraced especially by Black feminists, maternal rage similarly addresses the struggles and injustices of women as mothers in patriarchal society. Yet, unlike feminist rage, maternal rage has received scant attention beyond portrayals of nightmare or revenge and is nearly always embedded within the horror plot. Certainly, the threat of filicide and other acts of violence against one's own child never strays far from depictions of maternal rage. The Medea figure of the mother who kills her two sons to exact retribution for the deceit of their father haunts most depictions of maternal rage and its reverberations—the darker side of motherhood or, as Rich contends, a threat to the institution of motherhood.[60] *The Babadook*, *The Baby*, and *Pieces of Her* also contain reminders of this legacy, both directly and indirectly. Violence hangs in the air. These portrayals diverge from traditional representations in their rendering of the mother as a sympathetic figure given to anger for identifiable and comprehensible reasons. Her anger can be attributed to injustice and frustration; her snap often comes as no surprise at all. She is not a monstrous figure; she is rather a woman pushed to the brink. Rage becomes her only recourse and her only means of asserting her subjectivity.

Maternal rage courses through many of the films in this book and will return in snippets, especially in the analysis of shame and guilt. Lynne Ramsay's *We Need to Talk about Kevin* (2011), Maggie Gyllenhaal's *The Lost Daughter* (2021), and Alice Diop's *Saint Omer* (2022), discussed in later chapters, also allow maternal rage to show and even fan out. This chapter offers a cross-section of a broader, albeit not overly capacious, cadre of contemporary explorations of rage. Picking up after rage, this book moves to that other historically negative affect, shame. In many cases, shame transpires from acts of anger. Both are of a piece with responses to the institution of motherhood and its sapping, gendered scripts.

CHAPTER FOUR

Shame

In their essay "The Fantasy of the Perfect Mother," Nancy Chodorow and Susan Contratto posit that "blame and idealization of mothers have become our cultural ideology."[1] There is no middle ground in motherhood; a mother is either good or bad, and quite often these two judgments are inextricably linked. Compared to other emotions examined in this book, shame acts differently. Unlike regret, exhaustion, or rage, shame stems directly from the implicit shaming by society that mothers relentlessly face. Constantly under the watchful eye of others and held up to impossible standards, some mothers cannot cope and slip up; sometimes they even succumb to failure or worse. "Mothers operate under the gaze of society," as Jean-Anne Sutherland writes, "a society that has adopted clear characterizations of the 'good mother.'"[2] As though the pressures to be a perfect, devoted, and self-sacrificial mother were not enough, with failure come blame and shame. "[I]dealization and blaming are two sides of the same belief," Chodorow and Contratto conclude; where there is one, there is also the other.[3]

By idealizing and blaming mothers, the gaze of society plays a pivotal role in the mechanisms of maternal shame, for shame stems from exposure and perceived judgment. We might say this makes it particularly interesting for film. Yet, shame has seldom served as the object of film and film studies scholarship. No filmmaking era or genre practices plot shame as a defining quality, contrary to what we have seen, to some degree with exhaustion and rage. Films about maternal shame thus promise (new) generative studies of affect and form. The films in focus in this chapter, Maria Speth's *Madonnen* (Madonnas, 2007), Savanah Leaf's *Earth Mama* (2023), Maggie Gyllenhaal's *The Lost Daughter* (2021), and Alice Diop's

Saint Omer (2022), answer this promise in different ways. Fiction films, they all explore maternal shame through various modes of storytelling. All four follow mothers who leave their children. And shame permeates their worlds, even, in the case of *The Lost Daughter*, years after they have left. Though not an outlier, Diop's feature takes the portrayal of child abandonment to more drastic ends in its story of a mother who yields her infant daughter to the ocean tide with the knowledge that she will die. This act of infanticide is also a kind of abandonment, a giving up in the face of insurmountable pressure. Although shame is not unique to films about motherhood, its significant role in these four films hints at an unmistakable thematic affinity. Much like the other affects considered in this book, shame is everywhere, and most films of this book's assemblage demonstrate episodes of shame. The inescapable fantasy of the perfect mother ensures shame's presence. None of the mothers featured throughout the chapters of this book is perfect. Let's face it: no one can live up to such a fantasy. Thus, mothers fail. With feelings of failure comes shame.

But shame is more than just the corollary of presumed failure. It is a highly complex emotion with a rich, discursive history. Before we jump into the specifics of maternal shame, we must pay heed to the expansive theories of shame that inform this reading both directly and indirectly. Moving away from themes of motherhood and film, shame's trajectory takes broad strokes. Nonetheless, it provides a framework within which we may more profoundly traverse the presence of shame in these films from ontological reckoning to social breakdown. We begin with philosophy of the twentieth century, for it seizes on shame beyond morality and advances other ways of understanding shame as more than simply the consequence of deviating from the norm. One of the first thinkers to illumine shame as more than just a social matter, Emmanuel Levinas brought it to bear on being itself. For Levinas, shame marks the affective mode of being riveted to oneself, unable to ever escape, forever bound to a presence that is a body. Embodiment as the expression of our being cannot help but manifest a kind of nakedness, an exposure that is shameful. "Shame arises each time we are unable to make others forget [*faire oublier*] our basic nudity."[4] The shame of the exposure of the body to others presents a linchpin to subsequent philosophical work on shame.

Picking up from Levinas, Maurice Merleau-Ponty and Jean-Paul Sartre turn their attention to the encounter with the Other as means of further figuring our philosophical understanding of shame. This encounter similarly becomes an occasion of exposure that for them turns more specifically on sight. When exposed, we are subject to the gaze of the Other. Merleau-Ponty calls this "the alien gaze."[5] Exposed under the alien gaze, the body becomes object, as does the self. Yet, this encounter and exposure in which shame arises assumes a Hegelian dialectic for Merleau-Ponty. The gaze can, of course, be returned, at which moment the locus of shame also shifts. That is not to say that shame gets passed back and forth; rather, it expresses the very dialectic of being and its plurality.[6] Sartre, likewise, explores shame as a consequence of exposure to the penetrating gaze of the Other and the vulnerability of the self that this encounter inspires. He calls this ontology the "being-seen-by-the-Other." In that famous example in *Being and Nothingness*, Sartre paints the scene of shame in which he is caught in the act of looking—that is, while surreptitiously peeking through the keyhole of a closed door. Through this example, shame characterizes the recognition of self as the object of the gaze, what Sartre defines as a confession: "I am this being."[7] However, this example of being caught in the act of doing something illicit—looking when one should not—also summons judgment on the part of the Other. According to Sartre, "[Shame] is the recognition of the fact that I *am* indeed that object which the Other is looking at and judging."[8] I dare say that the residue of the social—if not the moral—imperatives of shame lingers even to some degree with Sartre's existential theory of shame. But let us leave this unorthodox thought aside for the time being.

For contemporary discussions of shame, we frequently turn to affect theories and the pioneering work of Silvan Tomkins. What endures is attention to vision and the body. Unlike his philosophical predecessors, however, Tomkins turns his focus to the psychology and physicality of shame, especially how it manifests in and affects a person. For Tomkins, each affect is associated with a bodily response. Categorically negative, shame stems from inner torment produced by external forces and shows itself through facial gestures, in particular, downcast or averted eyes and blushing. "Shame," Tomkins asserts, "is the most reflexive of affects in that the phenomenological distinction between the subject and the object of shame is lost." Rather than pointing to external objects, shame calls attention to the self through the face and eyes. Increasing one's visibility, it "generates the torment of self-consciousness."[9] Going beyond Sartre's reinforcement of the subject and object and even Merleau-Ponty's dialectical volleying, shame, for Tomkins, collapses subject and object, and, in this wreckage, communication also halts. Tomkins ultimately characterizes shame as, above all, ambivalent. In this ambivalence, there is also a source for recuperation, according to Eve Kosofsky Sedgwick.

Unlike affects such as anger, shame has not played a major role in feminist discourse and politics, but it has been crucial for queer studies, beginning most prominently with the work of Sedgwick. A recuperation of shame as an affect that regardless of its negativity stimulates collectivity, Sedgwick's approach and attention to the vicarious nature of shame are instructive to a study of motherhood and these films. Stressing the break in communication and the feedback loop at the site of shame, Sedgwick offers an allegorical illustration. She describes her own feelings upon an encounter with the denuded New York skyline in the wake of 9/11. The unreturned gaze of the void where the Twin Towers once stood becomes a source of vicarious shame for Sedgwick: "I was ashamed *for* the estranged and denuded skyline."[10] Her perceived assignment of a circumscribed object to shame—the missing Twin Towers—has also opened up her illustration to criticism. Joan Copjec insists, "Shame is intransitive."[11] Sedgwick's example certainly perplexes; however, it does not straightforwardly assign an object to shame. The missing Twin Towers are not the source of shame for Sedgwick; rather, the vicarious "for" matters here. Lauren Berlant instructively elucidates Sedgwick's scene of shame as "the experience of interest that a person holds toward an object after it turns its face away" or, simply, an "inexistent relationality and one-sided attachment."[12] Always occasioned by interest in another, shame attaches, but it does not directly reciprocate. Read within a longer history of shame, beginning with Levinas, Sedgwick's expressed shame *for* the denuded skyline may also present a metaphor for an encounter with nudity and exposure that is not one's own. Imagine the skyline were a disrobed person, bare where it was not before. Would that person not exhibit shame? Farfetched as it might seem, I dare us to ponder this possibility. In turn, the shame of exposure of that Other—be it person or thing—becomes contagious, not as an object (or illness) to be passed around but as a bodily performance that catches on.

Sedgwick's pursuit of shame as a performance that manifests itself on and by way of the body resonates with the medium of film. This chapter investigates the ways in which shame can perform on and with film. Not affixed to one body or even solely to the diegetic world, shame circulates in and beyond these films. Maternal shame is not about claiming an identity through shame the same way it has been for queer identity since Sedgwick; it does not constitute a recuperation of shame for political purposes or worldmaking. It mostly just crushes. Giving a stage to maternal shame, these films, nevertheless, provoke in their pursuit of a topic that does not hew to the fantasy of motherhood. If this fantasy requisitions an experience of motherhood defined by unconditional love, self-sacrifice, and happiness, these films tell the story of the collapse of these selfsame feelings, of self-interest, of deep unhappiness, and of a lack of unconditional love. And precisely at the wreck of the fantasy of motherhood accrues shame.

Frames of Shame

In the press booklet for *Madonnen* (Madonnas), German director Maria Speth describes her motivation for the film: "Everyone seems to know what a mother may or may not do. And the violation of these role expectations will be met with massive moral penalties."[13] The earliest film examined in this book, *Madonnen* presents an exploration of motherhood that predates both the onslaught of the regretting-motherhood debate in Germany and open discussions about the social pressures placed on mothers and the repercussions mothers face when they collapse under such pressures. *Madonnen* is essentially a film about bad mothering. The main character, Rita (Sandra Hüller, known more recently for her roles in *Tony Erdmann* [2016], *Anatomy of Fall* [2023], and *The Zone of Interest* [2023]), is a woman in her twenties and the mother of five children. She is unmarried. The children all hail from different, presumably brief, relationships. She has left the four eldest children, roughly between the ages of two and twelve, in the care of her own mother. Still an infant, only the youngest child remains with Rita throughout much of the film. Rita puts herself first, regularly partying, smoking, drinking, and consuming drugs. She borrows money from her mother allegedly to buy new shoes for her child but instead buys shoes for herself. Upon its release, newspaper headlines about the film read "Rabenmutter" (Raven mother), "Mama geht weg" (Mother goes away), and "In 'Madonnen' geht us um ein schwieriges Muttermodell" (Madonnas is about a difficult maternal model).[14] As chapter 1 discusses, the term "Rabenmutter" is uniquely German and serves as a rhetorical shaming device against mothers who not only abandon or neglect their children but who also might simply not hold the role of motherhood above all else or adhere to the sacrificial maternal role imposed on them by society. *Madonnen* is a portrait of a mother who experiences shaming and feels shame because she rejects this maternal role.

Speth complicates and critiques the idealized image of the mother beginning with the film's title. As she explains in an interview, the title should provoke and interrogate popular notions of motherhood: "The title of the film is meant to be provocative. Rita is a very different kind of mother than symbolized through the 'Madonna with child.' . . . In other words, the absolute embodiment of the mother. I wanted to place the character of Rita in tension with this."[15] Rita hardly represents a traditional madonna figure, but Kira Hussing draws our attention to the telltale madonna iconography in the film. Further scrutiny indeed reveals an occasion of shame. Rita evokes the nurturing *Madonna del Latte* (Nursing Madonna) in an early sequence while in France during a surprise visit to her estranged father when she dons a blue hooded housecoat reminiscent of Mary's light-blue robe in many representations.[16] In one striking scene, Rita sits on the couch next to her teenage half-brother and nurses her infant son, J. T. What strikes us is the public exposure of Rita's body and her absence of modesty, so often demanded of mothers. Rita appears to wear only undergarments underneath the housecoat. Although not in a public place, Rita's bodily exposure in the house of this family she has only just met and in view of her teenage half-brother, who repeatedly steals glances at her body, comes across as inappropriate. Mothers who breastfeed in public are frequently made to feel shame for not living up to the social standards set for mothers to be nonsexual and modest.[17]

The shame of the scene escalates when another iconographic image of the Madonna is evoked; namely, the *Lactatio Bernardi* or the *Lactation of St. Bernard*, a variation of the *Madonna del Latte*. In traditional iconography, Madonna performs a miracle by squirting breast milk (from a decorous distance) into the mouth of St. Bernard and curing him of an eye infection. In the film, the half-brother asks what breast milk tastes like and then if he may try. Unlike St. Bernard, he leans down and begins to suckle directly from Rita's breast, which makes her giggle. The miracle of rehabilitation turns sexual in this reperformance. When the boy's mother enters the room and catches sight of this act of lactation, she looks on with dismay and swiftly exits. The half-brother pulls away, head hanging in shame, and Rita quickly covers up. The act results in Rita's being kicked out of the house by her father and even deported back to Germany on account of her criminal record. Her father, we learn, is a policeman and uses his power to ensure that Rita will not return.

Madonnen conjures the epitome of maternal virtue through these painterly intertexts only to frustrate it at the same turn, not dissimilar to Angela Schanelec's maternal figure in *Ich war zuhause, aber...* (I was at home, but ..., 2019), explored in chapter 2. Exhorted to provide nourishment to their children but expected to do so modestly and privately, mothers constantly confront irreconcilable demands vis-à-vis breastfeeding. Engulfed by the shaming gaze, Rita's bodily response does not follow the characteristics described by Tomkins. Instead, she frequently puts on airs of indifference—as she does in the scene in which she is caught in the act of breastfeeding—or lashes out in anger. We are reminded of Levinas's discussion of shame as the affect that one seeks to hide both from others and from oneself.[18] Rita's refusal to corporeally respond to shame in common ways with head sunken, skin flushed, and eyes averted—dare we say, her shamelessness—leaves shame to diffuse into the scene and into the entire mood of the film. The tentacles of shame have a far reach. We feel ashamed for her.

"Are you ashamed of me?" Rita asks her mother during a brief, almost hostile, visit. Now back in Germany, Rita resides in a minimum-security prison for mothers. She receives no response to her question, leaving it hanging in the air. Does she also ask us? Certainly not oblivious to shame, Rita negotiates it and, at pivotal moments, hews to the role that society demands. Once released from prison, she needs both a place to live and a means to support herself. She looks for an apartment and lies to the rental agent about her marital status. Accompanied by a man who appears just once in the film, Rita explains that this is her husband but that the lease should be under her name. Thereafter, she seeks unemployment and childcare benefits, giving a fabricated story about a recent return from a failed marriage in the United States and claiming that she only has three children. As Hussing relates, though lying to the rental agent probably helped her situation, Rita does not have to lie about the number of her children, her marital status, or her prison sentence to the authorities. The state is obligated to provide her support.[19] Rita tells these lies out of shame or in the effort to evade the shaming gaze. She does not want the clerk in the public office to know that she is the mother of five children; that would be too many. She also doesn't want her to know that she is an unmarried mother; that would be improper. Finally, she does not want her to know that, as a mother, she also served a prison sentence; that would be criminal. Although any person, mother or not, might hide a criminal past out of stigma and shame, Rita's identity and performance of self—no matter how hard she fights it—are so entangled with her maternal role that it becomes difficult to determine the exact motivation for her behavior and actions. For over the first half of the film, Rita is hardly ever without J. T. Held in a front-facing baby carrier or later on her hip, J. T. is an extension of Rita's body. With no other options, she also brings him with her when she parties at night. *Madonnen* does not allow us to imagine Rita as anything other than a mother. At the same time, the film unapologetically presents Rita as a kind of outlaw and vagabond, reminiscent not only of Agnès Varda's Mona in *Sans toit ni loi* (Vagabond, 1985) but also of other figures Speth creates in her films, such as Lynn from *In den Tag hinein* (The days between, 2001) and the later character Ines from *Töchter* (Daughters, 2014).[20] Rita plays with expectations and challenges our perceptions of motherhood.

To be fair, Rita does attempt to turn over a new leaf after prison. She leases an apartment and eventually brings all of her children to live with her. With the help of a new boyfriend, Marc (Coleman Orlando Swinton), an American soldier posted at a base nearby, she briefly fashions a domestic world more in line with society's expectations. But quotidian family life quickly tires and bores Rita, and no sooner does this fragile world begin to fray does Marc also announce that he will soon return to the United States. In contrast to Rita, he is the one shown playing with the children, feeding them, and teaching them games and English words. So, Rita gives up. In a brief scene in a restaurant, photographed exclusively from outside and out of earshot of the actions and conversations indoors, we see Rita with her children and her mother seated together at a table, having a meal. Within less than a minute, Rita rises from her chair, places J. T. on her mother's lap, and moves toward the back of the restaurant, presumably to use the bathroom. Shortly thereafter, however, we see Rita leave the restroom and surreptitiously proceed toward the restaurant's side exit. Head down, she leaves without looking back. By leaving, she abandons her children—now all five—once again to her mother. Observing the scene from a distance and mediated through the deadening glass of the restaurant's windows, the image ostensibly eschews heavy emotion and judgment for Rita's actions. The image creates a palpable distance between itself and the scene of abandonment.

Throughout the entire film, the camera keeps its distance. Cinematographer Reinhold Vorschneider, Speth's regular collaborator and an important contributor to the German film movement the Berlin School (mid-1990s–2010s), to which Speth is also linked, is known for his aesthetic of observation and duration.[21] As Brigitta Wagner writes, "Vorschneider excels at long takes; static, contemplative shots with an often hand-held camera; subtle adjustments of focus; and gentle, sometimes imperceptible mobile framing that registers slight shifts in the relations between characters or between characters and the spaces they inhabit."[22] Vorschneider avoids proximity. Close-ups are rare, and if he does capture a figure in close-up, it is always from the side or the back. He also avoids shot-reverse-shot sequences that might give rise to connection or sympathy with the figures, Marco Abel further elucidates.[23] We are meant neither to sympathize nor judge. Speth makes this much clear: "It was very important to me to neither morally judge nor to emotionalize in a certain direction."[24] But shame works in mysterious ways. The more the camera retreats, severs communication, and averts its gaze from the action, the more shame actually accumulates in the film. Cinematography creates cinematic meaning. Vorschneider's awkwardly long takes unsettle and allow this shame to build. Wagner calls Vorschneider's frame "didactic," insofar as it instructs us how to look differently; but what if, at least in *Madonnen*, it is also "ashamed"?[25] Ashamed by what it observes? A return to Rita's earlier cited question presents a reevaluation: is perhaps *the camera* ashamed for her? Elspeth Probyn explains that the root of "shame" is *"Scham,"* the Old English as well as the contemporary German word for shame, meaning to cover the face.[26]

Shame's etymological act of covering finds form in Vorschneider's oblique gaze—from adjacent rooms, around corners, and through windows—as a frame of shame in *Madonnen*. One remarkable instance captures Rita and a fellow inmate at a distance through multiple diegetic frames as they are admonished and disciplined for staying out past curfew at the women's detention center (fig. 4.1).

The film's frames of shame document the life of a young mother unable to put her children's needs before her own and, therefore, unable to live up to the standards society sets for mothers. It does not ask about the fathers or linger on their absolute absence and lack of responsibility. To a large degree, society cares little about the paternal role and, if so, only representationally. Mothers continue to shoulder the burden of child-rearing. Different from the other films discussed throughout this book, including in this chapter, *Madonnen* also does not convey the toll of the burden of motherhood and the unrealistic expectations it places on Rita. If anything, the film shows this side of motherhood via Rita's mother (Susanne Lothar), who always appears drawn. It is she who must discipline the children when they throw a birthday party without parental supervision or when the eldest, Fanny, runs away to look for her mother. We never learn why exactly Rita abandons her children. Hussing proposes reading the film

FIGURE 4.1. The frames of shame in *Madonnen*. Directed by Maria Speth, 2007.

through the lens of maternal regret. However, according to Hussing, this regret turns on ambivalence: Rita is torn by her love for her children and her unhappiness in the maternal role.[27] I think it is fair to say that Rita likes the idea of being a mother but not the reality of such a responsibility. But the film ultimately does not permit access to Rita's heavily, even aggressively, guarded inner world. "You never speak about yourself," Marc says, "nor do you speak about the children." "Because there's nothing to tell," Rita responds indignantly. Rita remains inscrutable. Thinking about *Madonnen* through shame does not explain Rita's actions or her refusal to acquiesce to the expectations of motherhood. That is not the point. It does offer insight into the heavy mood of the film, so attuned to the microaggressions Rita battles. Attention to shame raises important questions about how we view mothers and—consciously or not—assign expectations about how they should act and care for their children. These impossible expectations borne of a fantasy of motherhood, of its institution, can only lead to feelings of shame.

Shame That Crushes

Oakland, California: A medium shot of a woman standing against the backdrop of a sparsely decorated room, to one side a white board, above a large scoring board. We learn later that this is the bare and cool interior of a community center. An off-screen voice almost provokes: "Why should we care if you make it?" There is no reverse shot; the camera stays fixed on the standing woman. She remains there, alone, the central point of our gaze and our scrutiny. The woman responds uncomfortably, avoiding the gaze of the camera, casting her eyes downward and to the side, hands in her pockets. She explains that she doesn't care if we care or not; this is her path, and no one will ever know what it feels like to walk in her shoes. Before the scene cuts out, she adds in a metacritical, even metacinematic, gesture of resignation: "When everybody got an opinion, judgment . . . like they God. Okay." With this establishing shot, *Earth Mama* (directed by Savanah Leaf, 2023) casts an observational documentary aesthetic of austerity. Filmed on 18 mm print, the image appears almost grainy, its colors muted.[28] More important, though, it establishes the mechanics of shame as an intrusive gaze and an anonymous—dare we say, acousmatic—voice that judges. The woman is exposed, made object to an "alien gaze," and rendered through the Sartrean logic: "I am indeed the object which the Other is looking at and judging."[29] She is rendered self-conscious. The woman does not appear again in the film; she serves to set the tone: a Black woman exposed and forced to account for herself.

Juxtaposed with *Madonnen*, British-American filmmaker Savanah Leaf's more recent debut drama, *Earth Mama*, about the struggles of a single Black mother of two children in foster care and expecting a third, presents a possible study of both what happens when systemic racism enters the picture and the distinction between two national contexts and systems of care: Germany and the United States. That would assume that these two mothers were otherwise similar and their experiences of a world that shames them alike. Basic plot and thematic parallels do invite some reflection, but ultimately *Earth Mama* takes maternal shame in a different direction.

Twenty-four-year-old Gia (played by first-time actress Tia Nomore) is in a losing battle to reclaim custody of her two preadolescent children and to maintain guardianship of her unborn child. She works part-time in a mall portrait studio, attends court-ordered group therapy sessions and drug rehabilitation meetings, takes regular urine tests, meets with her children for supervised visits, spends her last dollars on a crib for her baby. Gia never stops moving in this film, but it's never enough. She can't make child payments because she can't work more hours with the many meetings and sessions she is forced to attend. She is caught in a vicious cycle in a system designed to make her fail. The weight of the world she inhabits and the history she embodies, as *New Yorker* author Richard Brody puts it, by far surpasses that of her heavy pregnant belly.[30] As her friend Trina (Doechii) powerfully declares: "There's a lot of people expecting us to fail. My whole life, I had shit taken away from me. They tried to take our culture. They tried to take our homes. Tried to take our freedom. And you know they try to take our babies, too. Same shit that's happening to us right now happened to your mama, to my mama, and it happened to their mamas. That's exactly why we can't stop fighting for our kids, G. It's our God-given right to have our kids."

Broadly, *Earth Mama* is a film about what Dorothy Roberts appropriately calls "the family-policing system" and "benevolent terror" in the United States, child protective services (CPS), a system that disproportionately targets Black families and single Black mothers.[31] In her monologue, Trina tells of the longer history of aggressive intervention in Black family life, from which the methods of CPS stem, holdovers of a devastating past. Black motherhood is an identity long splintered by the history of slavery. To be enslaved was, according to Saidiya Hartman, to *lose your mother* and all that that entails: "To lose your mother was to be denied your kin, your country, and identity. To lose your identity was to forget your past."[32] From capture and enslavement to the nonlineage of being born into this institution, slavery refused the child a mother as well as the mother the experience of motherhood. Even before the United States stopped importing enslaved Africans in 1808 and the efforts to reproduce the enslaved population intensified, the mechanisms of control over the enslaved woman's body to ensure reproduction were coercive, violent, and dehumanizing. Enslaved women were treated as "breeders" of new generations of enslaved persons and not as mothers of children.[33] As Hortense Spillers importantly summarizes, the child did not belong to the mother under slavery; the enslaved family is not a family of kinship relations. Reproduction certainly continued—it had to for the structure of slavery itself—but the experience of motherhood, caring for one's child, was denied.[34]

Christina Sharpe demonstrates that in the afterlives of slavery, Black motherhood continues to be challenged, if not utterly negated. She attends to Aereile Jackson, a woman interviewed in Allan Sekula and Noël Burch's *The Forgotten Space: A Film Essay Seeking to Understand the Contemporary Maritime World in Relation to the Symbolic Legacy of the Sea* (2010), which troublingly labels her a "former mother." Presently residing in a tent city between two container freight lines in California's Almeda Corridor, Jackson has lost everything, including her children. They were removed from her care. No longer the caretaker to her own children, she apparently ceases to be a mother, now only "former." Jackson's story is one of erasure. Not only subjected to the tragic loss of her children, she is also deprived of her identity as a mother. In an interview, cited by Sharpe, Jackson clutches an assortment of dolls: "This is the only thing that I have to hold on to for me to remember my children. I lost a lot and I'm homeless and I haven't seen my children since I was unable to attend court because I had no transportation."[35] Rendered childless by the state for no other reason than poverty, Jackson, like Gia, represents one example of many Black mothers in a longer history whose motherhood is systematically negated. Following the narrative logic of Jackson's story, Sharpe frames the complexity of the history and continuity of the denial of motherhood to many Black women.

Jennifer Nash's *Birthing Black Mothers* picks up the pieces of the history of Black motherhood in the present—that is, in the era of Black Lives Matter (BLM). Black mothers face the all-too-frequent loss of children through state intervention and racialized violence; they also confront high death rates through medical racism and obstetric negligence. As a result, Black mothers have become "icons of trauma, grief, heroism, and death."[36] They live in crisis. In 2018 the *New York Times Magazine* published a long-form article, "Why America's Black Mothers and Babies Are in a Life-or-Death Crisis," by Linda Villarosa. Garnering much attention, the article documented and revealed the long-neglected and growing issues of the gross social injustice Black mothers face. According to Villarosa, "Black infants in America are now more than twice as likely to die as white infants," a racial disparity that was actually smaller in 1850, she observes. Furthermore, high Black infant mortality is entangled with "a crisis of death and near death of black mothers themselves."[37] The critically acclaimed 2022 film *Aftershock* (directed by Paula Eiselt and Tonya Lewis Lee) documents the crisis of Black mothers with a focus on the catastrophic rates of postpartum death in the United States. "I don't think people understand how incredibly scary it is to make the decision to have a baby as a Black woman in this lifetime right now," *Earth Mama*'s Nomore concurs.[38]

But while recognition of Black women's motherhood as marked by unrelenting violence, coercion, and criminalization is critical, so, too, is an understanding of what it means to be an "icon" of such tragedy, as Nash puts it. As I have discussed throughout, mothers frequently become mere images and symbols—highly visualized and even admired but not agents of their own lives and destinies. Cast as icons, Black mothers become the site and spectacle of admiration and fascination as well as trauma, violence, and crisis, not to mention death. The politics of representation with which Nash also grapples informs us of the risk of resorting to an objectifying and fetishizing gaze at Black women's suffering. Under this gaze, agency and nuance disappear. *Earth Mama* not only presents the unique struggles of Black motherhood but the film also explores and critiques the mechanisms of the gaze as it shapes the experiences of Black mothers.

Earth Mama does not fit neatly into the framework of crushing motherhood this chapter sets up or in this broader book, for that matter, in which a mother cannot bear the burden of childcare and collapses under the plinths of unachievable fantasy. The challenges Gia faces extend well beyond those of the seemingly capricious Rita. Recall the similar struggles the maternal figure Inez confronts in *A Thousand and One*, explored in chapter 2. Gia desperately wants to be a mother to her children; she does not appear to be bogged down with fraught emotions about her children as such nor about her identity as a mother. The negative feelings about motherhood arise as a result of external factors, specifically the insidious tentacles of the US foster-care system and its discriminatory modus operandi. The demand on Gia to show beyond doubt that she is a decent mother is not merely implicit; she must also prove this tangibly and legally, a task that proves overwhelming and besieged with shame.

In the same way the film opens with the interrogation of a woman under what appears to be the judging gaze of an anonymous interlocutor, Gia's quotidian existence comes under regular scrutiny. She has no freedom and no privacy. There is always someone watching, judging, shaming. She can only visit with her two children under the watchful eye of a case worker. She must submit to regular urine tests, observed by another. In one scene, Gia drives home only to find CPS employees knocking on her door and peering through the window of her house. The gaze of the foster-care system contrasts with her own as an employee of a portrait studio. As part of her job, she must construct tableaux of happy couples and families. She instructs her subjects on their bodily performance for the camera but also ensures that they are comfortable. She engages with them, reassures them, enters the frame herself to make adjustments and give compliments. Hers is not the alien gaze but a tender one. Gia's gaze complements the film's own cinematography. Notwithstanding the telling interrogative gaze that opens the film and returns in the first part, *Earth Mama* bears witness to the threatening and stigmatizing gazes within this diegetic world without replicating them. The camera responds to this external bombardment on Gia by closing in on itself, by centering on her in close-ups and shallow focus. Compared to Vorschneider's reluctant and furtive camera in *Madonnen*, which presents Rita as inscrutable and impenetrable, *Earth Mama* mostly eschews long shots. In their place, it creates an intimate world that tenderly embraces. Rethinking the gaze beyond its freighted legacy of power relations, Muriel Cormican and Jennifer Marston William propose the tender gaze, which stunningly befits the cinematography of this film: "To gaze tenderly is to be moved by something. It involves intentionality: to gaze is to look at someone and contemplate that person's interiority. It involves evaluation and judgment: to gaze tenderly at someone is to see that person in context, as part of an ongoing narrative, and thus to humanize."[39] The soundtrack, too, sonically insulates with mostly calm experimental jazz and, twice, the dulcet tones of Bettye Swann's "Then You Can Tell Me Goodbye." In interviews, Leaf indicates that she did not want to retraumatize her characters. The film provides some beauty and escape from the outside world, albeit minor.

To inhabit this world, as Gia does, however, means to be subjected to its apparatus of control. The shaming gaze and voice remain. One scene follows Gia to the park. First, she watches parents with their children out of focus but not out of earshot. Then, she furtively bends down at an empty stroller and steals several diapers. She is caught in the act and pursued by disembodied voices of other mothers. "I can't believe it. Is that your stroller?" "Excuse me?" "Excuse me." "Excuse me!" "Stop!" "Are you fucking kidding me?" "Hey!" Drowning out all other sounds, the voices judge; they shame. Hurrying toward her car, diapers under her arm, Gia tries not to look back, tries to shut out the voices. The sonic finger-pointing follows her to her car until the voices finally climax in the deafening, mechanical honk of a passing train somewhere in the distance. From inside the car, the camera captures Gia in a close-up profile shot, eyes cast downward; her shame is palpable.

Although the diegetic gaze bespeaks the mechanisms of shame in *Earth Mama*, the disembodied voice is similarly threatening and powerful. The interrogating voice that opens the film, the accusatory voices in the park, and finally, the blank robot voice that resonates each time Gia makes or receives a call to remind her of her diminishing cell phone balance and that she must make a payment. Much scholarship exists on the mechanics, politics, and ideology of the disembodied voice in cinema. Most famously, Michel Chion discusses the disembodied, nonlocalizable voice in cinema as acousmatic and assigns to it four powers: "[T]he ability to be everywhere, to see all, to know all, and to have complete power. In other words: ubiquity, panopticism, omniscience, and omnipotence."[40] The voice inserts itself into Gia's enclosed world and judges and shames.

For fear that the foster-care industry will also seize control of her unborn child, Gia begins to feel like she has no other choice than to consider open adoption. She is tormented by the decision, however, convinced that she would be abandoning her baby. Her friend Trina, who sees it as every Black mother's resolve to "fight for her kids," condemns her and judges her: "G, you're about to make the biggest mistake of your life. Turning your back on your fucking kids? Your dumbass don't even deserve no baby. . . . Step up and be a fucking mother!" Already torn by the idea of giving up her child, her friend's brutal reprimand becomes too much for Gia, and she desperately lapses into drug use before being rushed to the hospital to give birth. Now she is left with absolutely no choice. Drug test results come back positive, and as the sympathetic but reproving social worker Miss Carmen (Erika Alexander) informs her, she must either give her child up for adoption, or the state will take custody. Grasping at the last shred of agency and dignity, Gia hands over her child to the adoptive family. Alone with her baby for the last time, in a wrenching scene of extreme close-ups, she bids farewell and apologizes many times over. If we have no access to Rita's inner world, then Gia is an open book that invites overwhelming empathy and vicarious shame, something that returns in *The Lost Daughter* and especially *Saint Omer*. Yes, we feel the shame, too.

To compare Gia's coerced surrender of her child to an adoptive family to Rita's impulsive abandonment of her children in her mother's care seems out of place. For both, abandonment, nonetheless, becomes a source of shame, which they bear in different ways. Shame often attaches itself to the rubric of motherhood through the imposition of unrealistic expectation and fantasy. Without dismissing the stakes of necropolitical threat against Black motherhood, we note that the manifestation of shame does not recede. The imperative toward resistance and survival despite all odds pursues Gia. Her feelings of shame are borne of the feelings that she gave up in the face of adversity, that she failed, alas, to fight enough. In this way, motherhood becomes an oppressive, shaming structure.

Maternal Shame and the Sublime

A gnawing sense of bathos accompanies American filmmaker Maggie Gyllenhaal's drama and debut film, *The Lost Daughter*. In many ways, the film builds up to a suspenseful thriller that does not deliver. From the outset, the flash-forward to the (presumed) death of the main character, Leda (by a stab wound to the abdomen), which opens the film against the warning wail of a foghorn, propels us into a teleological scavenger hunt for the film's duration. Beset by mystery and increasingly ominous events and encounters, much of the film does, indeed, shore up its grim opening. Leda (played by Olivia Colman in the present and Jessie Buckley in flashback) is a middle-aged woman and professor of comparative literature. She arrives on a Greek island for a working holiday alone. Based on the short novel of the same name by Elena Ferrante, already there is a hint of the literary hanging in the heavy Mediterranean air. But the literary intertexts do not stop there. Thomas Mann's modernist novella *Tod in Venedig* (*Death in Venice*) also lets itself be felt. We anticipate sublime unraveling; yes, even a death. From the bowl of rotting fruit in Leda's holiday apartment to the brash and chaotic extended Greek American family that moves into this otherwise idyllic beachside town, disturbing Leda's (albeit uneasy) relaxation, something sinister percolates. Despite all the signs and the growing suspense, however, *The Lost Daughter* does not reveal horrifying trauma, abuse, or evil. Instead, the deep, dark secret that gradually surfaces is that Leda once abandoned her children. Are these not rather low stakes? But as much as the revelation of maternal abandonment might seem overplayed here, upon further thought perhaps it is not. In a review of the film, Adrian Horton from the *US Guardian* tells us that Leda's gradual confession that she left her children for three years to pursue her own desires and goals gets at one of the most enduring taboos of our culture. Mothers who prioritize their needs over those of their children are labeled selfish, uncaring, mean, and even unnatural, terms Leda also uses against herself.[41] Leda dares to assert that motherhood did not bring her unequivocal happiness and fulfillment; it consumed and crushed her. Leaving it behind was, she exclaims, "amazing." Unrepentant, she unravels the myth of motherhood, its institution, its fantasy. And yes, she will be punished for this past transgression.

Among the rowdy group of Greek Americans that has descended upon the town and its beach are a young mother, Nina (Dakota Johnson), and her toddler daughter, Elena. These two immediately catch Leda's attention and trigger memories of her own earlier years of young motherhood. In a parallel film of flashbacks, forming a kind of double-helix plot structure, we learn about Leda's struggles as a fledgling academic and mother to two adolescent daughters and married to a man too wrapped up in his own academic career to notice that anything is amiss, to say nothing of sharing the task of parenting. The presence of Nina and Elena forces Leda to confront her past. Feelings of both tenderness and shame materialize and show on Leda's body. In an early scene, Leda sees mother and daughter for the second time, playing on the beach. Enveloped by cinematographer Helene Louvart's tight framing and mobile camera, mother and daughter appear ensconced in their own world. At first, this scene evokes an expression of wistful affection and sentimentality on the observer's face. In a subsequent shot, however, Leda's soft smile tightens; she lowers her eyes and turns her head. She must avert her gaze. So overwhelmed by what she sees and its effect on her, she must leave the beach in search of reprieve and a glass of water. What is it that has agitated Leda so? We slowly learn that it is the involuntary memory of shame. Dramatic music swells, and the first of many flashbacks appears. Cutting in and out is a scene of a mother and two toddler daughters also apparently at the beach and caught in gauzy, extreme close-ups as they cuddle and share an orange. The shame that encapsulates this scene derives not just from peering into the private world of others and being "caught in the act" of such voyeurism but in the exposure of the self that can follow. Leda becomes ashamed because she is also put on display in all her vulnerability as a mother. The shame of her actions and perceived failure still haunts—even traumatizes—her.

As the relationship between Nina and her daughter begins to show its less harmonious sides, including the daughter's brief disappearance and Nina's desperation, Leda's flashbacks also become increasingly frequent. Always returning to a similar period in the past, when Leda is in her twenties and her daughters are still young children, we witness her heightening exhaustion, frustration, and exasperation. "Children are a crushing responsibility," she tells the heavily pregnant Callie (Dagmara Domińczyk), the aggressively nosy matriarch of the Greek American clan. Paying heed to the film's release in the wake of the COVID-19 pandemic, Lydia Kiesling of the *New York Times* describes *The Lost Daughter* as "captur[ing] with uncanny precision one version of the multitasking mother and arriv[ing] on the heels of a year that many women with children will remember as one of the hardest of their lives."[42] In one flashback, in particular, young Leda's toiling comes to a head. Trying to finally attend to some academic work, she is torn away by a whining child. On the phone in the next room, her husband refuses to take time from what he is doing to see to the incident and demands that she go, even though it is his turn. "I'm working," he patently proclaims. "And I'm suffocating," she retorts. Her daughter Bianca has cut her finger trying to peel an orange. She repeatedly begs her mother to kiss her wound: "Mama, please can you kiss it?" Leda cleans and bandages the finger but withholds a kiss or any comfort. Instead, she turns her back on both her distressed daughter, who continues to whine, and on the camera and leans briefly against the kitchen counter, her head down. "I can't leave you alone for one minute," Leda mutters in quiet desperation.

Shame resurfaces in the present when Leda accidentally encounters Callie, her husband, Nina, and Elena in a toy store. Still upset about the loss of her doll (which Leda stole on the beach earlier in the week), Elena fusses uncontrollably. Callie asks whether Leda's daughters gave her a hard time when they were little, and Leda claims with apparent annoyance that she cannot remember. Callie does not accept that answer: "Oh, no, you can't forget anything about your own children," she rejoins. The scene becomes tense. In close-ups, Leda shifts uneasily. Communication flags. Now an apparent spectacle to Callie, her husband, and Nina, looking on suspiciously and disapprovingly in reverse shots, Leda becomes vulnerable and ashamed of this exposure. The scene painfully evokes Tomkins's description cited earlier of the torment of shame that turns so sharply on visibility, exposure, and self-consciousness.[43] Betrayed by her face, her flushed cheeks, her averted eyes, Leda cannot hide her shame. Attempting to flee this public scrutiny, she gropes her way toward the store's exit. On the way, she knocks over some merchandise and can only mumble that she was very tired. A series of unsteady, shallow-focus shots frame Leda's shame until she finally clamors out of the store and bolts into the rain. But her escape brings only temporary reprieve, for there is no escape from shame. This would mean an escape from oneself. "What appears in shame," Levinas reasons, "is thus precisely the fact of being riveted to oneself, the radical impossibility of fleeing oneself to hide from oneself, the unalterably binding presence of the I to itself."[44] Leda's entire trip assumes an air of impossible flight. No matter where she goes, she is unable to escape herself and her past.

Leda's fondness and sympathy for Nina in her struggles as a young mother grow. Leda eventually confesses to Nina (and by extension to us) her secret. She abandoned her daughters. In a shaky close-up, Leda's face tightens, her eyes begin to water, and, choking on the words, she croaks: "I left." In a reverse shot, Nina stares at her in quiet disbelief. "When the oldest was seven, and the youngest was five, I left," Leda adds, now on the verge of tears. "I abandoned them, and I didn't see them for three years." Nina attempts to react with sympathy but cannot conceal her disapproval. "That sounds awful." Following this revelation, there is a flashback to Leda's last visit and farewell to her daughters. The sequence is highly emotional, framed tightly, and captured mostly in intimate, shallow focus. Roberta Flack's sad soul tune "I Told Jesus" resonates extradiegetically in melancholic overtones. Throughout, Leda remains stoic and resolute, even when her husband begs her to stay. In a final act, she performs a shared ritual at her daughters' request: she peels an orange in a serpentine spiral. Lingering only briefly, she then rises and leaves without a goodbye or even looking back. The young Leda shows no emotion, but the scene has followed her into the present. It haunts her. Subsequent scenes in the present suggest that Nina has shared Leda's story with her family. Shaming, even menacing, stares from this brutish clan seem to follow her everywhere. Leda is defenseless; Leda is totally exposed.

When Nina visits Leda in her apartment to borrow the keys for a clandestine rendezvous with a beach worker, Will, we witness the film's final episode of shame. Leda returns Elena's doll to Nina and declares that she stole it with the half justification: "I'm an unnatural mother." As cruel as this act of stealing a child's favorite toy may be, we do not blame Leda or hate her for it. When Nina stabs Leda with a hatpin, this seems like a far crueler and certainly more violent retaliation than deserved. But does not Leda orchestrate this punishment? Perhaps out of shame or even guilt? It cannot be a coincidence that she gifted Nina the hatpin on the very occasion that she revealed to her that she abandoned her children. Leda's shame and self-deprecation derive from internalized social expectations of motherhood. Leda deems herself an unnatural mother because she was unable to embrace the role of caretaker above all else; she was unable to compromise her full personhood for the institution of motherhood.[45] For a "natural" mother, Adrienne Rich teaches us, "is a person without further identity."[46] Beyond the act of stealing the doll, we are given to question what an unnatural mother is, or better, what a natural one is. According to Gyllenhaal, the film "exposes the myth of the 'natural mother.'"[47] It demands that we recognize that these categorical binaries of natural and unnatural, of good and bad, are creations of the institution of motherhood and far from the real experiences of mothers. As critic Shirley Li puts it, "Leda actively tests society's definition of a mother—she loves her daughters, but she can't devote her entire self to them—and for that she carries pride and shame."[48]

Shame clings to the film not as a moral judgment but as a reminder thereof. A woman feels ashamed about her past as a mother who was not always there. Her shame stems from an internalization of society's gaze and expectations of women and mothers. Nina and know-it-all mother-to-be Callie exist solely as living reminders of motherhood's impositions on one's own psychic and physical needs.[49] As memories surge, and Leda reveals bits and pieces from her past, rapture but also shame engulf her, lest we forget that motherhood, as Jeannette Catsoulis writes of the film, "can plunder the self in irreparable ways."[50] *The Lost Daughter* is not simply about a woman unable to live with her own past transgressions; it also gets at the unassailable burden placed on mothers to perform this role in certain ways. Rich explains, "Institutionalized motherhood demands of women maternal 'instinct' rather than intelligence, selflessness rather than self-realization, relation to others rather than the creation of self."[51] We might note that by comparison, the property manager, Lyle (Ed Harris), who also reveals that he left his children with their mother in Philadelphia when they were young to come to Greece, does not appear to be battling with the shame of this act of pursuing his own desires. There is no such thing as institutionalized fatherhood, no sacred calling for fathers. Lyle presents nothing less than a Beauvoirian specimen of the man who wants a home but also seeks freedom and adventure in new places.[52] The disparity of the gendered disposition toward parenting returns in the following chapter with a closer look at Beauvoir's philosophy of ethics.

Leda's gradual revelations are not met with understanding or empathy in the film. She faces renewed judgment and even violence by those around her; consider also the errant pine cone that strikes Leda in the back earlier in the film. But we are not immune to her shame and the power of its vicariousness. Noted throughout, moments of heightened shame are shaped by the film's cinematography. The lingering close-ups on Leda's face exhibit intimacy: they elicit our discomfort but likewise our empathy. Caetlin Benson-Allott interprets Louvart's cinematography as emphasizing Leda's opacity and, therefore, affording her privacy, in particular, when she is besieged by invasive questions from Callie.[53] Yet, its proximity also reveals Leda's shame. In close-ups, we witness her struggle to deflect the penetrating stares of others and to unavailingly suppress her own bodily responses. Much like in *Earth Mama*, Louvart's camera in *The Lost Daughter* is intimate, even tender, in its rendering of Leda.[54] The tender gaze calls up the vicarious experience of shame and what Alice Kuzniar calls "the redeeming role played by empathy in shame."[55] In its complex circuitry, shame clings, engulfs, and enraptures in this film, leaving us upended in its sticky residue. In the final scene, Leda awakens on the shore to the ebb and the flow of the sea. She appears to have survived the stabbing and the subsequent car crash that brought her down to the shore in the first place. Her cell phone buzzes, and on the other end are her two daughters, eager to ensure that she is "alive" and well. Out of nowhere, an orange appears, and Leda begins to ritualistically peel it. Is this a fantasy in death? Or a fantasy only possible in death? Although it is not impossible to imagine that Leda could have survived the assaults of the night before, the inconsistencies of this final scene suggest otherwise. The fantasy of motherhood comes at a high price. Shame finds company in disgust in *The Lost Daughter* in chapter 5, together rounding out my analysis of this film seething with bad feelings.

Vicarious Shame

Based on the 2016 court case of Fabienne Kabou, who was accused of infanticide, Senegalese French filmmaker Alice Diop's first feature film, *Saint Omer* (2022), opens with an image of a woman moving steadily along a beach. In the near darkness of this opening image, we can only make out the contours of the woman's hair, profile, and hand against an object held tightly at her chest, presumably a swaddled baby. Barely visible but manifestly audible, breath matched with the rush of waves fills the soundtrack. But it's just a dream; Rama (Kayije Kagame) awakens with a start. The sequence then gives way to a view of a large, hanging screen in a lecture hall. Upon the screen appears black-and-white archival footage of so-called *femmes tondues*, French women condemned to public head shaving. Once shorn, the women are then paraded through the streets, flanked by cheering and sneering crowds. These are images of women reduced to a public spectacle of shame in the aftermath of World War II as punishment for either collaborating with or courting Nazi officers. Against this silent footage, which derives from Alain Resnais's *Hiroshima mon amour* (Hiroshima, my love, 1959), a voice (we learn later that it is Rama's) resonates as she reads from Marguerite Duras's screenplay for the film. In reverse shots, women students (exclusively) are captured in shallow-focus, medium close-ups as they watch and listen with earnest expressions. In closing her lecture on Duras, Rama explains her choice of images: "This woman, humiliated, distraught, marked like a prisoner. . . . This woman, object of shame, becomes, thanks to the words of the author, not only a heroine but a human subject in the state of grace [en état de grâce]" (fig. 4.2).

FIGURE 4.2. The *femmes tondues* in *Saint Omer*. Directed by Alice Diop, 2022.

Saint Omer is a courtroom drama about Laurence Coly (Guslagie Malanda), a woman accused of leaving her fifteen-month-old daughter to be swept up by the high tide on the beach of Berck-sur-Mer. A professor of literature and author, Rama attends the trial with the intention of writing a book about the case. The opening sequence and the reference to the historical shaming of women, not to mention the closing words of redemption in Rama's lecture, shape this film as a universal tale of women's shame and the significance of recasting historical narratives. The evocation of the subject "en état de grâce" cannot help but summon the immaculate image of the Madonna again. If Duras's words return honor to the once-shamed woman of *Hiroshima mon amour*, simply named "Elle" (She), who had a tragic love affair with a Nazi officer in France, then perhaps Rama as author will do the same for Laurence. Or perhaps the filmmaker herself, who, like Rama, attended the actual court case, will restore subjectivity and humanity (and possibly even the sacred) to Laurence both in the film and in real life.

There are certainly challenges to addressing the universality of this film's narrative, as the opening does. Reception of the film has drawn attention to its important exploration of race and the tarrying racist structures of French society and its judicial system. Black motherhood brings forth its own history, one that is not necessarily determined by but also cannot be easily disentangled from histories of colonialism, diaspora, enslavement, apartheid, and segregation, as well as persisting issues of medical racism and state-sanctioned violence, as *Earth Mama* also saliently illuminates in this chapter. Implicitly evoking these histories, Diop positions Laurence's story within a broader maternal archive in which motherhood brings extreme unhappiness and isolation and, with these, shame.

Not unlike the others, in this film, too, a mother abandons her child because she is unable to care for her. Yet, here the conditions and consequences of abandonment are much more drastic, for Laurence does not leave her daughter with her mother, her husband, or an adoptive family. She leaves her alone on the shoreline of a beach to be carried away by the tide. Would she have left her daughter with her mother or her partner had those been a possibility? We cannot know. She is in France, whereas most of her family resides in Senegal. It becomes evident that Laurence does not have the same support system as Rita or Leda or even to some degree Tia, and they all certainly struggled as well. Cheryl L. Meyer and Michelle Oberman say that infanticide is often a crime of desperation: "As has been the case throughout history, infanticide in the twentieth and twenty-first centuries may be understood as a response to the societal construction of and constraints upon mothering. The sociocultural imperatives underlying the contemporary crime of infanticide include the fragmentation of the extended family and ultimately of the nuclear family as well."[56] In his reading of the film, Mario Telò correspondingly surmises that "infanticide takes shape as a desperate performance of care."[57] Cut off by her father and without means or support, some years prior Laurence finds herself dependent on a married man more than twice her age. She becomes pregnant and severely depressed. Her older partner pays scant attention. They live together, but he is often away. Pregnancy turns Laurence into an absolute recluse, and eventually she even gives birth all alone in her partner's apartment. Overall, the wrenching details of Laurence's experience of motherhood shock us. It comes as no surprise that when the judge pointedly asks Laurence if she wanted a child, she responds flatly, "No."

In spite of what we know about infanticide and its recurrent motivations, it persists in our imaginary as one of the most monstrous and inconceivable crimes. The nature of Laurence's crime as a mother who has killed her infant, or at least left her to die, no doubt determines the course of the trial. By means of interrogation and mechanisms of judgment, Laurence's entire life—her childhood, her upbringing, her relationships, her thoughts, her desires—becomes the object of scrutiny and punishment. She is exposed absolutely on the stand, forced to answer questions posed directly by the judge as well as by the trial attorneys, not to mention obliged to listen to the testimonies of her former partner, mother, and professor about her character: her capacity as well as failure as a mother, a lover, a daughter, a student. Under the penetrating and juridical gaze of the court and the law, Laurence is made vulnerable, rendered nothing more and nothing less than a Sartrean being-seen-by-the-Other, an ontology shaped by the shame of exposure. As a Black woman and mother, Laurence is caught in the aporia of white normativity: at once invisible and hypervisible. Courtroom etiquette shores up this exhibition. Laurence is led into the courtroom in handcuffs attached to a leash-like tether. Telò expounds that this judicial scene even "evokes a theater of slavery."[58] Whereas others sit, she must remain standing during much of the trial. Shame builds; yet, Laurence maintains stunning composure, as though draped in a pall of melancholic stoicism. Her responses are always measured and delivered with uncanny aplomb. Diop and her cinematographer, Claire Mathon, furthermore provide few close-ups of Laurence, which might betray her emotions or her interiority. This trial film is not Carl Theodor Dreyer's *La Passion de Jeanne d'Arc* (1928). Captured mostly in medium shots from behind the courtroom dock, Laurence maintains an emotional distance for much of the trial. The brown hues of her clothing, likewise, cause her to blend in with the wood paneling of the courtroom. Laurence performs pure exteriority.

The shame and humiliation imposed on Laurence in the stifling courtroom instead settle on Rama, who observes from the spectator seats with great affection. At the heart of *Saint Omer* lies the power of vicarious shame emplaced not just in an imagined spectator but one internal to the diegetic world of the film. Shame, we recall, is one of the most social of affects. Rama demonstrates how, in Tomkins's words, "the human being is capable of being shamed by another whether or not the other is interacting with him in such a way as to intentionally shame him, or interacting with him at all." Thus, even from a distance in the spectator seats and without directly interacting with Laurence, Rama "is capable through empathy and identification of living through others and therefore of being shamed by what happens to others."[59] As Sedgwick further elucidates, "one of the strangest features of shame ... is the way bad treatment of someone else, bad treatment *by* someone else, someone else's embarrassment, stigma, debility, blame or pain, seemingly having nothing to do with me, can so readily flood me."[60] Rama experiences Laurence's shame. It floods her and cleaves to her body. On the second day in court, when Laurence is attacked by the prosecutor for stringing the court along and apparently lying, the image focuses on Rama, now restive in her seat. She leans forward, casts her eyes first downward and then to her right, away from the spectacle of interrogation, and covers her mouth with her hand. Returning briefly to Laurence, the scene then cuts to a close-up of Rama back in her hotel room, lying on her side on the bed, her hands cradling her face. We learn that Rama is also four months' pregnant with her first child and apparently uncertain about her state. She neglects to tell her mother and sisters about the pregnancy. Later, she reveals that she fears becoming a mother similar to her own, who, as shown in flashbacks, was distant, inattentive, and even cruel at times.

As the trial progresses, the image ever more frequently cuts to Rama as spectator. Always in shallow focus, Rama and her reactions to the proceedings draw our attention. She is increasingly shown in close-up. In a final scene before again cutting out of the courtroom, Rama and Laurence make eye contact, and Laurence offers a small smile. In a reverse shot, Rama begins to weep. Back in her hotel room, she desperately packs her suitcase. She cannot take any more, it seems. Laurence's shame becomes Rama's, and it impresses on her to such a degree that it upends her. The film does not show Laurence between proceedings or in her cell at night. She exists only as a figure in the courtroom. Rama's life, struggles, memories, and emotions provide Laurence's missing interiority. Only near the end of the trial when, at last, the judge asks Laurence to describe the crime—specifically, when she abandons her daughter on the beach—does the image capture her in close-up. In the final shot of the trial, Laurence appears one last time and again in close-up. On this occasion her face is tear stained. Perhaps, there is an intertextual shimmer of Dreyer's Jeanne d'Arc, after all? *Saint Omer*'s dynamic of the empathetic gaze evokes even a double intertextuality: Jean-Luc Godard's *Vivre sa vie* (My life to live, 1962), whose main character emotionally watches Dreyer's film in the cinema, also comes alive. There must be a reason why Diop chose the telling place name "Saint Omer" for the title of her film? Does she seize on the homonymy of *mer* (sea) and *mère* (mother)? Sounded out, perhaps the title does not refer to the location of the trial but to the *saint aux mères* (saint to the mothers)?

Not exactly a martyr, Laurence does paint a rather tragic figure of a mother who, unable to cope, abandons her child and leaves her for dead: "*Medée naufragée*" (Medea castaway) is the name of Rama's planned book about the trial. One evening in the hotel, Rama even scrolls through Pier Paolo Pasolini's *Medea* (1969) on her laptop until she reaches the scene in which Medea affectionately bathes and then solemnly kills her sons, finally laying their small bodies out on their beds as though in slumber. María Ruido includes the same scene in her compilation film *Mater Amatísima: Imaginaries and Discourses on Maternity in Times of Change*, discussed in chapter 1. Once Rama reaches the murder scene, the diegetic screen of her computer fills the frame. For the duration of the scene, Pasolini's film becomes Diop's. Recalling Astrid Deuber-Mankowsky's analysis of Pasolini's rendition of Medea, the film refuses "to project Medea back into the realm of prehistory or into the circle of hysterical, irrational, and mad women and perverts."[61] The same can be said for *Saint Omer*. This brief screening of *Medea* precedes the final scene of the trial in which the defense attorney (Aurélia Petit) delivers a moving courtroom speech directly into the camera. With clarity, openness, and even poetry, she describes Laurence's struggles as a mother without support or resources who, in her absolute isolation and desperation, had little choice. Her appeal to our empathy—indeed, our shared shame—begins to manifest on the faces of those present in the courtroom. Similar to the opening sequence of the film, when Rama screens and lectures about the femmes tondues, here the image cuts to women in the courtroom in medium or intimate close-ups as they emotionally witness this scene: the judge, a juror, spectators, another attorney. All on the verge of tears or already overcome by them, these women respond to the defense attorney's universal call: "In a way, we women, we are all monsters. But we are terribly human monsters." Laurence, a Medea figure, demands her right as a human being.[62] Notwithstanding the grand gesture of this concluding speech and its universal appeal, if Diop's film restores Laurence's humanity, then it is through Rama's empathy and her capacity to share the shame. Rama performs the role of Duras, who transforms the femme tondue, the shorn and shamed woman, not only into a heroine but also into a human subject in a state of grace, something like the Pietà figure that appears in different forms throughout this book. She does not achieve this through her writing but through her bodily performance of shame on behalf of the Other.

Laurence's connection to Rama casts this story of a mother beyond straightforward universalism, an otherwise important topic in Diop's documentary filmmaking.[63] The whiteness of the courtroom, not to mention the town of Saint-Omer, where the trial takes place, is painfully evident. *Saint Omer* as a film makes room for a more nuanced understanding of the complexities not only of mothering but of what Nash provocatively refers to, at least in the US context, as "mothering while Black."[64] For Black mothers face tremendously more challenges and threats than white mothers do, both past and present; consider again Villarosa's revealing article.[65] Without falling into the representational trap of Black motherhood as either a "death world" or a site of power, however, Diop renders the stories of two women, two mothers, who do not or did not find unconditional happiness and self-fulfillment in the role of motherhood. Forging this connection between Laurence and Rama, Diop does not revert to straightforward categories of race and culture. Instead, she links these women through vicarious shame engendered by feelings of inadequacy as mothers and developed as a relation of interest that holds one's attention for another, even if only one-sided. Diop allows the public shame of Laurence's "failure" to live up to any kind of fantasy of the institution of motherhood to circulate and settle on Rama's body. Rama expresses shame in perceptible gestures and facial expressions. Not merely an attentive spectator, Rama harbors her own fears of motherhood and preemptively feels ashamed about her own failure as a mother-to-be. For ultimately, as Laurence's attorney reminds the court, her defendant did try to do the right thing as a mother: "She tried to fight, to keep going, but she lost."

This chapter does not simply explore cinematic representations of the failure of motherhood, of mothers who lost the battle of motherhood. That is part of it, however. To be sure, there are vast differences between leaving one's children with one's husband, one's mother, or another family and leaving one's child to die. What cuts across *Madonnen*, *Earth Mama*, *The Lost Daughter*, and *Saint Omer* and their portrayals of mothers is the shame that emanates from presumed failure. Shame plays out in singular ways in each of these films, but it is vividly present through performances of thwarted gazes, agitated bodily gestures, and uncertain camera frames. These films attest to the rich sensorium of shame for the cinema. As the medium of the look, cinema, in turn, serves as a dense site for shame. With an increased interest in maternal shame more broadly, cinema will no doubt play a critical formal role in its exploration and representation.

At first, a separation of maternal shame and maternal guilt seemed both challenging and disadvantageous because the overlap of the two feelings would only lead to repetition. Though this chapter and the next complement each other in their collective engagement with feelings of maternal failure, a distinct focus on guilt in chapter 5 invites the reader to explore the unsettling dimensions of a feeling and phenomenon that moves beyond bodily expression and penetrates the very core of being.

CHAPTER FIVE

Guilt

Motherhood is rife with guilt. "'Guilt, guilt, guilt' is the mother's real G-spot," Adrienne Rich proclaimed.[1] Guilt begins even before motherhood for many women: Women who choose not to have or cannot have children often feel guilty. Women who choose to have children outside of a traditional heteronormative union may experience guilt. With pregnancy, guilt sets in about diet, exercise, and lifestyle. Parturition can elicit guilt as well: Vaginal birth or C-section? In a hospital or at home? With anesthetic or without? Then comes the question of breastfeeding versus bottle-feeding, and where and how. The list goes on and on and on. Mothers who are ambivalent about or who regret motherhood often experience enormous guilt as well. Although the Guttmacher Institute reports that "relief" is the dominant emotion revealed by women who obtain abortions, the procedure is similarly socially embroiled with feelings of guilt.[2] In other words, abortion recipients are meant to feel guilty. Guilt becomes both the provenance and the effect of a vicious cycle of negative affect. Not in and of itself an affect, guilt is still closely related to negative affects, especially shame.

A pervasive element of maternal experience, guilt seeps into a whole host of contemporary films on motherhood, including many of those explored in previous chapters of this book. Yet, guilt does not necessarily shape all maternal narratives the way it does in the films in focus in this chapter. These include Alauda Ruiz de Azúa's *Cinco Lobitos* (Lullaby, 2022), Lynne Ramsay's *We Need to Talk about Kevin* (2011), and Xavier Dolan's *Mommy* (2014). Distinct in the stories they tell, the genres they follow, and their cultural contexts, all three dramas explore guilt as a defining experience for the maternal figures, something they indeed seem to feel much of the time. Guilt arises most prominently from feelings of inadequacy as a mother. In the case of the most recent film, *Cinco Lobitos*, guilt turns up when a new mother is unable to care for her infant alone and must move back home with her parents. In the other two films, maternal guilt is framed through the erratic and violent behavior of the mothers' teenage sons, which forces the mothers' hands in different ways. They feel responsible. The guilty mother is not necessarily the bad mother; the guilty mother is the mother who perceives herself as a bad mother—as a failure—and experiences her child's unhappiness and even misconduct as a rightful punishment.[3] At the same time, guilty feelings—well-grounded or not—cannot claim a rightful place in a mother's all-sunny sensorium. "Mothers are also expected to approach motherhood joyfully and completely," Ortal Slobodin observes. "The myth of motherhood makes it difficult for adverse feelings about motherhood to be expressed without shame, guilt or fear of being regarded as a bad mother."[4] A paradox of motherhood: mechanisms of guilt abound, but the feeling itself is unsanctioned. A mother feels guilty and then feels guilty for feeling guilty, and so it goes.

Although both guilt and shame propound a negative evaluation of self, following the previous chapter on shame, we might posit that guilt opposed to shame moves beyond affective attachment and into the realm of ethical and ontological responsibility. Guilt, unlike shame, Sara Ahmed affirms, implies action.[5] Certainly, in a court of law guilt as admission and indictment can have serious consequences. Donald L. Nathanson puts this into perspective: "Whereas guilt refers to punishment for wrongdoing, for violation for some sort of rule or internal law, shame is about some quality of the self."[6] In the context of motherhood, however, guilt operates somewhat differently. Guilt may well not issue directly from an identifiable wrongdoing or violation but, rather, from a sense of inadequacy, which, not unlike shame, reflects on a perception of self. Though certainly not unthinkable, none of the mothers in these films is in truth guilty of abuse or neglect of her children. They are, nevertheless, burdened by guilt.

A return to the philosophical writings on guilt from Friedrich Nietzsche and Martin Heidegger as debt and to Emmanuel Levinas and Simone de Beauvoir on the ethical situation of the mother provides insight into the complexity of this feeling and its pervasiveness. Though this is not an altogether novel genealogy, Claire S. LeBeau similarly draws our attention to the intractable role of both ontological guilt and ethical guilt for mothers in her approach to clinical psychology. She, too, hearkens back to Heidegger and Levinas to understand that which she phrases "the fundamental structure of care," both for one's own existence and for that of the Other.[7] But what makes the mother's situation unique? LeBeau turns to clinical case studies to develop her argument. I seek to expand on this philosophical argument with particular attention to Beauvoir and an ultimate turn to film. Although Beauvoir does not write extensively about guilt, her pursuit of the ethical situation of the mother extends the work of Heidegger and Levinas in important ways for the present chapter.

There is something inescapably German about the philosophical heritage of guilt, or *Schuld*. Meaning both guilt and debt, Schuld turns on personal responsibility, according to Nietzsche, who saw it as "the oldest and most primitive personal relationship of all." He illumines: "[T]he relationship between buyer and seller, creditor and debtor: here for the first time person confronted person, here a person first *measured himself* against another person."[8] This early relation of indebtedness to others becomes the origin of bad conscience for Nietzsche from which ressentiment also develops. Guilt, we might say, lies at the root of morality. Nietzsche's approach to guilt does not directly account for care, but it does propose a structure of personal responsibility as foundational for our relation to others. Beginning with Nietzsche, the complexity of guilt even at the level of language influences subsequent thinkers.

Heidegger also recognizes the relational importance of "being-guilty" (*Schuldigsein*) as "owing," "having something due on account," or "having debts." Being-guilty, he elaborates in *Being and Time*, "is a way of Being with Others in the field of concern, as in providing something or bringing it along."[9] But for Heidegger this relation is not so much moral as it is intrinsically ontological. His notion of *Dasein*, literally "being-there," hinges upon both being-in-the-world and being-with-Others (*Miteinandersein*).[10] Heidegger understands being-guilty then not as the consequence of indebtedness, as Nietzsche does, but, rather, as that which *gives rise to* indebtedness. The very basis of being, guilt is *the* ontological condition, insofar as it ushers in the awakening of conscience. Being-with-Others means being-guilty: "[It] constitutes the Being to which we give the name 'care,'" what he calls *Sorge*.[11] We are thrown into a relation of care constituted through the guilt of existence. Heidegger refrains from delving into the ethics or particulars of care and, as scholars note, he ultimately yields to an indifferent mode of being-with-one-another in favor of solicitude.[12] His central positioning of this relationality for both ontological and phenomenological thought, nevertheless, becomes critical for both Levinas and Beauvoir and, finally, for thinking about the situation of the mother. As Sarah LaChance Adams indicates, "Care ethics validates the inquiry into familial relationships against traditional philosophical disinterest in these concerns."[13]

Building on and departing from Heidegger, Levinas understands Dasein not as constituted through a mere coincident being-with-Others (*Miteinandersein*) but, instead, as an imperative of being-for-the-Other.[14] A prepositional distinction denoting, on the one hand, coexistence and, on the other, a state of submission, even sacrifice, Levinas's subject becomes inextricably linked to the Other in an inescapable relation of responsibility and indebtedness, not just *to* the Other, as Nietzsche had it, but more importantly *for*. Contra Heidegger, for whom the relation to the Other is ontological and, therefore, reducible to mere representation, Levinas conceived of this relation, instead, as deeply ethical; what he even calls "religion." Much more than representational, the Other has an identity, albeit universal: "That being is a man," he writes, "and it is as a neighbor that man is accessible: as a face."[15] Notwithstanding the overall limited and archetypal nature of Levinas's approach to the feminine and the maternal, his broader understanding of subjectivity as intractable—even oppressive—responsibility toward as well as sacrifice to the Other brings into sharp relief the ethical condition of motherhood.[16] Is not motherhood "often thought of in terms of idealisms related to self-sacrifice, unconditional love, unyielding devotion, warmth, and strength verging frequently on stoicism[?]" LeBeau cannily asks.[17] Indeed, Levinas evokes maternity as a metaphor for being-for-the-Other.[18] Lisa Baraitser similarly intones, drawing on Levinas, that the mother, or certainly maternal subjectivity, is "'called into being' through the relation to *the child* as 'other.'"[19]

Tracing guilt's recasting into an ethics of care through philosophy, we come finally to Beauvoir. "Beauvoir," LaChance Adams plainly states, "provides one of the most important contributions to understanding the ethical life of mothers" because she grasps "that our ethical obligations often outstrip our ability to meet them, that others tax our reserves, and that one may *justifiably* need to assert one's own well-being over another."[20] Thinking with Beauvoir about motherhood is not a straightforward matter; it, nevertheless, can lead us far. To begin, we note that Beauvoir is one of the first thinkers to demystify motherhood as not just total fulfillment. She unapologetically articulates the unhappiness, bitterness, and dissatisfaction that plagues many mothers.[21] Motherhood might be a "marvelous privilege" for some, but for others it is also oppressive, "a kind of slavery."[22] To propose that Beauvoir views motherhood as a wholly negative activity would be inaccurate. She maintains an ambiguous position that finds form in her approach to ethics. Distinct from Levinas, Beauvoir understands ethics as situated rather than universal. According to Beauvoir, our social, political, and biological situatedness shapes our freedom and ability to make ethical choices and pursue ethical freedom. This conviction ushered in her feminist philosophy.

Woman's situatedness has historically established her as the alienated Other to man's subjectivity—*le deuxième sexe* (the second sex), as it were—a relation that has "suited [his] ontological and moral ambitions."[23] Men have reaped the possibilities of freedom and the pursuit of projects in a transcendence beyond mere biological life. Women, by contrast, have been forced to toil in immanence and dedicate themselves to repetitive tasks, such as domestic labor, including childbirth and child-rearing (chapter 2 discusses Beauvoirian immanence in greater detail). This is not to say that women do not have ethical freedom or that they exist outside of ethical life in Beauvoir's philosophy. The relationality of man and woman, subject and object, transcendence and immanence is dialectical and, therefore, inherently wrought with tension and ambiguity.[24] However, woman's situatedness has given rise to attendant challenges in her pursuit of ethical freedom and, certainly, transcendence.

Already precarious, woman's ethical freedom comes under further duress with the onset of motherhood. Invoking Beauvoir, Jacqueline Rose plainly states, "When a woman becomes a mother, she loses her freedom."[25] Bound to the obligation to support the well-being and flourishing of her child, she often finds herself hindered from pursuing her own freedom. Beauvoir regarded the mother as further alienated both in body and social dignity.[26] The peril of motherhood's absolute being-for-the-Other to woman's hard-won freedom and self are central to the maternal conflict, which Beauvoir articulates in all of its dimensions and violence: "[The mother] feels hostility for this little individual who threatens her flesh, her freedom, her whole self."[27] The challenge of squaring not only one's own freedom, needs, and desires but even one's very being with those of another often proves impossible for the mother. She must, therefore, sacrifice herself. Beauvoir's understanding of the sacrificial nature of motherhood endures. Rich confirms that motherhood demands "selflessness rather than self-realization, relation to others rather than the creation of self."[28] Orna Donath echoes, "The mother is portrayed as naturally self-sacrificing, endlessly patient, and devoted to the care of others in ways that almost demand she forgets she has her own personality and needs."[29]

At this juncture, nearly all the films that fill these chapters become objects of study and even others not mentioned. Maternal self-sacrifice is central. Of particular relevance is A. V. Rockwell's *A Thousand and One*, discussed at length in chapter 2, an unmatched tale of self-sacrifice about a woman who devotes herself to the upbringing of a child she found abandoned on the street. The absolute being-for-the-Other, Inez gives up her dreams of becoming a hairstylist, tolerates the philandering and bouts of absence of her husband, and stays put—a fixture of the private household—to create a stable life for her unofficially adoptive son, Terry. A working-class, for all intents and purposes single, Black mother in New York, Inez struggles in and outside the home. The scale of her sacrifice defies measurement. But Inez does not give herself over to guilt, as the mothers in this chapter are wont to do. For her, failure is not an option.

Self-sacrifice all the time is hard, to say the least. Failure or, at the very least, feelings of failure settle in as a constant corollary. Beauvoir recognized the inevitability of failure in any ethical relation. There is "[n]o ethics without failure," she holds.[30] Already a constituent part of ethics, failure hangs over the mother-child relationship like a cumulonimbus. Confronted first with the dictate to sacrifice oneself completely and then faced with the threat of failure to fulfill the same, mothers must endlessly question their acts and decisions.[31] Although Beauvoir does not directly discuss guilt as part of her ethics, both the maternal obligation to the child (a *Schuldigkeit*, or an indebtedness by dint of relation, or even simply gender, as in the case of Inez) and the dogging sense of failure present a wanton brew that leaves many mothers nowhere else to turn. Indeed, is not guilt the faithful companion of failure?

The threat of failure and the oppressive feeling of guilt pervade *Cinco Lobitos*, *We Need to Talk about Kevin*, and *Mommy* in different ways. In all three films, the mothers wrestle with guilt and the conviction that they are bad because they cannot balance their own freedom with the obligations of care for their children. They perceive their mothering as flawed. It is solely their fault that their children will either have problems in the future or already do at present. In *Cinco Lobitos*, this feeling of guilt overwhelms as unmanageable responsibility for an infant. In the latter two films, *We Need to Talk about Kevin* and *Mommy*, the respective mothers feel at fault for producing troubled or even deviant offspring. At fault is not the mother, however, but the oppressive institution and ideology of motherhood, which, according to Sara Ruddick, "defines maternal work as a consuming identity requiring sacrifices of health, pleasure, and ambitions unnecessary for the well-being of children."[32] Perhaps, more than any other emotion examined in this book, guilt is powerfully entangled in narrative and, in the case of two of the films, in the genre of melodrama. Not yet (or, perhaps, simply not to be) redeemed by scholars of film and feminism, we cannot bring a generative cinematic history of guilt to bear on these films. If anything, we must continue to take care not to fall into the trap of psychoanalytic theory's positioning of the woman as the "guilty object" to be punished or saved, instrumental in earlier film and typified in film noir. For this warning, we are, of course, beholden to Laura Mulvey.[33]

The Mother-Daughter Plot of Guilt

The debut film of Spanish Biscayan filmmaker Alauda Ruiz de Azúa, *Cinco Lobitos*, presents a reflection on transgenerational motherhood and the central role women must continue to play in domestic life and the rearing of children. The film reestablishes the woman and mother as the primary caregiver both to the home and to the screen. If early twenty-first-century European cinema about women problematized domesticity, what Barbara Mennel describes as "the notion of women's innate maternal and domestic nature," often in a shift away from representations of women in the home toward the workplace, *Cinco Lobitos* curiously returns us there in a willful embrace of what Mennel critiques as "the specter of domesticity."[34] I do not wish to analyze this film solely within a Spanish—or European, for that matter—context, but such an approach does provide an important entry point into this film and an analysis of maternal guilt. As briefly explored in chapter 1, Spain's long history of fascism under Francisco Franco sedimented the trope of the mother in the national imaginary as the *ángel del hogar* (angel of the hearth), what Lindsey Reuben Muñoz discusses as "a female figure constructed into the servitude and sanctitude for the needs of the working man," originally a product of early capitalism.[35] Certainly, this role has been troubled in Spanish cinema; just consider the influential oeuvre of Pedro Almodóvar. Reuben Muñoz elaborates that many films made during the transition era (the restoration of democracy in the late 1970s, after Franco's death) represent the home as a place of oppression for women but also often devalue domestic labor.[36] Although this immediate backlash to Francoist ideology no longer dominates cinema, the role of the mother in Spanish cinema remains fraught.

Cinco Lobitos portrays a thirty-five-year-old woman, Amaia (Laia Costa), in the early throes of first-time motherhood. She and her partner work on a contract basis, she as an English-language editor and he as a theatrical lighting designer. The film begins with the postpartum return to their Madrid apartment, newborn in tow, and flanked by Amaia's well-meaning but overbearing parents, Begoña (Susi Sanchéz) and Kolda (Ramón Barea), visiting from a coastal town in the Basque region. Despite the familial assistance and fawning, the film shows how Amaia struggles. Sapped of energy, she expresses acute physical pain from the incision after her C-section and grimaces in agony each time she must breastfeed, something she quickly abandons. The ambivalence of motherhood immediately manifests itself in a tangle of exhaustion and frustration as well as delight and joy. Soon, Amaia's parents leave, and then her partner, Javi (Mikel Bustamente), receives a contract with a theater in another city and, against her wishes, decides to leave for several weeks, too. In an earlier scene, Amaia herself regrettably declines a work opportunity. The explicit gender disparity in their parental roles rears its ugly head with great haste. In the absence of her partner, Amaia must essentially bear the burden of single-parent caretaking.

She becomes divided between her own pursuit of autonomy and freedom and her responsibility to and for her young daughter. Not yet prepared (and no doubt unable) to fully sacrifice her career to motherhood, Amaia also attempts to get back to work and finally accepts an editing assignment. Trouble ensues. As she plugs away at the computer one evening, her baby, Jone, begins to wail relentlessly. She has a fever. Then, as Amaia briefly turns her back to call a doctor, Jone slides off the sofa and hits the floor with a thud. Amaia rushes her to the hospital in a panic. Wracked with guilt, she calls her colleague from the hospital to resign from the project. She fails to balance her career with child-rearing and struggles to reconcile herself to the self-sacrifice of motherhood. If "[a] woman must choose between the affirmation of her transcendence and her alienation as an object,"[37] as Beauvoir speculates, then as a mother with an absentee partner, Amaia has no choice. Her resentment mounts; so, too, does her guilt.

In the wake of the incident, Amaia slides further into emotional and physical depletion. Desperate and defeated, she makes a lachrymose phone call to her mother and soon finds herself on her way back to her childhood home with her father. The move back to her parents' house and the recognition that she still needs them after all this time are difficult truths that settle uneasily. Amaia feels like a bad mother: inadequate, irresponsible, incompetent. Entangled in these feelings of guilt, she also cannot square motherhood with her desire to pursue her career. Throughout the film, Amaia frequently talks on the phone with a colleague about various new projects that she must ultimately decline and does so with perceptible equivocation. As she explains to her mother, the more she declines work, the less likely she will be contacted for work in the future. Neoliberal reality creeps in with all of its assaulting vectors. That both Amaia and Javi do creative contract work positions them directly within the precarization of cultural workers, no longer a chosen path of alternative and resistant work patterns with the benefits of autonomy and flexibility but a harsh neoliberal condition of insecurity and struggle.[38]

Positing the origins of the good and bad mothers construct in psychoanalysis, E. Ann Kaplan informs us that its "purpose is to manipulate women in, or out of, the work-force, in accordance with capitalism's needs."[39] Women are made to feel guilty for not living up to the "powerful ideology of the masochistic, angelic, all-sacrificing mother."[40] *Cinco Lobitos* demonstrates how this manipulation continues into the contemporary neoliberal world. Although the COVID-19 pandemic is never mentioned in this 2021 film, its exacerbation of gender disparity in the home haunts. The "stay home" imperative presented a crisis for mothers, to whom the vast majority of care and household work fell.[41] Many mothers were compelled to leave the workforce and dedicate themselves full-time to care work. Within this context, Andrea O'Reilly warns, "It will be a long time before we return to normal—whatever that may be in a postpandemic world."[42]

In a final phone conversation with her colleague, who offers Amaia an amazing opportunity to work with her on a project, Amaia says she'll think about it but already knows the answer. At this point, Amaia is also caring for her mother and father after her mother's stroke. To her mother, she remarks on the terrible timing of everything and what a lousy life she has. Her mother assures her that other lives always seem better than the one dealt. Her bromides seem to placate Amaia. Indeed, coming from a woman who is ill, the will to live on in spite of everything could not be more compelling. Yet, it also strikes the viewer as resigned. Certainly, there is immense value in care work, familial connections, and interdependence, but why must Amaia shoulder this all on her own? Why doesn't her father, Koldo, do any of the cooking or cleaning? Why does he not even know which medication Begoña needs? And where is Javi? Why does he only come for visits between projects when it is convenient for him?

The film juxtaposes two familial generations: Amaia's parents and Amaia and Javi. From Francoist Spain to the neoliberal present, little has changed for mothers, who continue to bear the brunt of care work. Amaia's mother, Begoña, awakens before dawn to prepare breakfast. She does the cooking, the shopping, and the cleaning. When she becomes ill, not Koldo but Amaia takes up these tasks. And on Begoña's deathbed, she requests that Amaia find *una chica* (a girl) to perform housework for the father. The men, though kind and loving, are caught up in their own projects and mostly oblivious to the struggles of the women. *Cinco Lobitos* celebrates the strength of these women. Amaia overcomes her initial uncertainty about motherhood by becoming a mother to her own mother. Unspoken guilt, however, still lingers in this mother-daughter bond. I do not read this phenomenon through psychoanalysis as a result of the daughter's maintained primary identification with the mother, a plot that often turns on the pathological in popular representations and especially melodrama.[43]

Instead, I turn again to Adrienne Rich. In her essay "Motherhood and Daughterhood," she presents a highly personal and devastating meditation on transgenerational motherhood that in many ways hinges on guilt. "I know now as I could not possibly know then," she writes, "that among the tangle of feelings between us, in that crucial yet unreal meeting, was her guilt. Soon I would begin to understand the full weight and burden of maternal guilt, that daily, nightly, hourly, Am I doing what is right? Am I doing enough? Am I doing too much? The institution of motherhood finds all mothers more or less guilty of having failed their children."[44] Amaia gives up her career, at least for the time being, to parent and perform care work, not unlike Begoña, who once gave up the chance for love. We learn that when Amaia was just five years old, her mother had an affair, which she presumably surrendered in order to perform her duties as wife and mother.

After Begoña's stroke and on the eve of her death, she and Amaia do have that "crucial meeting" Rich only imagined with her mother, at least briefly. After watching a home-video compilation Koldo prepared of Amaia as an infant and child on the occasion of Amaia's daughter's first birthday, Begoña asks Amaia how she was as a mother, if Amaia remembers. She responds, "I remember that you were very organized. You were always very busy. And I recall that you were not very loving. You got angry if I misbehaved or fell down. If I did not greet your friends, you would pinch me." Confronted with this, the mother is horrified: "How horrible!" Amaia tries to reassure her: "But you really took care of me, Ama."[45] Begoña's guilt renders her incapable of continuing the conversation. It becomes too much. She abruptly breaks off and asks Amaia to fetch her medication.

Maternal guilt in *Cinco Lobitos* is multigenerational, as are hardship and renunciation; maternal guilt circulates. Guilt shapes a world captured by expressive suffering. At the beginning, Amaia feels guilty for not performing the role of mother the way she believes she ought to: without frustration, without exhaustion, and without anger. She both resents not being able to continue her career and feels guilty for this resentment. She thinks she is a bad mother. When she finally has no choice but to return to her parents for support, the never-ending guilt amplifies. Amaia could not hack it on her own—she needs her mother. As Amaia begins to settle in with her parents, her mother's own oppressive guilt slowly surfaces: her guilt about her affair, about her unhappiness in her marriage, about her strict mothering. When her stroke comes, we are left to wonder if it is not what Rich refers to as "a lancet of guilt and pain" running through her body.[46] Is it embodied maternal guilt? Alongside the strength and resilience of the mothers, the film also taps into deep reservoirs of guilt passed down from one generation to the next, like the lullaby from which the film derives its title, which only the mothers sing and seem to know: "Cinco Lobitos" (five little wolf cubs). *"Cinco lobitos tiene la loba..."* (The female wolf has five little wolf cubs...). What a burden, indeed!

Maternal Guilt like No Other

Scottish filmmaker Lynne Ramsay's *We Need to Talk about Kevin*, based on the homonymous 2003 novel by Lionel Shriver, is a cinematic portrayal of maternal guilt like no other. Maternal guilt is not simply the frame story to a tale about a Columbine-style American tragedy with a nod to films such as Gus Van Sant's earlier *Elephant* (2003); this *is* the story. As Kelli Fuery puts it, "The film shows that who we really need to be talking about is Eva and therefore what it really is to experience motherhood."[47] A very different approach to maternal guilt compared to *Cinco Lobitos*, *We Need to Talk about Kevin* finds form in the generic frame of the psychological thriller. Set mostly in suburban northeastern United States, more or less contemporary with the film's making in the aughts, Eva (Tilda Swinton) is confronted with every mother's worst nightmare: a monstrous child who turns homicidal. A tale told between two trenches of time—the past and present, or before and after the event—Ramsay's film offers what Sarah Louise Smyth formulates as "an intense rendering of the mother's perspective."[48]

Through present struggle and traumatic flashbacks, Eva attempts to piece together the narrative of horror, a teleology that could proffer answers: why and how did this happen? Just before his sixteenth birthday, her son, Kevin (Ezra Miller), embarks on a murdering spree. He kills his father and younger sister before heading to school and taking the lives of numerous fellow students and a teacher. The film begins with Eva's memory of discovering her husband and child prostrate in the backyard. This memory will return later on with fuller clarity. For now, it serves as an opening to a mysterious nightmare, which moves even further into the past during the Tomatina festival in Buñol, Spain, before Kevin's conception. From a bird's-eye view, a tangled throng of red-soaked bodies undulates in slow motion. In the thick of these bodies, Eva appears for the first time, hoisted in the air with arms splayed as though a crucified figure. Signs of guilt in *We Need to Talk about Kevin* come in many different forms. This visually Christian introduction to Eva, a Christlike figure who atones for the guilt of the world, provides at the very least an evocative opening contour. The mother as martyr has a long history. Her name, Eva (not only of a piece with "Eve" but also its equivalent in a number of other languages, including German and Spanish), also personifies the mother of humanity and the figure who brought sin and guilt into the world in the first place and for which she must suffer through childbearing.

Cutting to the present, in the extended aftermath of the terrible event, a red glow illuminates the messy living room of a small, rickety, clapboard house. Passed out on the sofa after an evening of copious wine and pills, evidenced through a sweeping pan of the coffee table, Eva slowly comes to. There are many signs of disturbance in this opening sequence. But the pervasive red pouring through the windows introduces this tale of guilt and accompanies it until the final sequence of the film. Gallons of crimson paint have been splattered upon the facade of Eva's house: the door, wall, windows, front steps, even on the front windshield of Eva's car. The house looks like a site of cinematic gore; that's the point. Yet, Eva hardly reacts to the disturbing vandalism. She looks, pauses, and then returns inside. Her apparent indifference is not one of analytic realism à la Jean-Luc Godard—"It's not blood, it's red"—it is instead one of guilt, a guilt long internalized, a guilt to which she has fully consigned herself.[49] An unrelenting reminder of her guilt and her own demand for punishment, Eva will labor throughout the duration of the film, bound by the well-nigh Sisyphean task of scraping, scrubbing, and sandblasting the red paint day in and day out. There is a sense that not only has such vandalism happened before but also that it will happen again. Painting over the red does not appear to be an option; that would be far too easy. After each afternoon spent scouring away at that damn spot, crimson sticks to her clothing, hands, and face, a constant reminder of the massacre and her role as both witness and responsible party.

Eva has committed the worst crime a woman can commit: she has failed as a mother, and this has brought about detrimental consequences. Su Epstein states the obvious: "When the son becomes a killer, the mother becomes a suspect."[50] Without fail, Beauvoir rejected this idea in her earlier essay, "Pyrrhus and Cineas": "To bring a child into the world is not to found him."[51] In other words, as LaChance Adams also iterates, if the son turns out to be a killer, the mother is not responsible for the crime.[52] She is right, of course, but guilt always seeks a scapegoat, and no one befits the role better than the mother.[53] Eva continues to blame herself for Kevin's horrible crimes, now two years after the fact, and allows others to do the same. She lost her property and wealth in a civil suit, apparently found guilty of parental negligence.[54] Spurned by the community, she nonetheless remains in the town, despite or perhaps owing to the recurring hostility and violence she experiences. This arrives in the form of brutal assault, insults, and menacing stares, even the sabotaging of her carton of eggs in the grocery store. Again and again, without resistance, Eva submits to the cruelty of others. Ostracized and alone, she lives out her everyday through rituals of punishment, both self-imposed and from without, for her guilt. At one point, two men in suits knock on Eva's front door. Suspecting further harassment, she hesitates to answer. When the two men reveal themselves to be Jehovah's Witnesses keen to ask whether she knows where she will spend the afterlife, Eva seems relieved and answers with insouciance: "Oh, yes, I do as a matter of fact. I'm going to burn in hell. Eternal damnation. The whole bit."

The thing is, Eva was not a terrible mother to Kevin. Even through her guilt-addled recollections of the past and her search for telltale incidents of his emerging monstrosity, she hardly surfaces as the malefactor one might expect. We learn of occasional outbursts of anger and one episode of violence. Emotionally distant with her child, Eva was hardly abusive. She "nonetheless reminds us," Vivenne Muller contends, "that mothering is never 'good enough.'"[55] In the novel, Eva narrates in first person through a series of letters to her late husband. Early on, she writes: "I have no end of failings as a mother, but I have always followed the rules."[56] If Eva is a bad mother, then it is mainly because, in Sarah Arnold's words, she "reject[s] her traditional function of self-sacrifice and devotion."[57] Presented in early flashbacks as a traveling, hedonistic city dweller, she seems to become pregnant more out of societal wont or whim than out of any real personal inclination to parent. Prior to motherhood, she was an adventurer and entrepreneur who started her own travel-writing firm and took frequent trips abroad. Like Amaia in *Cinco Lobitos*, Eva struggles to give in to the sacrifices of motherhood expected of her and still desires the freedom to pursue her projects; she feels burdened by the needs of her child. At one point, she barks at the colicky baby Kevin: "Mommy used to be happy before little Kevin came along. Now she wishes she were in France!" Fuery avers that Beauvoirian ambiguity paints Eva's existence before motherhood as one of "'bad faith' freedom—the idea that being free is equitable with having no responsibility, confusing licence to do what you want, when you want, with being free."[58] But this does not fully account for Eva's subsequent struggle with maternal responsibility and sacrifice. Thus I ask here: does Beauvoirian ambiguity, the conflict between self-sacrifice for the Other and pursuing one's own freedom, suffice as evidence of bad mothering?

Molly Ladd-Taylor and Lauri Umansky observe that "throughout the twentieth century, the label of 'bad' mother has been applied to far more women than those whose actions would warrant the name.... It can be found as well in the guilt feelings of working women who have internalized the 'bad' mother label."[59] Eva has certainly internalized these feelings of guilt and convinced herself that she failed as a mother. Kevin, she believes, is proof of that. But mother-blaming also has a stake in all of this, and in the conservative American society in which the film is set, this politics of blame is central: mothers get blamed for everything.[60] Why? "Is it just that mothers are *there* at the center of the nuclear family? Is it that no one can live up to the sentimentalized good-mother ideal? Or is mother-blaming merely a symptom of our society's misogyny?"[61] Yes, yes, and yes. Monique Plaza indirectly responds in the affirmative: "I suspect the vast apparatus of hatred of the Mother of being one of the most prodigious and effective bastions of misogyny."[62]

Save for its horrific conclusion, Eva's experience of motherhood echoes many of those explored in this book, especially the early stages of motherhood. In her critique of the film for the *London Guardian*, Esther Walker writes, "*Kevin* is, of course, a film that makes real the fleeting thought that every parent has at least once, that their child might be evil. Or at least, that it hates them particularly."[63] Pregnancy is alienating to the point of abjection for Eva. In a striking memory sequence, Eva sits restively in what appears to be a changing room following a stretching class for pregnant women. Positioned centrally in a strange tableau of bulging bellies, Eva stands out. She is the only woman fully clothed, unsmiling, and disengaged from the unctuous conversations buzzing around her. Both part of this group of white, upper-middle-class, and able-bodied mothers-to-be and separate, Eva appears filled with the anxiety that she is the only one suffering. She has already, perhaps intuitively, embraced what Barbara Almond identifies as "the fear that one might produce a monstrous offspring," if not through nature than through nurture.[64] Notes of *Rosemary's Baby* flavor the sequence. If pregnancy edges on the abject, the scene of parturition—or better, dystocia—is pure horror, too. A sound match from the present and the yelling of an inmate being restrained by guards during a visit to Kevin in prison bridges the two scenes of violence. A distorted close-up image of Eva's stretched face and gritting teeth reflected in double on the overhead surgical lamp accompanies her screams. This unsettling montage of noise continues as soundtrack to a postpartum image of Eva again centrally positioned, this time in a hospital bed, with a demeanor of exhaustion and disdain as her husband, Franklin (John C. Reilly), cradles the screaming baby. There are no fawning relatives or friends, bright bouquets of flowers or balloons as part of this hospital setting. Brief and without dialogue, this image reveals so much about the trauma of birth for many women and the wrenching feelings of ambivalence that can accompany early motherhood. Eva is anything but "blissfully happy."[65] This ambivalence becomes a source of guilt for her (fig. 5.1).

Guilt

FIGURE 5.1. The misery of the postpartum in *We Need to Talk about Kevin*. Directed by Lynne Ramsay, 2011.

Swinton's washed-out performance of Eva is the picture of emotional ambiguity, or what Smyth calls her "flat affect," borrowing from Lauren Berlant. Her performance not only detaches the film from the melodramatic, still churning in *Cinco Lobitos* and in *Mommy* as well, but also lends to the icy and distant veneer perceived by those around her and at times by the audience, too.[66] Those toothy smiles she feints in an attempt to placate a screaming baby Kevin chill to the bone. But any viewer can see that Eva has her work cut out for her from the beginning. As a baby, Kevin screams bloody murder without pause, eliciting dirty looks from passersby as Eva desperately pushes his stroller through the New York City streets and eventually must drown out his wails by positioning herself proximate to a pounding jackhammer at a construction site. He also refuses to nurse or take the bottle from her. Although both she and her husband work full-time, primary caretaking falls to her. Like so many husbands and fathers in this book, hers is likewise clueless and expresses no empathy or understanding for Eva's trials with motherhood. When she begins to express concern about Kevin and his alarming nature, Franklin gaslights her and offers disturbing, gendered platitudes: "Eva, he's just a boy. He's a sweet little boy. That's what boys do." But, perhaps, she could have tried harder? At least, that is what the present Eva seems to think. Perhaps, she could have prevented the impending tragedy.

Incomparable to Amaia's or Begoña's maternal guilt in *Cinco Lobitos*, Eva's guilt does not exactly accord with what Rich characterizes as "the guilt of Everymother."[67] Eva's guilt stems from the conviction that she created a monster that killed people and, by extension, that she killed people. In brief episodes from the period of the trial in which Eva is put on the stand for negligent mothering and, apparently, pleads guilty, we see only her courthouse departures among a pack of journalists and enraged families who are all too eager to indict her for Kevin's crimes: "You murderer!" "You killed my baby!" they screech in the background. Yet, maternal guilt is maternal guilt is maternal guilt. It always emanates from amplified feelings of responsibility and the sense of failure in the face of this responsibility, regardless of whether one's child turns out rotten or not. *We Need to Talk about Kevin* takes maternal guilt to an extreme but coincidently tells a very common story.

The mother-son relationship of this film presents a subgenre of its own, what Tamara Moya names the cinema of "madres incorregibles e hijos imposibles" (incorrigible mothers and impossible sons), among which she includes such titles as Juan José Campanella's *El niño que gritó puta* (The boy who called bitch, 1991), Santiago Lorenzo's *Mamá es boba* (Mom is silly, 1997), Christophe Honoré's *Ma mère* (My mother, 2004), Xavier Dolan's *J'ai tué ma mère* (I killed my mother, 2009) and *Mommy* (2014), Ramsay's *We Need to Talk about Kevin* (2011), Anthony Chen's *Ilo Ilo* (Mom and dad are not home, 2013), Gracia Querejeta's *15 años y un día* (15 years and one day, 2013), and Jennifer Kent's *The Babadook* (2014).[68] Certainly, the figure of the diabolic son and the resultingly fraught maternal-filial relationship have a firm place in cinema, but not all of these films focus on or give space to the experience of the mother, emphasizing, instead, that of the son. *The Babadook*, *We Need to Talk about Kevin*, and *Mommy* are important exceptions. All three also portray maternal guilt, the latter two in particular.

Good *Mommy*/Bad *Mommy*

Concerning his pursuit of maternal figures in his films, Xavier Dolan echoes Beauvoir: "It's just that mother figures inspire me and they are rich characters and they're a solid foundation to start writing about and to, you know, write a story on. Mothers have sacrificed dreams and projects and ideas and maybe even values and a part of themselves to become moms."[69] Dolan has, indeed, emplaced the maternal character centrally in contemporary Quebec cinema in implicit critique of the hitherto "burdensome legacy of motherhood and its impacts on the contemporary Québecoise society."[70] To be sure, the oppressive rule of the Catholic Church until the 1960s and the long struggle for sovereignty in Quebec have shaped, not to mention often systematically excluded, representations of maternal experience in uniquely national ways on the screen.[71] Some of the most influential in contemporary cinema, Dolan's explorations of motherhood also engage us in stories of struggle and guilt that extend well beyond Quebec, or even Canada, for that matter. *Mommy* returns to the topic of his first film, *J'ai tué ma mère* (I killed my mother, 2009), but this time with a greater focus on the struggles of the mother. As film critic Peter Bradshaw of the *London Guardian* quips, "[N]ow it's the mother who feels like doing the killing."[72] *Mommy* is a film about Die, short for Diane (Anne Dorval), who is mother to a hyperactive, unruly, and violent teenage son with attention deficit hyperactivity disorder (ADHD), Steve (Antoine-Olivier Pilon). Die is a recently widowed, working-class mother, who is tough, loud, and brash but also warm-hearted.

Mommy is set in the outskirts of Montreal in a slightly distant and fictional future, in which a controversial new law allows parents to turn children with behavioral problems over to state care to be placed in government-run psychiatric hospitals. Introduced in a title card at the opening of the film, the law looms over this story of mother and son. Die and Steve are reunited after Steve is expelled from a juvenile facility for setting fire to the cafeteria and injuring a fellow youth. This reunion ultimately turns Die's life upside down. Already struggling to make ends meet, she must quit her job because Steve requires full-time care and homeschooling. On top of that, she faces the constant threat of harm at the hands of Steve, whose capacity for both affection and violence is oceanic. Dolan intimates the impact of Steve's homecoming through the framing device of a car crash in an early scene, in which an oncoming car slams into Die's at an intersection. Shaken but unscathed save for a cut on her forehead, Die emerges from the wreck of her car enraged at the careless driver that struck her and hollering profanities in thick Joual.[73] Yet, nothing is quite the same in the wake of a crash; it always unsettles time and space. Much literature exists on the trope of cinematic crashes as a space of opening and possibility in which characters persevere on borrowed time after unbidden brushes with fate.[74] In the context of *Mommy*, I am inclined to read the crash more pragmatically as a brutal onslaught to a series of impacts and assaults. At the site of the crash comes a phone call on Die's mobile, presumably about Steve and the incident at the juvenile facility. This saga of mother and son is doomed from the start.

Not dissimilar to *Cinco Lobitos*, maternal guilt is elusive in this film, too; it circulates between mothers. *Mommy* is Die's story, as an opening title card clearly establishes. The film's first image renders her plucking an apple from a tree branch; her inveterate link to guilt (recall Eva in *We Need to Talk about Kevin*) requires no further introduction. But guilt in *Mommy* also attaches to another maternal figure, Kyla (Suzanne Clément), whose excessively emotional performance casts her as a kind of surrogate to Die, who, by contrast, appears to have neither time nor energy for guilt. The two women come to complement each other, fill in the gaps, and shoulder the burdens the other cannot, to some extent resembling the attachment between Laurence and Rama in *Saint Omer* discussed in the previous chapter. Die is a strong, self-possessed, and pragmatic woman. Kyla is sensitive, shy, and nurturing. Their bond begins with the episode of the car crash, which Kyla witnesses from her own car in the position of the viewer. Only later do the two meet as new neighbors, but the film connects them immediately through the shock effect of this original violent event.

These two different mothers embody to a certain degree the ideologically good and bad identities of cinematic mothers so entangled in discourses of maternal guilt. Die epitomizes what Loïc Bourdeau describes as Dolan's strategies of *"unmothering"* women, through which he "let[s] them express their own desires and subjectivities outside of the realm of motherhood."[75] According to Arnold and Ladd-Taylor and Umansky, precisely these pursuits would lead to Die's designation as a "Bad Mother."[76] Die is "unmotherly" in many ways. She chain-smokes, drinks, tokes, dresses like a teenager with her short skirts and heavy makeup, swears, and flirts and is sexy.[77] Beyond that, she lets her son drink and smoke (at least a little) and engages in obscene public sparring matches with him. She leaves a trail of disapproving stares and comments in her wake, but she mostly brushes them off. Not impervious to the burden of guilt tethered to the status of the bad mother, Die simply doesn't show it. In her excessive presence, there is a note of Barbara Stanwyck's maternal figure, Stella Dallas, from King Vidor's 1937 classic melodrama by the same name, whose tawdry style contributes to her tragic failure to achieve the status of good mother.[78]

Juxtaposed with Die, Kyla hews to the sacrificial paragon of motherhood in all of its melodramatic rue. She is the mourning mother who only knows suffering in the wake of a lost son, a boy slightly younger than Steve. So severe is her internalization of guilt that speech almost eludes her. She stutters terribly. Her near–speech impediment evokes melodrama's muteness. An expressionistic form, melodrama's sense deprivation must necessarily be speech; ergo, muteness is the problem of melodrama, according to Peter Brooks.[79] Upon their first encounter, Kyla can hardly pronounce even her own name when asked. The impediment began two years ago, she eventually explains to mother and son. We are only given to speculate that this also marks the death of her son, whom she never mentions in the film but whose portraits adorn her bedroom dresser. The embodiment of self-sacrifice and devotion, Kyla evokes the classic cinematic "Good Mother," who punishes herself out of guilt for what happened to her son.

Such a strict contradistinction of the two women does not hold, however, just as the categories of good and bad designed to manipulate and blame women contain more than just a taint of the false.

As Die and Kyla's friendship develops over boxed wine and laughs on the back porch, so, too, does their interdependence. A high-school teacher, Kyla (currently on leave, we learn), assumes the role of tutor for Steve during the day so that Die can go to work; Die helps Kyla to relax and forget. Gradually, her stutter also starts to fade. Spending time with and helping Steve serve to also assuage her guilt. But these blissful moments of apparent equilibrium and maternal codependence are numbered once Steve begins to spiral again. First, he nearly slits a man's throat, and then he attempts to take his own life. Wrenchingly dramatic and public, Steve's attempted suicide marks a turning point in the film. Discovered by a panicked Kyla, Steve lies prostrate in the aisle of a store next to a pool of blood. Die and Kyla must carry Steve's limp body from the store. Dolan slows down the image and allows the soundtrack to mark their toil and suffering. Captured from a slightly high angle, the image also seizes on their strength. But Die has had enough. The grim "option" she vehemently refuses at the beginning of the film when she collects Steve from the juvenile center—that is, to sign her son over to the state to be placed in a psychiatric care—becomes in the course of time her only real option (fig. 5.2).

FIGURE 5.2. Mothers united by strength and guilt in *Mommy*. Directed by Xavier Dolan, 2014.

In an extended sequence, Kyla solemnly prepares a picnic lunch, and Die returns home with a rented SUV. The three of them will take a road trip together, so goes the story. We learn this is a mere ruse to deliver Steve to an outlying psychiatric institution. A drawn-out and horrifically violent scene of Steve's resistance to restraint concludes the sequence, in which both Kyla and Die break down. It's too late. Eventually rendered unconscious with a taser, Steve is overtaken and committed to the psychiatric hospital. After everything, we can hardly blame Die for her decision. But the guilt of giving up a child and to such conditions overpowers. As much as she tries to reject its grip, she cannot. This is the only time in the film she shows her full emotions. In an interview, Dorval has described the character Die as a "strong woman who does not feel sorry for herself, who never incites pity, despite all the blows life throws at her."[80]

The film cuts ahead after the event to what seems like a period of days, possibly even weeks. Accomplices to each other's guilt, Die and Kyla have apparently avoided each other during this time. In the wake of this new trauma, Kyla seems to have reverted to her old, stuttering self. Shuttered inside, she sits at a partially covered window, silent and nervously popping the bubble wrap loosely folded around framed photos of her son. She means to prepare for a move but cannot accomplish anything. Her distant husband, Patrick (Alexandre Goyette), enters, opens the blinds, and brusquely yanks the frames from her hands with a disapproving look. Throughout the film, they barely exchange a handful of words. With his one-dimensionality, his character serves as a mere judging presence and a reminder of what Sharon Hays calls the "guilt gap." According to Hays, "No matter how much time fathers spend watching the children, they almost never spend as much time worrying about them as mothers do."[81] Mothers experience guilt far more often and to a greater extent than fathers.

Kyla finally visits Die to bid her farewell. She, her husband, and daughter are moving to Toronto. Always tough, always practical, Die maintains a brave face for her friend and responds with feigned excitement at Kyla's news: "It's extraordinary! Extraordinary!" she repeats. Kyla understands the act and the pain this excitement must be masking. With great effort, she stammers, "I-I-I can't just a-a-abandon m-m-my family." Unintentionally laying blame and evoking Die's own abandonment of her son, Kyla catches her words. What she meant was that she is sorry that she cannot stay, stay here with Die. But there is no undoing what she said. The register changes. Die is forced to address the issue she has been skirting. Now in close-up, she appears to gather herself through pained facial restraint. Resisting a confession of guilt, she, instead, delivers a hollow speech about hope. In a reverse close-up shot, Kyla averts her eyes, now welling with tears. The experimental 1:1 aspect ratio Dolan employs throughout much of the film makes these arresting close-ups incredibly close, even claustrophobic. Intimacy swells, and the scene in all of its intensity and taxing emotional restraint becomes almost too much to watch. Only after Kyla leaves and, upon crossing the street, turns around to mouth an inaudible "*merci*" (thank you), does Die now at the upstairs window nearly fall to guilt—and grief. Fighting her emotions, refusing expressive suffering, she actually performs just that bodily and gestural inflation. Her face violently contorts in an explosion of gestural intensity. The film fully surrenders to its melodramatic frame.

Not in thrall to bodily expression until the latter part of the film, Die's guilt resonates most with the ethical situation of the mother as run through Levinas and Beauvoir. She finds herself in a state of submission and total sacrifice to her teenage son on account of his ADHD. Steve requires constant care; he is intensively and demandingly present, in love and in violence. Die becomes an absolute being-for-the-Other. This inescapable relation of responsibility for Steve fills Die with guilt because of the impossibility it presents. A life with Steve is unendurable. In an episode shortly after Steve's homecoming, he goes out on his longboard for the afternoon and returns with groceries and gifts. Die is skeptical and demands to know where he got this stuff and with what money. Steve grows enraged at what he perceives as her ungratefulness and attacks her. Pushing his mother against the wall, he begins to choke her. She can only escape by responding in violence, hitting him over the head with a framed picture. He continues to pursue her. She pulls down a bookshelf to block his way and locks herself in a closet. The brutality of the rivetedness of being-for-the-Other reaches new heights in this scene in which the mother must hurt her child to defend herself. Rich links this maternal responsibility to guilt: "She became a scapegoat, the one around whom the darkness of maternity is allowed to swirl—the invisible violence of the institution of motherhood, the guilt, the powerless responsibility for human lives, the judgments and condemnations, the fear of her own power, the guilt, the guilt, the guilt."[82] The guilt that Eva feels after throwing toddler Kevin across the room in an outburst of frustration and violence when he seems to intentionally defecate in his freshly changed diaper stands out here, too. Guilt does not always accompany violence, but the latter certainly answers the mother's terrible "fear of her own power."

Mining the depths of maternal guilt becomes a radically vast endeavor. So complex is this guilt that it rests at the very core of one's being, a being determined by our relationality to and for others. Nietzsche called this debt, which Heidegger ontologized as a relation of care. In different ways,

Levinas and Beauvoir devised their philosophy of ethics in engagement with this system of care as indebtedness. Ontology came to mean a relationality of perpetual surrender. If I may make some provisions here: a giving-over to guilt. It takes no leap of imagination to draw a line between the ethics of care and the relationality of mother and child shaped by responsibility and indebtedness. This line is guilt, motherhood's right, red hand. Many films attend to the grating presence of maternal guilt; *Cinco Lobitos*, *We Need to Talk about Kevin*, and *Mommy* track it in all of its ontological and ethical complexities. Guilt bears out over exceedingly different stories of mothers and children in these films, who, measuring themselves against the unattainable paragon of the "Good Mother," are left with the feeling of inadequacy, failure, and even blame. They acquiesce to the status of "Bad Mother," so keenly assigned them by others and promptly internalized.

This chapter has taken us away from the affective realm, strictly speaking. If anything, guilt presents a dizzying vortex of affects but cannot be called one on its own. This does, however, not conclude here; rather, the final chapter returns to a more conventional, albeit deviant, affect, so as not to linger too long in the melodramatic pathos of guilt. Instead, ready your eyes and your nose to the repulsive and the abject. The final chapter explores the mother's experience of disgust.

CHAPTER SIX

Disgust

In her landmark study on negative feelings, Sianne Ngai contemplates disgust as the "ugliest" of what she calls "ugly feelings."[1] She relegates disgust to an afterword, including but also structurally excluding it from her affective taxonomy. A return to Julia Kristeva and her influential study on abjection provides further insight on this thwarted affect. Disgust haunts the boundaries of subjectivity, not to mention logical thought, not as object but as abject. "It is something rejected from which one does not part, from which one does not protect oneself as from an object."[2] Of particular importance to the present chapter, Kristeva's *Powers of Horror* was not only one of the first extended studies on disgust—what she calls "the abject"—it furthermore takes up the matter of the maternal body as one of the primary sites of disgust: "The abject confronts us . . . with our earliest attempts to release the hold of *maternal* entity even before ex-isting outside."[3]

Lochia, shit, breast milk, the postpartum body, moldering fruit, and oozing wounds: to begin, this chapter is particularly interested in the objects that have come to shape our imaginary about maternal disgust theorized first by Kristeva. In this way, it follows in the discursive tradition of cinematic disgust established through horror film studies and the writings of Noël Carroll and Barbara Creed, in particular, both of whom are also indebted to Kristeva. Creed's work becomes especially relevant in its focus on the monstrous feminine and, specifically, the maternal body. "Virtually all horror texts represent the monstrous-feminine in relation to Kristeva's notion of maternal authority and the mapping of the self's clean and proper body. Images of blood, vomit, pus, shit, etc., are central to our culturally/socially constructed notions of the horrific."[4] Yet, what

Linda Williams famously designates as a body genre, horror concerns itself with the response of the viewer—here, the disgusted or fearful viewer.[5] Though horror's emotive configuration has long relied on identification with a central character for response cues, the maternal figure has largely defied this kind of identification.[6] Thus, horror films about mothers almost exclusively foreground the *disgusting mother*, frequently a trait of what Sarah Arnold denominates as the "bad mother" in cinema (consider, for instance, the mother as corpse in Hitchcock's *Psycho* or the mother with multiple external wombs in Cronenberg's *The Brood*, and the list could go on).[7]

But we do not even have to go to the extremes of horror, a genre already saturated in affective modes of disgust, to find visualizations of the revolting mother. One of the most unforgettable images of the disgusting mother arrives in Xavier Dolan's first feature film, the drama *J'ai tué ma mère* (I killed my mother, 2009). Likewise starring Anne Dorval as the mother, Chantale, and similar to *Mommy* (2016), examined in the previous chapter, this film explores a troubled mother-son relationship but more explicitly from the perspective of the teenage son. In the opening montage, following the son's (played by Dolan himself) admission that he cannot possibly be her offspring, there is a series of extreme close-up shots in slow motion focused on his mother's mouth as she bites first into an orange whose zest sprays and then into a bagel slathered with cream cheese. The images are crosscut with extreme close-up reverse shots of the son's eyes watching and then shifting away in horror. Their sheer size alone makes these shots of messy consumption monstrous. In *Bigger than Life*, Mary Ann Doane reveals, "The close-up presented two threats to the norm of the mimetic body: first, it was perceived as aesthetically offensive in extreme ways—as monstrous or grotesque, an excessive display of disproportion in scale; and, second, as an untenable fragmentation of the human body."[8] Magnified and fragmented from the rest of the face, not to mention the body, the mouth becomes monstrous by virtue of its scale alone. That this monstrous mouth also messily consumes food, the elementary form of the unclean for Kristeva, and furthermore enacts the opening of the body's borders between inside and out, intensifies the monstrosity of the image.[9] When the image zooms out, the son, seated adjacent to his mother, first shudders in disgust, then emits an "ugh!" Unable to look at her now, he reproaches her for her manner of eating. *J'ai tué ma mère*, like so many films in the history of cinema, presents the mother as the source of disgust. Seldom do films take into account her perspective and subjectivity with regard to disgust. The possibility of a *disgusted mother* remains an anomaly of cinema.

Not adhering to a specific genre, in the films studied in this chapter—Emily Atef's *Das Fremde in mir* (The stranger in me, 2008), Bess Wohl's *Baby Ruby* (2022), and Maggie Gyllenhaal's *The Lost Daughter* (2021)—it is the mother who experiences disgust at (her own) maternity. A number of films explored throughout this book contain elements of (self-) disgust, but these three provide exemplary portrayals. The mother in each of these films repels at the sight of her baby, at her postpartum body with its oozing fluids and sagging flesh, or in retrospect at the near-traumatic reminders of these objects years later. Perhaps more than any other feeling explored in the chapters of this book, disgust in these films demands a focus on the subjectivity of the maternal figure and her horrified perspective of motherhood. This final chapter thus presents a study of disgust that departs from all previous studies insofar as it is not one of masculine imagination and concerned with the male gaze upon "the disgusting attributes of female sex."[10] The woman, specifically the mother, looks at, smells, touches, even tastes motherhood.

In search of models for the disgusted mother in cinema, let us consider the fuller life and history of this affect before delving into this chapter's case studies. Disgust has a significant history within philosophical aesthetics. In his genealogical study of disgust, Winfried Menninghaus locates the birth of a discourse about disgust in the eighteenth century with the emergence of modern aesthetics. But always an outsider, this strong sensation exceeded the conditions for aesthetic judgment. Disgust was deemed anti-aesthetic. As Menninghaus illumines, "The 'aesthetic' is the field of a particular 'pleasure' whose absolute other is disgust: so runs its briefest, its only undisputed, yet almost wholly forgotten basic definition." Borne of a discourse that simultaneously rejected it, disgust became the misfit of aesthetic theory. This starts to change in the nineteenth and twentieth centuries with the turn away from metaphysics toward the material and the body with the ideas of Friedrich Nietzsche, Sigmund Freud, Georges Bataille, and finally, Julia Kristeva. In different ways, all of these theorists argue that disgust wields the power to repel as well as attract. Thus, Menninghaus presents three critical features as a starting point for his study: "(1) the violent repulsion *vis-à-vis* (2) a physical presence or some other phenomenon in our proximity, (3) which at the same time, in various degrees, can also exert a subconscious attraction or even an open fascination."[11] This general definition not only takes heed of the changing reception of disgust since the eighteenth century but also accentuates the experience of disgust, which impels an undeniably visceral response of shuddering and turning away.

Sometimes thought to act as a bridge between the two philosophical camps of metaphysics and materialism in the genealogy of disgust, Aurel Kolnai's 1929 essay, *Der Ekel*, presents a phenomenological treatise on disgust that centers on bodily experience without completely forsaking aesthetic judgment. "[F]rom the very beginning," he writes, "there is shuddering and turning away from the object, and nausea, either real or intentional. These phenomena may increase in intensity with the continued presence of the disgusting object." Disgust is bound up with bodily phenomena and conditioned by one's proximity to the object. It extends peripherally in a reach to the subject "along the surface of his skin," what Kolnai calls "a kind of secondary intention," and without pervading the totality of the subject. Aesthetics enters with Kolnai's perception of the disgusting or alien object as in possession of stock qualitative or essential features, its specific *Sosein*, or so-being.[12] His primary example of this ontology is the object that lies in putrefaction. This disgusting state of things reaches the eyes, the nose, and the tactile surface of the skin, the three senses capable of perceiving disgust.

Bringing this to bear on film, a nod to Eugenie Brinkema is in order. She speculates the Sosein of disgust in Kolnai's philosophy as the potential link back to film, which similarly possesses stock qualitative features for the visual representation of different feelings, such as, she notes, the quality of the close-up to isolate and magnify objects. But as she herself recognizes, Kolnai's approach to disgust relies, above all, on olfactory responses, and in her formalist universe beyond subject and body, the contemplation of smell, unlike vision, requires a significant and protracted theoretical sleight-of-hand.[13] I find a direct link back to film through Kolnai's vivid description of the visceral response to disgust, which I read as still very much present in his philosophy. Contra Brinkema's argument, Kolnai maintains the visceral, instinctive, and unmediated nature of disgust as a "rejection, expulsion, revulsion, and Nietzschean 'No'-ness," through his characterization of disgust as a defensive reaction.[14] The embodied subject—here the disgusted mother—repels the alien object: eyes averted, nose burrowed, body cringing against the physical proximity of the baby, she is even given to retching. There is nothing quite as unmediated and expulsive as the gag as a response to something disgusting. Inverting Kristeva's matricidal "I feel like vomiting the mother," in these films, the mother feels like vomiting motherhood.[15] If Brinkema returns to the a priori Sosein of disgusting objects as a means of foreclosing the subject, this study follows Imogen Tyler's intervention of "abject criticism" to interrogate the violent premise on which Kristeva's theory of abjection is grounded and proposes a reparative return to the response of disgust by a subject long ignored—the mother.[16] For as Lisa Baraitser similarly exhorts, "Kristeva's position seems to destroy the potential for maternal subjectivity at the point that it appears to rescue mothers from their silence."[17]

"To feel disgust is human and humanizing," William Ian Miller tells us.[18] Why is it then that mothers are not supposed to feel disgust about their children or about motherhood? Does maternity trump humanity or suggest a loss thereof? Recall the dilemma that the figure of Medea invokes, discussed in chapter 1: she does not represent humanity. Disgust is, perhaps, even more taboo for mothers than regret, exhaustion, rage, shame, or guilt because it seems so self-alienating. And, yes, there exists even less literature on the topic of maternal disgust than on the other affects. But mothers are human, too. They may be disgusted by blood, shit, and vomit, for instance, just as anyone else. For the simple reason that disgust has long been entangled with objectifying perceptions of the mother does not mean she herself cannot feel disgust. This, furthermore, does not mean that she has merely internalized her own objectification. Instead, we might say she is exercising her humanity.

"The Stranger in Me" (What More Can One Say?)

"Disgust hovers like an unwelcome guest over the maternity room," Colin McGinn provokes.[19] French German Iranian filmmaker Emily Atef's 2008 film *Das Fremde in mir* (The stranger in me) does not begin in the maternity room, but its tale of disgust does. Roughly eight and half minutes into the film, Rebecca (Susanne Wolf) gives birth to her first child. This scene of labor is decidedly vivid and intimate. At the same time, it resists graphic and gynecological images of the female body and focuses with astounding attentiveness on the lived experience of Rebecca, who diligently follows the instructions of the doctor to breathe, hold her breath, and then push in a repeated pattern. At first the scene of parturition evokes no horror or trauma. However, the obstetrician immediately places the infant face down on Rebecca's chest, and she repels. Coated in a layer of fetal blood and mucus, the gleaming infant appears like a blob of claret flesh. Seemingly unbothered by pregnancy, Rebecca's moment of encounter with her body's inside, and what Kristeva describes as the "collapse of the border between inside and outside," gives rise to her disgust.[20] The infant is nothing if not the alien object, the "stranger in me" of the film's title. But it is also quite literally the abject, "the jettisoned object" from the mother that threatens defilement.[21] The image rests on Rebecca for the remainder of the scene. Eyes wide and lips puckered, her facial expression verges on gagging. She raises her hands but cannot bring herself to touch this object on her chest. When the doctor asks from off-screen how she is, she offers no verbal response. Childbirth challenges the autonomy of the subject and its borders. Both the film's title "The stranger (or strange/foreign object) in me" and this scene of parturition evoke Beauvoir and Kristeva.[22] Engaging the two, Jacqueline Rose writes, "To be a mother, to give birth, is to welcome a foreigner, which makes mothering simply 'the most intense form of contact with the strangeness of the one close to us and of ourselves.'"[23]

No longer a visual taboo, portrayals of labor in cinema and elsewhere in public culture have become increasingly commonplace and graphic. As a result, Tyler and Baraitser contend that the "diverse field of 'maternal aesthetics' has transformed previous notions of beauty, taste and disgust around reproductive bodies and practices." But they are careful to also note that "disgust, revulsion, horror, or distaste still circulate" in visualizations of childbirth.[24] Indeed, if the goal of increased visualization has served as a subjective embrace of childbirth away from sterile medicalization, then a recognition of the disgusted mother is just as important as that of the "ecstatic" mother. The disgusted mother has not simply internalized objectifying maternal disgust; in films such as *Das Fremde in mir*, she expresses disgust in a manner that goes against the grain of social expectation. For even with the increased visualization of childbirth, women are still not frequently empowered to respond negatively. In an interview, Atef attests to the difficulty of expressing the crushing negative emotions that can accompany the experiences of motherhood and the pressure for women to delight in the birth of their children, no matter what. "Women are expected to be happy and thankful after delivering a healthy baby," she explains, "but that is not always the case. Even if they want to, they can't say that they wish they didn't have a baby. Even after a difficult birth, a woman cannot say, 'Oh! I feel like shit!'"[25]

One of a spate of recent films about women who suffer from postpartum depression, this slightly earlier example documents the story of Rebecca, a florist and young mother who feels overwhelmed by the responsibility of motherhood and resentful of the fact that she must give up her work in order to stay home with the baby. (The housewife model rears its ugly head—again!) By contrast, her husband, Julian (Johann von Bülow), has increased his work hours ostensibly to support the new family and is hardly present. Rebecca's negative feelings become unbearable, and, eventually, she attempts suicide. Atef's portrayal of postpartum depression stands out for its attention to the manifestation of visceral loathing that some mothers experience. In this film about the struggles of early motherhood, disgust provocatively looms.

Rebecca's initial maternal response of disgust in the hospital lingers. In repeated scenes following the birth, she avoids looking at her baby as much as possible and only reluctantly holds him as a necessary means of pacifying him, mostly unsuccessfully. Not presented as an overly fussy or difficult baby that keeps Rebecca up at all hours, Lukas's mere presence disturbs. In an attempt to find normalcy after the birth and its upheaval, Rebecca decides to reopen her flower shop. She brings Lukas along. But in one scene she becomes so disgusted by his gaze and then the gurgling sounds he makes that she first turns his baby carrier around to remove him from her view, then finally brings him into the back room—out of sight and sound. In the establishing shot of this scene, Lukas sits in his carrier, pacifier in mouth, and intently gazes up at Rebecca. Caught at a lower angle with his head tilted backward, he appears strange, however. His fixated stare verges on menacing. In a reverse shot, Rebecca glances only briefly his way and with aversion as she prepares a bouquet of pink peonies. We learn from an earlier scene when she is still pregnant that Rebecca's arrangements are an art form exacted with precision and a careful aesthetic. Subsequent shots in this later scene position Lukas behind the flowers that Rebecca carefully arranges, creating a compelling contrast between what Rebecca clearly perceives as disgusting versus what she perceives as beautiful. The scene evokes early aesthetic debates about the incommensurability of beauty and disgust. "Nothing is so much set against the beautiful as disgust," Immanuel Kant straightforwardly writes in *Observations on the Feeling of the Beautiful and the Sublime*.[26] Although Kant would later take a more nuanced approach to disgust as not the opposite of beauty but, rather, the quality that renders an object incapable of beauty, even through artistic representation, his repudiation of disgust as altogether unaesthetic endures.[27] According to Menninghaus, the "foundation of modern aesthetics can be described negatively as a foundation based on the prohibition of what is disgusting."[28] That Rebecca is a florist and creator of beauty serves to emphasize the rift that motherhood presents for her. In this scene, she cannot design something beautiful in the presence of Lukas, whom she regards with disgust and disdain.

Rebecca's postpartum body becomes a source of the revolting to her as well. Her swollen, seeping breasts that nonetheless stubbornly resist attempts at breastfeeding and later pumping have acquired a yellow pigment resembling jaundice. Not only does Rebecca exhibit feelings of frustration and failure because she is unable to breastfeed, she manifests detestation at the sight of her oozing breasts and the evident discomfort of the manual breast pump with which she pulls and rings her nipple only to ultimately extract a meager few drops of milk into the bottle. She eventually throws it aside in revolt and apparently gives up on breastfeeding altogether. Not dissimilar to the scene of childbirth, films increasingly show mothers hooked up to electric breast pumps. These representations, including in *Tully* (2018), discussed in chapter 2, and in *Baby Ruby* (2022), to be discussed later in the present chapter, render visible the toll motherhood can take on a woman's body, which is no longer hers alone. Connected not even to a baby but to a machine that sucks nourishment from her body to feed another, the mother becomes *disembodied* in these scenes. Graphic in its portrayal, *Das Fremde in mir* shows Rebecca's struggle with the manual pump to intensify the agony of her experience. Fully exposed, we view with transparency the action of the pump and its physical assault of the nipple. Perched on the rim of the bathtub, Rebecca hunches over, straining against the discomfort of the pumping action. She grits her teeth. Finally, abandoning the pump, her breast continues to leak as she hangs her head in disgust and despair. Evidently perceived as even more obscene than childbirth, the direct visualization of the lactating nipple is still rare in cinema. Consider Pedro Almodóvar's *Madres paralellas* (Parallel mothers, 2021), whose controversial original promotional poster contained nothing but an extreme close-up of a lactating nipple, which was swiftly censored on social media and replaced in advertisement for the film in the United States and elsewhere with a much more "palatable" image of the two central maternal figures in an embrace. (Almodóvar's film does not actually contain any images of lactating breasts, or even naked breasts, for that matter.) *Das Fremde in mir* does not deem it too obscene to show. The film does not aim to provoke, however. Instead, it presents an altogether realistic and physical portrayal of the travails of postnatal life for this mother and the continued strain on her body.

Repelled by her son and by motherhood and afraid of what actions these negative feelings could further incite after nearly drowning Lukas in his bathwater, Rebecca leaves the house early one morning, travels to the edge of the city, and abandons herself to death in the woods. By chance, a group of teenage boys stumble upon her unconscious body, and she is brought to the hospital. It is unclear how long she had lain there. Now thin, weak, bruised, and wounded, the maternal body resembles the corpse. Once a source of life, now life has nearly been sucked from Rebecca's body. Kristeva describes the corpse as the falling (cadaver, from *cadere*, to fall) of the body beyond its limit.[29] If we follow the telos of disgust presented in *Das Fremde in mir*, we cannot help but also draw a through line between the maternal body to the corpse: both positioned at the borders of the self, both abject. By attempting to shake off motherhood—and life—Rebecca actually brings herself closer to precisely the abjection she attempts to flee. For Kristeva, both the maternal body and the corpse body are "waste bodies"; they are bodies that excrete waste, blood, life.[30] They are sites of excretion, abjection, and defilement. Creed, too, characterizes the corpse as *the* image of abjection: "whole and mutilated, followed by an array of bodily wastes such as blood, vomit, saliva, sweat, tears and putrefying flesh."[31] The film recalls this slippery imbrication. In a scene in the hospital after her suicide attempt, a nurse carefully washes Rebecca's still body as though in funerary preparation. Rebecca is conscious but weak and silent. The evidence of her pregnancy and childbirth still marks her body. To the nurse's comment about her postnatal state, she does not respond. Rebecca has rejected her body, this "revolt of being."[32]

The film does not end with Rebecca's falling body, however. Atef seeks to show how a mother can overcome the incredible challenges of postpartum depression and disgust. If the first half of the film presents Rebecca's escalating struggles, which culminate in her attempted suicide, then roughly midway through, the narrative begins to pursue her gradual healing. Rebecca does overcome disgust. But a film can be about disgust without staying with it. *Das Fremde in mir* offers a truthful and realistic depiction of disgust as a strong component of the admixture of postpartum negative feelings. Through its recurrent use of flashback during roughly the first half of the film as Rebecca recalls the latter stages of her pregnancy, childbirth, and then her struggles with early motherhood while tramping through the woods and then waiting to die, the film presents a purposefully subjective perspective. We only experience motherhood through Rebecca's intimate experience and the memory of this experience, which is a far cry from the expectations of unconditional love and affection.[33] This earlier film sets an important example that indirectly influences later films in its lifting of taboos about the exploration of the disgust felt by mothers.

Shit, Blood, and Tears

American filmmaker Bess Wohl's debut feature, *Baby Ruby*, presents a tale of disgust that similarly manifests first in the maternity room. A horror-thriller, the film conjures the expectation of disgust from the beginning. Likewise a first-time mother, Jo's (Noémie Merlant) perfect life as a well-to-do lifestyle influencer and vlogger is rent asunder by early motherhood. Rendered as a nightmare of dystocia from which she breathlessly awakens, the scene of labor is a brief but gory flashback of echoed screaming, struggle, and blood, lots and lots of blood, entirely from Jo's perspective. McGinn taxonomizes the repugnance of pregnancy and parturition without mincing words: "[T]he cramped and coiled fetus swamped in fluid;

the wormlike umbilical cord; the grisly birth process with its blood and placenta; the dilated uterus, sometimes ripped and bleeding; the pain and wailing. The onset of life is almost as bathed in disgust signals as its termination."[34] Hints of *Rosemary's Baby* once again accompany the postpartum scene in *Baby Ruby*. Lumbering out of the hospital bed, Jo hesitantly moves to check on her baby, asleep in a bassinet, apparently unsure of what she might find in the wake of her nightmare. But she is abruptly intercepted by a surly voice resonating through a crack in the door: "Is everything OK?" Followed by: "Did you poop yet? You can't leave until you poop." Likely the voice of an attending nurse, its disembodiment renders it strange. The voice from the nonvisualized source always maintains an element of power and perversity. Unprompted and unpreceded, even in this postnatal context the demand that Jo "poop," furthermore, seems less uncaringly medical than simply grotesque. Not only does Jo become reduced further from maternal body to defecating body—a mere digestive tract—the brutal logic of the scatological inquiry and pronouncement infantilizes, stuns, and, yes, disgusts.

The scene invokes an earlier one in Jason Reitman's *Tully*, discussed in chapter 2, in which the mother, Marlo (Charlize Theron), lashes out at a nurse who demands that she urinate before she can be released from the hospital. In several films considered in this book, the postnatal body becomes an oozing site of excrement that must be brought under control. Kristeva identifies shit as one of the most threatening and polluting forms of the abject next to menstrual blood.[35] Though Kristeva draws an ontological line between shit and the maternal as the filth that becomes defilement, *Baby Ruby* immediately aligns the postpartum body with excrement in this longer sequence. A cut to Jo's midriff as she sits on the toilet in an attempt to fulfill the demand of the nurse captures her blood-soaked padded undergarment. Then a series of jump cuts reveals her pain-stricken mien as she tries to shit. The jump cuts give the impression of a protracted bout of constipation over hours or even days. Eventually she rises from the toilet seat. Another shot of her midriff reveals her inner thighs now smeared with leaking blood. Nearly gagging in disgust, she pulls back the elastic band and peers into her lochia-saturated underwear (figs. 6.1 and 6.2).

The image of her convulsed expression then cuts to the toilet bowl as it flushes. A cesspool of blood and excrement, the revolting close-up image of the toilet is no stranger to the cinema. Most famously, the horrifying eruption of blood from the toilet bowl in Francis Ford Coppola's *The Conversation* (1974) demonstrates a stubborn tarrying or reemergence of excrement desperately condemned to an obscene beyond—the toilet.

FIGURES 6.1 and 6.2. The revolt of the postpartum body in *Baby Ruby*. Directed by Bess Wohl, 2022.

Slavoj Žižek interprets the toilet as the domain of "the horrifyingly-sublime Beyond of the primordial, pre-ontological Chaos into which things [are supposed to] disappear."[36] When things do not disappear into the toilet, horror mounts as the threat of defilement from the beyond quite literally percolates. The close-up of the bloody cesspool within the toilet bowl in *Baby Ruby* lingers in a prolonged flush. Blood and shit introduce us and Jo to motherhood and initiate a strange and disgusting series of occurrences in her postpartum experience, beginning in the hospital and continuing well after her discharge. Upon departure from the hospital, she is accosted by a nurse who delivers to Jo her nearly forgotten placenta in a cooler: "I thought you wanted to eat it . . . it's all nutrients," the nurse gushes from off-screen. Evidently in recoil from this cannibalistic proposal, Jo nonetheless accepts the cooler and its contents. Indeed, the placenta will make its return later in the film when we are given to speculate that Jo not only eats it herself but feeds it to her husband and mother-in-law in the guise of a spaghetti Bolognese.

A film ostensibly about the severity and horror of postpartum psychosis, a rare but real condition, *Baby Ruby* explores the place of disgust that clings to the experience of early motherhood with horrifying stickiness.[37] Thus, despite the medicalizing frame of the film—Jo suffers from psychotic episodes and hallucinations—it does not altogether pathologize the broader reality of her maternal struggles. Attention to disgust, in particular, Jo's expression of disgust, opens up this portrayal of motherhood as experiential and not entirely exceptional. With sleep deprivation in the first weeks of motherhood and long hours spent alone at home while her husband is at work, her delusions appear to intensify. Baby Ruby's chronic colic saps her of all her energy. Against Ruby's howls, lengthy sequences of jump cuts, split screens, and mirror images of desperate rocking and shushing sessions day and night visualize Jo's exhausting postpartum reality as a hallucinatory nightmare. Hours turn into days and then weeks. Jo loses track of time, and her grasp on reality loosens. Her experience of disgust registers most prominently as her recoil against her own postpartum body: her shit, her blood, her afterbirth, her shedding hair, and her sagging, stretch-marked skin.

In front of the bathroom mirror and attached to a mechanical breast pump, Jo inspects her body. In extreme close-up, we see her hands vigorously move over her soft, excessive flesh. She pinches and then kneads the thick knots of loose skin at her abdomen, encasing her navel. The broken red lines of skin stretched beyond its limit serve to mark it. Similar to the earlier close-up of the toilet bowl, the intensifying shot scale that magnifies the object here again serves the effect of disgust. Jo's postpartum flesh becomes isolated and amplified. A formal cinematic design of disgust, the close-up brings us into proximity with the object. The disgusting object is that which gets too close for comfort, what Menninghaus refers to as "a nearness that is not wanted."[38] Caught in close-up, objects become larger than life and, therefore, often monstrous in their surrealization, Doane reminds us in her reading with Jean Epstein.[39] Despite the mechanics of the close-up, exclusively for the viewer, for Jo herself does not see her flesh at such close range, her hands feel what the viewer sees. It is furthermore her reaction that arrives in the form of a reverse shot. The image cuts back to Jo in the mirror. With a look of repulsion, her reflection becomes fixed as she continues to perform minor actions. This surreal scene of disgust evokes her own disembodiment, a splitting of the self through the sickening with the self. When the border between the self and the disgusting object collapses, we seek to escape from ourselves. Here Jo first confronts and then pulls away from herself in loathing.

Not dissimilar to Rebecca in *Das Fremde in mir*, Jo's vocation is to produce beautiful things. *Baby Ruby* opens with Jo's own planning of her baby shower, which must be perfect. Her vlog, *Love, Joséphine*, contains stylish images and tips on lifestyle, travel, fashion, and cooking from her, Jo, "a French girl in America." As she announces at her baby shower, she does not anticipate her baby changing her work or lifestyle in any way. If anything, her baby, which she describes in entrepreneurial terms like a little "brioche," will provide the necessary accessory to help her expand her band of followers in the vlogosphere, as she makes what she foresees as an effortless transition from lifestyle to mommy vlogger and momfluencer. Without directly evoking the terms, the "have-it-all" perfectionism and neoliberalism of both postfeminism and new-momism hang heavily in the air. Susan Douglas and Meredith Michaels interpret the two concepts as inextricably intertwined: "The new momism has become the central, justifying ideology of what has come to be called 'postfeminism.' . . . Postfeminism means that you can now work outside the home even in jobs previously restricted to men, go to graduate school, pump iron, and pump your own gas, as long as you remain fashion conscious, slim, nurturing, deferential to men, and become a doting, selfless mother."[40] This postfeminist, neoliberal intensification of mothering fixates on perfection. And, "[t]he perfect," Angela McRobbie elucidates, hinges "most fully on restoring traditional femininity, which means that female competition is inscribed within specific horizons of value relating to husbands, work partners and boyfriends, family and home, motherhood and maternity."[41]

Some mothers do appear to have it all in *Baby Ruby*. The gauzy troupe of beautiful mothers Jo encounters on several occasions while jogging or once gathered at an organic farm proffer the fantasy of new-momism that she strives so hard to achieve. "You guys look so happy and relaxed and rested. And your babies are so quiet. They don't even cry. What's your secret?" she asks, to which one mother replies imperiously and without pause: "Trust your instincts." Indeed, the institution of motherhood demands instinct over intelligence. Jo begins to doubt herself as a mother, but so caught up in the cruel fantasy of new-momism, her hold on reality slips further. An attachment that becomes its own obstacle, the fantasy of new-momism presents a variation of Lauren Berlant's "cruel optimism."[42] Even as Jo begins to accept that not all is rosy in motherhood, the grip of new-momism remains. In one of the film's most powerful scenes, Jo's overbearing but well-meaning mother-in-law, Doris (Jayne Atkinson), tries to convince her that her maternal struggles are real and understandable.

In a gesture of camaraderie, she reveals her own past toils as a mother and her secret fantasies to even harm her son when he was a baby. But Jo forcefully rejects her advice. "Stop! Just stop! . . . You have to stop!" she repeats with hands over her ears and eyes tightly shut. "Yes, and that's the problem!" Doris exclaims. "We can't talk about these things, not even to each other. We can't admit it. We can't even look at it! And so, it grows stronger." Jo's "mask of motherhood," to speak with Adrienne Rich, does not crack through. She refuses to engage in Doris's discussion of the taboos that keep mothers silent.[43] Cruel optimism dies hard.

Yet, Jo cannot return to her vlog. Disgust manifests at once as a consequence of fantasy and a hindrance to the same in *Baby Ruby*. Jo finds her postpartum body and new lifestyle repulsive because she aspires to an image of the thin, sexy, and stylish mom who has everything under control. But her feelings of disgust do not cohere with the implicitly affirmative and joyous attitude of motherhood: is this not supposed to be the most amazing experience in the world? Already positioned "at the outer limit or threshold" of ugly feelings, as Ngai proclaims, disgust takes the experience of motherhood to the edge.[44] There is no room for ambivalence in disgust in this film. There are no conflicts or equivocations. Disgust is the imperative to expel. It crushes given notions of maternal love and care. As hard as Jo tries, any moments of connection or even tenderness between mother and child in the film strike the viewer as contrived. On two occasions when Jo cuddles Ruby, the consequences prove detrimental. The seemingly toothless infant viciously bites Jo's breast when she attempts to nurse her, and at a later point she grasps Jo's earring so tightly that it violently rips out of her ear. The film offers reminders of Lucy Gaymer and Siân Robins-Grace's horror-comedy series, *The Baby*, and its murderous tot, explored in chapter 3. As hard as she tries, Jo finds no reprieve.

In a culminating near-fatal car crash—similar to the tipping point in *Tully*—Jo is forced to confront the reality of her paranoia and psychoses as more than just gaslighting, of which she has accused her husband and mother-in-law and which certainly holds precedent in the films explored previously in this book. Jo seeks treatment. Like *Das Fremde in mir*, *Baby Ruby*'s story develops, climaxes, and then appears to find some resolution for Jo, who, after a stint in the hospital and in therapy, returns home. But the film ultimately leaves much open. In a final sequence, Jo confronts her split self in an oneiric standoff in the woods, but where exactly she lands remains unclear. So much of Jo's experience, real or imaginary, is bound up with feelings of disgust. The shaping and conditioning of postpartum psychosis through visceral disgust present a pervasive sickening mood that sticks, to borrow Sara Ahmed's descriptive verb for the affect, to the narrative even beyond potential resolution.[45]

Disgusting Memories of Motherhood

Whereas *Das Fremde in mir* and *Baby Ruby* portray disgust in the immediate postpartum period of motherhood and as part of the encompassing medicalized experiences of depression and psychosis, making a second appearance in this book, *The Lost Daughter* explores disgust years after the throes of early motherhood have long passed. I return to the film in this final chapter because as much as it presents a tale of maternal shame (chapter 4), it also powerfully explores maternal disgust. Moldering fruit, insects, oozing wounds, and vomiting dolls: disgust permeates this film as the inescapable memory of motherhood that haunts, even tenaciously pursues, the middle-aged Leda through symbolic objects. In her reading of Elena Ferrante's novel, upon which the film is based, Stiliana Milkova goes so far as to propose that disgust constructs motherhood in *The Lost Daughter*.[46] Kristeva's theory of the abject notwithstanding, if any fiction writer has boldly tackled the topic of maternal disgust, then it is Ferrante.[47] Most important, Ferrante leaves room for maternal subjectivity vis-à-vis disgust. It is impossible to separate disgust from motherhood in this story about a mother still burdened by her earlier abandonment of her two young daughters. As Milkova indicates, Ferrante's "female protagonists are constantly rent by repulsion, repugnance, and revulsion. . . . Bodily fluids and bodily orifices, insects and reptiles, ugly or slimy surfaces take center stage in her narratives."[48] Ferrante allows borders to open.[49]

But before the plot offers glimpses into Leda's past, disgusting objects strangely begin to populate her world in this otherwise beautiful Greek seaside setting. On just the second evening of her stay, Leda reaches into the resplendent fruit bowl positioned centrally on a table of her holiday rental to find that, concealed inside, the fruit has all spoiled (fig. 6.3). The dark, soft rot clinging to peaches, apples, and oranges hidden from first sight produces a sign of disgust all too familiar. In his taxonomy of disgust, Kolnai highlights rot as "disgust aroused by putrefaction, or by a sticky, dirty mishmash."[50] Kristeva generalizes and approaches all food, in the state of rot or not, as potentially disgusting: "Food loathing is perhaps the most elementary and most archaic form of abjection."[51] Determined to feast on this fruit, Leda is assailed by its sight and, judging by her crinkled nose, its smell. In the description of this scene in the novel, even the taste disgusts Leda. "I discovered that under the beautiful show figs, pears,

FIGURE 6.3. The assailing *natura morta* in *The Lost Daughter*. Directed by Maggie Gyllenhaal, 2021.

prunes, peaches, grapes were overripe and rotten. I took a knife and cut off large black areas, but the smell disgusted me, the taste, and I threw almost all of it in the garbage."[52] In the film, Leda first raises a peach, caught in close-up (fig. 6.3). A reverse shot reveals a countenance of disgust as she gasps an "ugh!" Then there is a cut back to the bowl as she raises an orange in a similar state of rot, which elicits from Leda an "oh, my god!" Finally, she picks up the entire tray and moves off-screen. Although she does not attempt to salvage the fruit, as her literary counterpart does, she still consumes the decay through this miasmatic encounter. According to Eugenie Brinkema, the power of the olfactory already introduces decay into the body in a manner of consumption: "To smell decay is to welcome into the body the softening of flesh, to touch that softness in the nerves of the nose and to lose any sense of which skin it is that festers."[53] Catching a whiff of this putrefaction, Leda cannot help but ingest the black rot. In chapter 4, I suggest parallels between *The Lost Daughter* and Thomas Mann's *Tod in Venedig* (Death in Venice, 1912). Are these decaying fruits reminders of the overripe, contaminated strawberries in Mann's novella that very likely killed him in the end?

The image of the bowl of fruit evokes a still-life painting. In the novel, Ferrante provides this description on an earlier page: "The tray shone as if in still-life." Milkova returns us to the Italian original: "Il vassoio brillava come in una natura morta."[54] The Italian for still-life, *natura morta* (quite literally, "dead nature") is much more evocative of this scene of decay.

Infused with the notion that art can, if not conquer death, then at least parry it a while, the *vanitas* (vanity) quality of the still-life so popular in seventeenth-century Dutch painting suspends its objects—fruit, flowers, sometimes shellfish or game—at the immortal threshold of decay.[55] In both novel and film, however, death and decay cannot be kept at bay; they are not frozen in time as on the canvas. From aesthetic to gastronomic, the rotten fruits in *The Lost Daughter* assume a life and death of their own and remind us of disgust's most elemental manifestation. What appeared upon arrival in Greece as a shining and inviting tray of fruit reveals itself to be a disgusting reminder of mortality. Fruit will return multiple times in the film both through flashbacks and in the final scene as a symbol of Leda's connection to her children, for whom she used to frequently peel oranges, thus deepening the symbolism of the encounter within the context of this film about motherhood.

On a subsequent evening, Leda awakens to the shrill buzzing of a large cicada perched on her pillow as it secretes a yellow fluid. The sight causes her to visibly recoil. "I felt disgust," Leda narrates in the first person of Ferrante's novel. According to the novel, the massive insect has presumably burst its stomach from gorging on olive-tree sap and now empties the contents onto Leda's pillow. Disgust heightens at the recognition of what Milkova refers to as "this act of violating natural borders and letting the interior slime ooze out uncontained."[56] The horror within, Kristeva might describe this scene with the cicada as "the collapse of the border between inside and outside." The skin "a fragile container, no longer guaranteed the integrity of one's 'own and clean self' . . . and gave way before the dejection of its contents."[57] A bursting stomach that dejects its contents strongly summons a vision of maternity and especially parturition, reduced in this scene to the insect world of slime and presumed death. With a look of repulsion, Leda picks up the pillow and hurls the cicada out the open window. Returning to bed, she hides her face under the covers in a direct turning away from the site of disgust.

The burst stomach of the cicada not only serves as a revolting reminder of pregnancy and birth, it also foreshadows Leda's own wounds in the film. First, she is hit in the back by a wayward pine cone in the woods while leaving the beach, the unknown provenance of which serves the film's mystery. Inspecting her wound in the bathroom mirror back in her apartment, she glimpses a swath of flesh reddened by abrasion, which seeps blood. Near the end of the film, Leda also sustains a severe abdominal wound, stabbed by Nina with the very hatpin Leda gave to her as a gift. Yelling obscenities, not least calling Leda a "fucking sick cunt," Nina inflicts a wound both physical and verbal in the scene. The assault on Leda unsettles further in its brutal sexualization and maternalization of her body. Motherhood and femininity are met with violence and pathologization: y.o.u. f.u.c.k.i.n.g. s.i.c.k. c.u.n.t. Nina's attack on Leda is an attack on motherhood. She evokes a long and deeply misogynist tradition of what Menninghaus characterizes as the trope of the *vetula*, or "the disgusting old woman," in aesthetic culture, and Kristeva, the maternal abject.[58] Not quite burst open, Leda's abdomen does ooze, not sap but blood. The boundary of the body has been forced open, and as we will see, refuses to close. Prompted by Leda's confession that she was the one who took Nina's daughter's doll, the stabbing ultimately enacts a disproportionately violent punishment for Leda's cruel and strange act of theft and admission that she is an unnatural mother. It comes as no surprise that the doll also figures centrally in this film's taxonomy of disgust.

Roughly a quarter of the way through and in the midst of a commotion caused by Nina's daughter's brief but distressing disappearance on the beach, Leda steals the child's doll. It is unclear why she does this. In flashback, we learn that Leda also had a doll she cherished as a child and which she lovingly passed on to the eldest of her own daughters, Bianca. Unenthused by this old plastic doll, Bianca takes a marker to it. Upon discovering this, Leda flies into a rage and flings the doll out of the apartment window. Crashing against the street below, the plastic figure shatters into pieces. Evocative of a painful memory of motherhood and maternal struggle, one would imagine Leda would keep her distance from the doll. Certainly, cinematic representations of dolls almost exclusively belong to the realm of horror, ineluctably uncanny and revolting because, as William Ian Miller notes, they look human but are not.[59] Elena's doll becomes a locus of disgust in Leda's possession. After bringing it back to her apartment and inspecting it, Leda presses the doll tightly to her breast in a maternal embrace, only to be spewed upon with a slimy flow of muddy seawater. We might read this act of vomiting as the doll's manner of ejection of the self, its own separation of being, and, perhaps, as a surrogate for Leda. The novel certainly goes in this direction: Leda narrates, "Nani, with her black spittle, resembles me when I was pregnant for the second time."[60] In the film, the doll's expelling and splattering remarkably invoke the real messiness of early motherhood, to which Leda responds in disgust. This maternal act of embracing the doll ends in Leda's repugnance and another drone of "ugh!" Awakening with a start in a subsequent scene, Leda's left breast is still soiled light brown from the doll's murky ejection. The blotch resembles the remains of a lactating breast and, again, a recollection of motherhood. Turbid water is just a prelude to an even more vomitous seepage from the doll's dark cavity. Paced several scenes and days apart in the film, Leda is confronted by a long, thin, black worm that slithers from the toy's open maw. Upon noticing the darkness, which emerges as the slimy reptile, Leda reacts with loathing and throws the doll onto the bathroom floor. Giving birth to a living object, the doll now wholly assumes a maternal form. But why then does Leda steal the doll, this object of absolute disgust, in the first place? Leda cares for the doll. She cleans it and buys new clothing for it. Does she attempt to cleanse what she perceives as unclean? Rub out the abject nature of the doll and, therefore, that of motherhood? The doll clearly holds an allure for her. In one scene, she believes she may have misplaced it and frantically searches her apartment. Leda's relationship to the doll models Menninghaus's conceptualization of disgust as that which both repels and attracts.[61] This paradox of disgust similarly captures Leda's coinciding fascination with and aversion to motherhood, what Kolnai calls a "macabre allure."[62]

The paradox of disgust that manifests in *The Lost Daughter* operates differently than it does in a horror film, in which disgust, not unlike fear, appeals to the viewer as a means of visceral, sadomasochistic thrills.[63] Here, instead, disgust occasionally bumps up against the beautiful. Although the beauty of the film's setting on a Greek island and the intimate cinematography does not dispel disgust and, indeed, often brings us too close for comfort, it prevents the film from succumbing completely to disgust. A notable case of the paradox of disgust for Kolnai is haut goût. In Brinkema's comprehensive reading of Peter Greenaway's *The Cook, The Thief, His Wife, and Her Lover* (1989) through the affective form of disgust, she also scrutinizes the possibilities of haut goût: "The paradox of disgust—its blend of aversion and attraction—results in a heightened sensual experience, one that is in the best taste, and that tastes best, by retaining its link to the revolting. Decay accentuates, exaggerates, alluringly brings out characteristics by subjecting them to the force of rot's state changes; decay can bring into existence new qualities—even vitality of the new as such."[64] This passage returns us to the rotting fruit in *The Lost Daughter*. Though the moldering peaches, apples, and oranges are not the same as the dishes explicitly enjoyed in the state of decay, such as gamey pheasant, we cannot deny their aversion and attraction. Upon arrival, Leda acknowledges the platter with a nod of approval and runs her hand over the surface of the fruit. In the darkness of the evening, the fruit shimmers in deep colors, as though painted by Caravaggio's brush.

The film's final scene brings the paradox of disgust to the fore. Leda awakens on the beach, lapped by the incoming tide. The night before, her car went off a cliff. She stumbled from the wreck and collapsed on the beach. The surreal note in this final scene subtends its tone of disgust. Is

Leda actually dead? Upon waking, dazed and confused Leda first inspects her stab wound, which has stubbornly secreted in blots of crimson, staining her white blouse and leaking onto her prodding fingers. What some might read as a saccharine ending, first with its cut to a flashback of Leda as a young mother enjoying an intimate moment with her daughters and then a phone call between present-day Leda and her two adult daughters, I read as the film's culmination of disgust. Suddenly, an orange appears in her hand, and in close-up her bloodied fingers begin to peel it. A nurturing symbol of her connection with her daughters, the orange also stands as a reminder of rot, violence, and decay in the film. Captured in close-up from Leda's perspective, her burgundy-stained fingers pulling at the orange's flesh in this penultimate shot give rise to disgust. This is not an image of nurture and storgic love but one of revolting gore.

A mother's feeling of disgust moves this chapter. Often cited as the source of disgust and certainly abjection, the mother's own subjectivity in this affective experience has long been ignored. *Das Fremde in mir*, *Baby Ruby*, and *The Lost Daughter* all explore disgust from the perspective of the mother. The first two begin their tales of disgust in the maternity room at the scene of parturition. Ever more frequently portrayed on the screen, childbirth presents the apeiron of disgust. Visualized or not, the carnage and bodily waste of the event are inexorable. Beyond the visceral horror of labor, childbirth directly challenges the mother's bodily freedom and self through the thrusting open and unmaking of flesh's borders. The subsequent seeping postpartum body of the mother endures into early motherhood. Both mothers in *Das Fremde in mir* and *Baby Ruby* struggle with early maternity and postpartum demands on their bodies. *The Lost Daughter* takes us to a later period of motherhood, in which disgust registers through memory objects associated with being a mother. Suppurating wounds, rot, blood, as well as insects, reptiles, and dolls: these objects make up the diegetic world of *The Lost Daughter* in its turn on maternal disgust. Perhaps even more than the previous two films, *The Lost Daughter* moves away from the perilous objectification of the mother as the source of disgust, in particular, in her postpartum state, to reinforce the subjective experience of disgust still felt by the mother even years later. With a return to *The Lost Daughter* and its igniting confession of the crushing responsibility of motherhood, I conclude this final chapter and leave us in the squalor of the most ugly of affects.

CONCLUSION

Warning: Mothering Can Crush!

Cinema of Crushing Motherhood assembles films that challenge the demands of happiness placed on mothers. The films break with taboos about motherhood by presenting maternal figures who experience a range of negative feelings. To borrow Adrienne Rich's stunning phrasing: these films dive into the wreck—the wreck of the myth of perfect motherhood. Motherhood is not only hard; it can also be downright miserable. These cinematic representations unapologetically visualize this misery—often to an appalled audience. Tracking the steady swell of films invested in maternal bad feelings, this book presents an updated version of what Lucy Fischer terms "cinematernity," or cinema conjoined with maternity. The circumstances of this new cinema range widely and appear to be increasing. In this book I do not dwell too heavily on the impacts of the COVID-19 pandemic—certainly significant but still very recent—on mothers and motherhood. I do trace the radical turn toward the exploration and affirmation of regret in maternal discourse in the 2010s and its direct and indirect influence on these films. If nothing else, this latter phenomenon has created an aperture for unconditional maternal complaint. Regret goes as far as acknowledging some mothers' wishes to undo motherhood, to turn back time and say "no." Probing these films through regret and concomitant negative feelings permits a closer and more rigorous look at what it means to be a mother and to be in a terrible state.

What does it mean to be crushed by motherhood? The act of crushing can be so violent that it can cause an object to lose shape or, worse, break into pieces. Motherhood crushes. It squeezes and deforms mothers; it violently alters their bodies and their very beings. But the films in this book do not offer portrayals of crushed mothers alone. The dual significance of crushing here describes the films as radical objects themselves, which also participate in the intensity. The films *crush* motherhood and the terrorizing institution it has long upheld. They force our recognition of motherhood as anything but ever pleasant, joyful, and fulfilling. Mothers in these films are regretful, exhausted, enraged, ashamed, guilt-ridden, and even disgusted. This cinema pushes the boundaries of maternal representation through its pursuit of maternal regret and bad feelings like few other media and, perhaps, no other audiovisual media. The new cinematernity that unfolds in this book reveals sides of motherhood long relegated to the shadows. Giving these arcane yet rife experiences image, body, and sound, it advances other ways of mothering and being outside of the trite and harmful ideal of the maternal, which—let's face it—is simply dressed-up white patriarchy, as Rich has taught us.

A conclusion here can offer only a summary and a survey of the chapters, which cannot be stacked on top of one another according to teleological or chronological sequence. Although structurally similar and overlapping in theme, each chapter is a unique study of a particular feeling, its history, its properties, and its systematic interpretation over time. Certain voices do echo throughout the book, such as those of Beauvoir and Rich, but each chapter asks in its own way what it means to feel regret or exhaustion or rage or shame or guilt or disgust. This book's series of affective studies wades through the philosophy of these feelings to eke a path toward understanding the deep ontological and ethical imperatives of motherhood at work in this cinema. Without inviting a linear arc, *Cinema of Crushing Motherhood* does pursue comprehensive pathways of thinking and approaching film. It partakes of film philosophy, an interdisciplinary field invested in the important exchanges and engagements between film studies and philosophy. Taking philosophy to bear on the questions of cinema, it reveals the rich philosophical layers of these films and in turn (I hope!) also inspires us to think differently about topics in aesthetics, ethics, and ontology more broadly.

A collection of philosophical and affective studies of film that crisscrosses along circuitous paths of Western thought, *Cinema of Crushing Motherhood* takes maternal feelings seriously. It recognizes mothering, inter alia, as the absolute being-for-the-Other and the ethical dilemma to which that gives rise. The sacrifice of motherhood is oceanic. It can feel like a hostile takeover of the body and the self. In multifaceted ways, this book provides contour to the maternal struggles we see on-screen; it sharpens our approach to contemporary images of motherhood. Diverging in genre, mode, and cultural provenance, the book's somewhat motley ensemble of films and series expanding across drama, horror, thriller, and documentary shows collectively what the experiences of both mothering and motherhood can look, sound, and even smell like, most important, *for the mother*. She is the active feeling subject both of this new cinema and of this book.

I did not set out to write a book of new feminist cinema. Such a grandiose pursuit would intimidate even the most ambitious of authors. The subtitle of this book, *A New Feminist Cinema*, as it so often does, came much later as a solicited shorthand or elucidation. But it fits. This is a study that explores films—in many cases, debut films—mostly by women directors about a shared experience from the perspective of women.[1] What is it then if not feminist? And what are these films if not likewise feminist? Notwithstanding the complexity and discursive slipperiness of feminist cinema as a concept, genre, mode, or movement difficult to define, most would agree that it emerged as both practice and theory with the women's movement in the 1970s and developed through the 1980s and 1990s.[2] At its outset, it aspired to present audiences with a picture of the ordinary details of women's lives, their thoughts, and the challenges they face from the perspective of women, a picture not previously shown and explored on the screen.[3] Feminist cinema was and continues to be primarily what Patricia White refers to, drawing on Claire Johnston, as a "countercinema by and for women."[4] The interventional nature of this cinema operates on different levels. Certainly, it is about presenting new perspectives and stories on screen, but it also goes deeper than that. In her early, foundational essay, "Women's Cinema as Counter-Cinema," Johnston clarifies that this cinema calls for a Marxist rethinking of the very tools and techniques of cinema itself, which she deems "an ideological product—the product of bourgeois ideology."[5] For one, a feminist cinema seeks to challenge the founding idealisms of desire, fantasy, and romanticism and especially of woman as spectacle within this nexus. The films that comprise the cinema of crushing motherhood follow in the footsteps of earlier feminist or women's cinema. At the same time, they stretch the possibilities of earlier feminist cinemas further with a crushing intensity that catapults the bourgeois housewife model and its fantasies of sacrificial maternity. Yes, this is categorically a feminist cinema.

Even just a gloss of the history of feminist cinema demonstrates its critical (if indirect) engagement with Marxist calls for family abolition, recently revisited by contemporary feminist and queer scholars. Although not central to this book, family abolition provides an important frame. Similar to the discourse of regretting motherhood, family abolition presents a contemporary revolutionizing of kinship against the private family shaped by violent traditions of colonialism and capitalism, which can isolate and sometimes brutalize. Rather than focusing on motherhood, however, this discourse moves toward a more gender-inclusive critique of the family. In this concluding chapter I am thus inclined to reflect on my project and its approach to the maternal that focuses on women. Indeed, is not a study about women's films and women's experiences of motherhood too narrow, too essentialist, too obsolete? In a defense of her own choice to focus on and name "women's cinema" in her book *Women's Cinema, World Cinema*, White helpfully cites Alison Butler's definition of women's filmmaking that rejects the reproval of gendered essentialism. "The distinctiveness of women's filmmaking is . . . not based on an essentialist understanding of gendered subjectivity, but on the position—or positions—of women in contemporary culture."[6] Originally written over two decades ago, Butler's words still ring true. For better or for worse, with the cycle of recent films about motherhood that form its basis, *Cinema of Crushing Motherhood* emerges from the (unique) *positions* of mothers and women in contemporary culture, which are still so enmeshed in systematically assigned social roles and stereotypes. From beginning to end, I follow the insights of the films and ask what they do and tell us about motherhood. They guide this study. So many women filmmakers find inspiration in stories of the experiences and burdens of motherhood, and for many this becomes their first foray into filmmaking. We do not see the same thing happening with fatherhood. Let's face it, a survey of recent films presents far fewer examples that explore the experiences and burdens of fatherhood on men. Perhaps these are yet to come. The response to a question posed to the editors of *Mothers of Invention: Film, Media, and Caregiving Labor* (2022) about why none of their chapters look at fatherhood brings this into perspective: They did not receive any contributions about fatherhood, despite initial attempts to broaden the scope of the volume to look at parenthood more generally.[7]

On a related and final note, as I put the finishing touches on this book in late summer of 2024 the US Surgeon General issued an advisory about the hazards of parenting on mental health. It called attention to parenting as a critical public health issue. Its warning states: "Over the last decade, parents have been consistently more likely to report experiencing high levels of stress compared to other adults. 33% of parents reporting high levels of stress in the past month compared to 20% of other adults. When stress is severe or prolonged, it can have a harmful effect on the mental health of parents and caregivers."[8] Significantly impacted by the COVID-19 pandemic, parents certainly do shoulder an incredible responsibility that has only accreted the world over. Public recognition and the call for more support are important steps. By the same token, such a warning comes belatedly, dare we say even centuries late. Indeed, why is that as soon as we open up the category of caregiving and begin talking more about "parenting" rather than "mothering" suddenly public recognition for its crushing responsibility becomes possible? Imagine if the advisory stated: "*Mothers* have been consistently more likely *to experience* [though not report] high levels of stress compared to other adults." Or simply: "Warning: Mothering Can Crush!" No such public statement exists, nor likely ever will, but collectively, the films that make up this study unapologetically offer such a warning.

Notes

Preface

1. Biss, "Of Institution Born," xiv.
2. Ruddick, *Maternal Thinking*, xxvii.

Introduction. A New Cinematernity

1. Rich, *Of Woman Born*, 25.
2. *Oxford English Dictionary Online*, "crush," accessed January 17, 2025, https://www.oed.com/search/dictionary/?scope=Entries&q=crush.
3. Milton, *Paradise Lost*, 118 (book 6, line 340).
4. This book interprets film broadly to include serial productions on streaming platforms.
5. The international Wages for Housework movement is still relevant today. See Federici, *Wages against Housework*.
6. O'Reilly, "Trying to Function," 8.
7. Flynn, "All-Consuming."
8. Mayer and Columpar, *Mothers of Invention*, 2.
9. Arnold, *Maternal Horror Film*, 68.
10. Kaplan, "Case of the Missing Mother," 128.
11. Kaplan, *Motherhood and Representation*, 45, 110–12; Ladd-Taylor and Umansky, *"Bad" Mothers*, 2.
12. Ruddick, *Maternal Thinking*, 189.
13. Kaplan, *Motherhood and Representation*, 45.
14. Kaplan, "Case of the Missing Mother," 128; Creed, *Monstrous-Feminine*.
15. Ladd-Taylor and Umansky, *"Bad" Mothers*, 2.
16. Quiney, "Confessions," 23.

17. Lubecker, *Feel-Bad Film*, 2. "Ugly feelings" I have, of course, from Sianne Ngai, *Ugly Feelings*.

18. Fischer, *Cinematernity*, 4–5.

19. Consider especially Williams, "Something Else."

20. I explore this further in chapter 1 of this book with reference to two newer films, *Stories We Tell* (Sarah Polley, 2012) and *The Arbor* (Clio Barnard, 2010). See Kaplan, "Case of the Missing Mother," 126–27; Rich and Williams, "Right of Re-Vision," 212–19. B. Ruby Rich is most notably linked to the term "cinefeminism." See *Chick Flicks*, 1–2.

21. Baraitser, *Maternal Encounters*, 4.

22. Fischer, *Cinematernity*, 4.

23. Guevara-Flanagan and Lusztig, "How to Do Everything," 66. Another compilation/documentary film one could take as a starting point is Elizabeth Sankey's recent *Witches* (2024). Culling clips from an extensive archive of fiction cinema, this film explores the long history of stigmatization of postpartum depression and psychosis. Due to its late release in November 2024 on the streaming platform MUBI, I unfortunately could not include it in this study, but it attests to the continuing relevance and interest in this topic.

24. Rémy, "Yours in Sisterhood."

25. Eichhorn, *Archival Turn*.

26. Landry, "Searching for a Storyteller," 114.

27. Baer, "Remediations of Cinefeminism," 144.

28. Mulvey, "Women Making History," 29, 31.

29. Torlasco, "Against House Arrest," 40.

30. Hamacher and Lusztig, "Conversation," 66.

31. I speculate that Sophie Lewis's Euro-American connection has provided the impetus for her reference to regretting motherhood within her own work on the abolition of the family. Lewis, *Full Surrogacy Now*, 6.

32. Gill, "Affective," 619. See also Brady, *Mother Trouble*, 6.

33. Douglas and Michaels, *Mommy Myth*, 25.

34. Gleeson and Griffiths, "Kinderkommunismus."

35. Marx and Engels, "Manifesto," 487.

36. Gleeson and Griffiths, "Kinderkommunismus."

37. Lewis, *Abolish the Family*, 6.

38. Weeks, "Abolition."

39. Landman, *Regret*, 36.

40. Donath, "Regretting Motherhood," 360.

41. Karklin, "Exhaustion," n.p.

42. Hamacher and Lusztig, "Conversation," 68.

43. Rich, *Of Woman Born*, lxi.

44. O'Reilly, "Mothering against Motherhood," 165.

45. Gumbs, Martens, and Williams, *Revolutionary Mothering*, 9.

46. Hartman, *Lose Your Mother*, 85.

47. Sharpe, *In the Wake*, 28.

48. Collins, "Shifting the Center," 45.
49. Ruth Quiney notes the phenomenon of confessional maternal memoirs popular in the early twenty-first century and their "subjective experience and personal politics." As Jennifer Nash illumines, these were predominately authored by white, middle-class mothers. See Quiney, "Confessions," 19; Nash, *Birthing Black Mothers*, 136.
50. Nash, "Political Life," 711.
51. See Ahmed, *Living a Feminist Life*, 162.
52. Kristeva, *Powers*, 47.

Chapter 1. Regret

1. Beauvoir, *Second Sex*, 565, 556.
2. Rich, *Of Woman Born*, 1, 30, 25.
3. Parker, *Torn in Two*, 1.
4. Almond, *Monster Within*, 1.
5. LaChance Adams, *Mad Mothers*, 35.
6. Almond, *Monster Within*, 4.
7. Berlant, *On the Inconvenience*, 27.
8. Donath, *Regretting Motherhood*, xix.
9. Donath, *Regretting Motherhood*, xix.
10. Donath, "Regretting Motherhood," 360.
11. Donath, *Regretting Motherhood*, xx.
12. Heffernan and Stone, "#regrettingmotherhood," 338.
13. Göbel, "Sie wollen ihr Leben." See also Kaiser, *Das Unwohlsein*, 21, and Bock, "Racism and Sexism."
14. Wildenthal, *German Women*, 79, 91, 103.
15. Rich, *Of Woman Born*, 33.
16. Heffernan and Stone, "#regrettingmotherhood," 349.
17. Heffernan and Stone, "#regrettingmotherhood," 349.
18. Donath, *#regretting motherhood*, 13, my translation.
19. Duden, "Rabenmutter," accessed January 18, 2025, https://www.duden.de/suchen/dudenonline/rabenmutter.
20. Ladd-Taylor and Umansky, *"Bad" Mothers*, 2.
21. Wellershaus, "Rabenmutter."
22. See Göbel, *Die falsche Wahl*, and Mundlos, *Wenn Mutter*.
23. Landman, *Regret*, 5.
24. Landman, *Regret*, 15.
25. Landman, *Regret*, 36.
26. Price, *Theory of Regret*, 5.
27. Price, *Theory of Regret*, 8.
28. Spelman, *Fruits of Sorrow*, 107; Ahmed, *Cultural Politics*, 118–19.
29. Ahmed, *Cultural Politics*, 119.
30. Donath, "Regretting Motherhood," 345.

31. Donath, *Regretting Motherhood*, 222.
32. Donath, *Regretting Motherhood*, xix, original emphasis.
33. Lesage, "Political Aesthetics," 507.
34. Lesage, "Political Aesthetics," 508.
35. Hoffmann and Grimme, *Regretting Motherhood*.
36. Thornham, "Impossible Subjects?" 263.
37. Rich and Williams, "Right of Re-Vision," 215.
38. Patricia White comments that even well-meaning feminist documentary traditions of self-presentation and self-narration can serve the exploitative desires of a consuming public keen on witnessing up close and personal the suffering of another. See White, "Documentary Practice," 217.
39. I have altered the English slightly from that of the subtitles to produce a more literal translation.
40. Nichols, *Introduction to Documentary*, 139. Robin Curtis and Angelica Fenner remind us of autobiography's genealogical link to confession, with the literary precursors by St. Augustine and Jean-Jacques Rousseau. See Curtis and Fenner, *Autobiographical Turn*, 11.
41. Walker and Waldman, *Feminism and Documentary*, 2.
42. I have altered the English slightly from that of the subtitles to produce a more literal translation.
43. Rangan, *Immediations*, 134.
44. Rangan, *Immediations*, 105.
45. Cartwright, *Moral Spectatorship*, 6.
46. Rangan, *Immediations*, 139.
47. Certainly, in the case of Spain, the rule of Franco endured much longer and until more recently than that of Hitler in Germany, but this history and its influence on motherhood apply to both national contexts. Heffernan and Stone, "International Responses," 125.
48. Heffernan and Stone, "International Responses," 125.
49. Pérez Nieto, "Motherhood."
50. Russell, *Archiveology*, 21.
51. Leyda, *Films Beget Films*, 13.
52. Nichols, "Remaking History," 150–51.
53. Mulvey, "Women Making History," 29.
54. Mulvey does not address the situationist movement in her article, but the artistic concept of "détournement" is frequently associated with the movement's radical repurposing of objects. Mulvey, "Women Making History," 29, 31.
55. Columpar and Mayer, *There She Goes*, 2. See also Putnam, *Maternal*, 55.
56. Ruido, "Mater Amatísima."
57. O'Brien, *Family Abolition*, 45.
58. Because there was some discrepancy between what Sophie Rois says in German and the subtitles in English, I have altered the translation slightly to produce a more literal translation.

59. Euripides, *Medea*, 35.
60. Lombardo, "Medeas," 25.
61. Astrid Deuber-Mankowsky makes an argument specifically for Pasolini's film, but I contend that the same can be said for Trier's later version. See Deuber-Mankowsky, "Cinematographic Aesthetics," 256.
62. Cited in Kerrigan, *Revenge Tragedy*, 109.
63. Pérez Nieto, "Motherhood," 207.
64. S. I. Johnston, Introduction, 6.
65. Pérez Nieto, "Motherhood," 209.
66. Rosario Porto, who had a history of depression, was found dead in her cell in 2020 in an apparent death by suicide.
67. Pérez Nieto, "Motherhood," 209.
68. L. Fischer, *Cinematernity*, 23.
69. Chodorow and Contratto, "Fantasy," 62.
70. The abusive and at times extremely violent comments that circulate in social media about mothers who express regret and comments about Donath herself attest to this. Donath, *Regretting Motherhood*, xvi.
71. Donath, *Regretting Motherhood*, 189.
72. This text is spoken in voice-over in Spanish. The same text can be found in English translation on Ruido's website in a description of the film. Ruido, "Mater Amatísima."
73. Similar to the previous quote, this text is spoken in voice-over in Spanish. The same text can be found in English translation on Ruido's website in a description of the film. Ruido, "Mater Amatísima."
74. As Heffernan and Stone reveal, beyond its place of origin in Israel, the regretting motherhood debate has found traction in Europe, North America, and South Korea. Heffernan and Stone, "International Responses," 123n2.

Chapter 2. Exhaustion

1. Baraitser, *Maternal Encounters*, 11.
2. Rich, *Of Woman Born*, 25.
3. Beauvoir, *Second Sex*, 644, 73–75, 639, 568, original emphasis.
4. Lori J. Marso's recent declaration that Beauvoir uses a specifically cinematic method is illuminating here. Marso, "Phenomenology in the Kitchen," 56–57n4.
5. Deleuze, *Cinema 2*, xi, 189.
6. See Landry and Landry, "Torlasco's 'Philosophy in the Kitchen,'" 465.
7. Deleuze, *Cinema 2*, xi.
8. Deleuze, "Exhausted."
9. A host of authors has called attention to this gendering of the time-image, particularly, as it pertains to Italian neorealism. See Torlasco, "Philosophy in the Kitchen"; Casarino, "Images for Housework"; Landry and Landry, "Torlasco's 'Philosophy in the Kitchen.'"

10. Deleuze, *Cinema 2*, 1–2.
11. Bazin, *What Is Cinema?* 77.
12. Deleuze, *Cinema 2*, 1–2; 12.
13. This builds on an article I cowrote with Christinia Landry, "Torlasco's 'Philosophy in the Kitchen.'"
14. Gorfinkel, "Weariness," 324.
15. Deleuze, *Cinema 2*, 142.
16. Beauvoir, *Second Sex*, 640.
17. Deleuze, *Cinema 2*, 274. Gilles Deleuze also considers becoming at length in his works with Félix Guattari.
18. Beauvoir, *Second Sex*, 640.
19. Deleuze, *Cinema 2*, 189, 196, 276; see also Gorfinkel, "Weariness," 313.
20. Gorfinkel, "Weariness," 313.
21. Aviva Briefel makes this important point. See Briefel, "Parenting," 3.
22. Baraitser, *Maternal Encounters*, 67. See also Putnam, *Maternal*, 31.
23. Compared to the other films examined in this chapter, there is a plethora of secondary literature on *The Babadook*.
24. Arnold, *Maternal Horror Film*, 1–2.
25. Creed, *Monstrous-Feminine*.
26. Still, "Abject Relations," 24.
27. Briefel, "Parenting," 13.
28. MacInnes, "Babadook."
29. Zhang, "All about Repetition."
30. Howell and Baker, *Monstrous Possibilities*, 29.
31. Baraitser, *Maternal Encounters*, 57–58. See also Putnam, *Maternal*, 32.
32. Quindlen, "Playing God"; Almond, *Monster Within*, 185–90.
33. Quindlen, "Playing God."
34. Sobchack, *Carnal Thoughts*, 79.
35. Rich, *Of Woman Born*, 24.
36. Donath, *Regretting Motherhood*, 31, 39.
37. Rich, *Of Woman Born*, 37.
38. Donath, *Regretting Motherhood*, 31.
39. Mundlos, *Mütterterror*, 11, my translation.
40. Bradshaw, "Tully Review."
41. Beauvoir, *Second Sex*, 638.
42. Doane, *Desire*, 71.
43. Berlant, *Cruel Optimism*, 24.
44. Hirsch, *Mother/Daughter Plot*, 14.
45. Spelman, "Woman as Body," 39, 40.
46. Hirsch, *Mother/Daughter Plot*, 166.
47. Beauvoir, *Second Sex*, 484.
48. Tasker, *Working Girls*, 145. Certainly, many other scholars have also argued this. Betty Friedan even notoriously referred to the home as "the

comfortable concentration camp" for women in that feminist tome. Friedan *Feminine Mystique*, 282.

49. O'Brien, *Family Abolition*, 25.
50. Hornaday, "A Thousand and One."
51. Beauvoir, *Second Sex*, 640.
52. Collins, "Shifting the Center," 47.
53. Nash, "Political Life," 701.
54. Nash, "Political Life," 711.
55. A. Walker, "Writer," 99. See also Nash, *Birthing Black Mothers*, 137–42. Nash brings our attention to a different essay by Walker, "One Child of One's Own: A Meaningful Digression within the Work(s)" (1979). This slightly later essay still maintains some of the ambivalence of the first but is not as expressive of the interruption of motherhood.
56. Roberts, *Torn Apart*, 20.
57. Hartman, *Wayward Lives*, 90–91.
58. This is something I explore in an article on several of Schanelec's films. See Landry, "Gendered Suspension."
59. Quinlivan, *Place of Breath*, 3.
60. Quinlivan, *Place of Breath*, 119.
61. Tremblay, *Breathing Aesthetics*, 24. See also Williams, "Film Bodies."
62. Irigaray, *Between East and West*, 47.
63. Deleuze, *Cinema 2*, 193–94.
64. Gorfinkel, "Weariness," 316.
65. See Landry, "Gendered Suspension."
66. See, for instance the description of the film, "Ich war zuhause, aber," *filmportal.de*, https://www.filmportal.de/.
67. Pethö, "Between Absorption," 41.
68. Bordwell, *Figures*, 67. See also Thompson and Bordwell, "Observations on Film Art."
69. Brinkema, *Forms*, 101.
70. Peucker, *Material Image*, 55.
71. Landry, "Gendered Suspension," 176.
72. Ziegler, "Michelangelo."
73. Peucker, *Material Image*, 62.
74. Brinkema, *Forms*, 98.
75. Kaplan, *Motherhood and Representation*, 97.
76. Kristeva, "Stabat Mater," 133.
77. Kristeva, "Stabat Mater," 135.
78. Kaplan, *Motherhood and Representation*, 4.
79. Rich, *Of Woman Born*, 21.
80. Rich, *Of Woman Born*, 18.
81. Nancy, *Fall of Sleep*, ix, 1.
82. Nancy, *Fall of Sleep*, 3.

Chapter 3. Rage

1. Rich, *Of Woman Born*, 30.
2. A slew of new books that focus on feminist rage have been published in the last decade: Brittney Cooper's *Eloquent Rage* (2018), Soraya Chemaly's *Rage Becomes Her* (2018) and Rebecca Traister's *Good and Mad: The Revolutionary Power of Women's Anger* (2018) and the edited volume *Burn It Down: Women Writing about Anger* (2019).
3. Tomkins, *Shame*, 197.
4. A number of authors have pointed out this important trajectory, myself included. See Ngai, *Ugly Feelings*, 182; Landry, *Theatre of Anger*; Cherry, *Case for Rage*.
5. Aristotle, *Nicomachean Ethics*, 73.
6. Kim, *On Anger*, 45.
7. Dubin, "Rage."
8. Hirsch, *Mother/Daughter Plot*, 170. A note also on language: Throughout, I employ the terms "anger" and "rage" interchangeably. Although "rage" does tend to leverage more intensity than "anger" and is often considered anger's evil twin, most feminist authors view the terms analogously, and I follow this model.
9. Creed, *Monstrous-Feminine*, 47.
10. Ahmed, *Promise of Happiness*, 68.
11. Modleski, *Women*, 24.
12. McHugh, "Prolegomenon," 13.
13. Clover, *Men, Women, and Chainsaws*, 164.
14. Arnold, *Maternal Horror Film*, 28.
15. Creed, *Monstrous-Feminine*; Kaplan, *Motherhood and Representation*, 107–23.
16. Rich, *Of Woman Born*, 5, 13.
17. Ahmed, *Cultural Politics*, 174.
18. Ahmed, *Cultural Politics*, 174–75.
19. Ahmed, *Cultural Politics*, 174–75.
20. Lorde, *Sister Outsider*, 124, 127.
21. Ahmed, *Cultural Politics*, 175.
22. McHugh, "Prolegomenon," 14–15, 21n51.
23. Rich, *Of Woman Born*, 13.
24. Rich, *Of Woman Born*, 3.
25. Balanzategui, "Babadook," 27.
26. Creed, *Monstrous-Feminine*, 139–40.
27. MacInnes, "Babadook."
28. Howell and Baker, *Monstrous Possibilities*, 33.
29. Chodorow, *Reproduction of Mothering*, 77–91; Kaplan, *Motherhood and Representation*, 45.
30. Pyles, "Centring," 171; Almond, *Monster Within*, 190.

31. Rich, *Of Woman Born*, 5.
32. Barone, "Year's Best?"
33. Mangan, "Baby Review"; Hess, "When Motherhood Is a Horror Show."
34. Archer, "What Overturning Roe v Wade Could Mean."
35. O'Brien, *Family Abolition*, 6, 237, original emphasis.
36. Trister Grace and Anderson, "Reproductive Coercion," 371.
37. Mundlos, *Mütterterror*.
38. Mangan, "Baby Review."
39. Beauvoir, *Second Sex*, 524, 532.
40. Rich, *Of Woman Born*, xxxv.
41. L. Fischer, *Cinematernity*, 75.
42. L. Fischer, *Cinematernity*, 76.
43. Hirsch, *Mother/Daughter Plot*, 3.
44. Frye, *Politics of Reality*, 88.
45. Ahmed, *Cultural Politics*, 177.
46. Frye, *Politics of Reality*, 88. See also Austin, *How to Do Things*, 22.
47. Frye, *Politics of Reality*, 89.
48. Hirsch, *Mother/Daughter Plot*, 169.
49. Hirsch, *Mother/Daughter Plot*, 169–70.
50. Almond, *Monster Within*, 198.
51. Ahmed, *Living*, 162.
52. Almond, *Monster Within*, 190.
53. Ngai, *Ugly Feelings*, 175.
54. Ngai, *Ugly Feelings*, 179.
55. Rich, *Of Woman Born*, 3.
56. LaChance Adams, *Mad Mothers*, 24.
57. Cooper, *Eloquent Rage*, 174.
58. Petersen, "Burn It Down."
59. Lesage, "Women's Rage," 420.
60. Rich, *Of Woman Born*, 30.

Chapter 4. Shame

1. Chodorow and Contratto, "Fantasy," 65.
2. Sutherland, "Mothering."
3. Chodorow and Contratto, "Fantasy," 65.
4. Levinas, *On Escape*, 64–65.
5. Merleau-Ponty, *Phenomenology*, 193.
6. Merleau-Ponty, *Phenomenology*, 193.
7. Sartre, *Being and Nothingness*, 345–50.
8. Sartre, *Being and Nothingness*, 350, original emphasis.
9. Tomkins, *Shame*, 133, 136–37.
10. Sedgwick, *Touching Feeling*, 36, emphasis added.
11. Copjec, "Object-Gaze," 167.

12. Berlant and Edelman, *Sex*, 37.

13. Speth, "Madonnen," my translation.

14. See, for instance, Schnelle, "Rabenmutter"; Nicodemus, "Mama geht weg."

15. Speth, "Interview," my translation.

16. Hussing, "Regretting," 79.

17. Taylor and Wallace, "For Shame," 90.

18. Levinas, *On Escape*, 64.

19. Hussing, "Regretting," 80.

20. I discuss Lynn at length in my study of the Berlin School. See Landry, *Movement and Performance*, 98–101.

21. In his pathbreaking monograph on the Berlin School, Marco Abel does not single out Speth, but there is some mention of *Madonnen*. In my own study on the Berlin School, I dedicate significant space to Speth's earlier film *In den Tag hinein* (The days between). See Abel, *Counter-Cinema*, and Landry, *Movement and Performance*, 97–107.

22. Wagner, "Vorschneider," 62.

23. Abel, *Counter-Cinema*, 117.

24. Speth, "Interview," my translation.

25. Wagner, "Vorschneider," 62.

26. Probyn, "Writing Shame," 72.

27. Hussing, "Regretting," 78–79.

28. This feature film is based on the 2020 documentary short Leaf codirected with Taylor Russell, *The Heart Still Hums*, about mothers struggling against the foster-care system in Sacramento, California. The unnamed woman captured here appears in the earlier film. Aesthetically, the two films are distinct. The earlier short is visually highly stylized with black-and-white, deep-focus images.

29. Sartre, *Being and Nothingness*, 350.

30. Brody, "'Earth Mama.'"

31. Roberts, *Torn Apart*, 12, 16, 20.

32. Hartman, *Lose Your Mother*, 85.

33. Marie Jenkins Schwartz offers a comprehensive study of the history of Black motherhood under slavery. See her chapter "Procreation," in Schwartz, *Birthing a Slave*, 9–31.

34. Spillers, "Mama's Baby," 74, 80. See also Landry, "Motherhood That Is *Einfach anders*," 77–79.

35. Sharpe, *In the Wake*, 28.

36. Nash, *Birthing Black Mothers*, 3.

37. Villarosa, "Why America's Black Mothers."

38. Lawrence, "It's Incredibly Heavy."

39. Cormican and William, *Tender Gaze*, 4.

40. Chion, *Voice*, 24.

41. Horton, "How the Lost Daughter Confronts"; Benson-Allott, "Film and the Right," 59.
42. Kiesling, "Hollywood."
43. Tomkins, *Shame*, 136.
44. Levinas, *On Escape*, 64.
45. Benson-Allott, "Film and the Right," 60.
46. Rich, *Of Woman Born*, 3.
47. Li, "Movie."
48. Li, "Movie."
49. Benson-Allott, "Film and the Right," 61.
50. Catsoulis, "'Lost Daughter' Review."
51. Rich, *Of Woman Born*, 5.
52. Beauvoir, *Second Sex*, 484.
53. Benson-Allott, "Film and the Right," 61.
54. Cormican and William, *Tender Gaze*, 4.
55. Kuzniar, "Sublime Shame," 501. I also borrow my section title from Kuzniar's article.
56. Meyer and Oberman, *Mothers Who Kill*, 13.
57. Telò, "Medea," 422.
58. Telò, "Medea," 420.
59. Tomkins, *Shame*, 159.
60. Sedgwick, "Queer Performativity," 14, original emphasis.
61. Deuber-Mankowsky, "Cinematographic Aesthetics," 256.
62. In Alexander Kluge's 2008 *Nachrichten aus der ideologischen Antike—Marx/Eisenstein/Das Kapital* (News from ideological antiquity—Marx/Eisenstein/The Capital), Sophie Rois discusses the Medea figure in chapter 1.
63. Diop established herself first as a documentary filmmaker, and her films have focused on the lives and struggles of migrants in France. Diop, "Entretien."
64. Nash, *Birthing Black Mothers*, 136.
65. Villarosa, "Why America's Black Mothers."

Chapter 5. Guilt

1. Cited in LaChance Adams, *Mad Mothers*, 187.
2. Guttmacher Institute, "One Week Later."
3. Almond, *Monster Within*, xxii.
4. Slobodin, "Between the Eye," 218.
5. Ahmed, *Cultural Politics*, 105.
6. Cited in Ahmed, *Cultural Politics*, 105. Jean-Anne Sutherland's article "Mothering, Guilt, and Shame" also presents an insightful study on the differences and similarities of guilt and shame. See Sutherland, "Mothering."
7. LeBeau, "Ontological," 334.

8. Nietzsche, *Beyond*, 258, original emphasis.
9. Heidegger, *Being and Time*, 327.
10. Heidegger, *Being and Time*, 325.
11. Heidegger, *Being and Time*, 332–33.
12. Heidegger, *Being and Time*, 157–58; Bauer, "Beauvoir's Heideggerian Ontology," 74.
13. LaChance Adams, *Mad Mothers*, 24.
14. Levinas, *Entre Nous*, 213.
15. Levinas, *Entre Nous*, 7–9.
16. LaChance Adams, *Mad Mothers*, 78–79.
17. LeBeau, "Ontological," 339.
18. Levinas, *Otherwise Than Being*, 104.
19. Baraitser, *Maternal Encounters*, 8, original emphasis.
20. LaChance Adams, *Mad Mothers*, 12, original emphasis.
21. Beauvoir, *Second Sex*, 565.
22. Beauvoir, *Second Sex*, 532, 568.
23. Beauvoir, *Second Sex*, 159.
24. Keltner, "Beauvoir's Idea," 201.
25. Rose, *Mothers*, 132.
26. Beauvoir, *Second Sex*, 539.
27. Beauvoir, *Second Sex*, 551.
28. Rich, *Of Woman Born*, 25.
29. Donath, *Regretting Motherhood*, 32.
30. Beauvoir, *Ethics of Ambiguity*, 10.
31. LaChance Adams, *Mad Mothers*, 187.
32. Ruddick, *Maternal Thinking*, 29.
33. Mulvey, "Visual Pleasure," 35.
34. Mennel, *Women at Work*, 25.
35. Reuben Muñoz, "Biopolitics," 1154. One can recall the longer discourse on the ideal of the angelic mother that E. Ann Kaplan indicates was often pitted against the "evil" witch opposite (just consider any fairy tale). See Kaplan, *Motherhood and Representation*, 9.
36. Reuben Muñoz, "Biopolitics," 1158.
37. Beauvoir, *Second Sex*, 59.
38. Puar, "Precarity Talk," 164.
39. Kaplan, *Motherhood and Representation*, 45. Some scholars locate the origins of these concepts even earlier in history and attribute them not to psychoanalysis but to scientific Darwinism. See Ladd-Taylor and Umansky, *"Bad" Mothers*, 9.
40. Kaplan, *Motherhood and Representation*, 45.
41. O'Reilly, "Trying to Function," 7.
42. O'Reilly, "Trying to Function," 23.
43. See Chodorow, *Reproduction of Motherhood*, 95–99; see also B. R. Rich, *Chick Flicks*, 213.

44. A. Rich, "Motherhood," 112.
45. The film does not have subtitles. I have translated from the Spanish.
46. A. Rich, "Motherhood," 113.
47. Fuery, *Ambiguous Cinema*, 190.
48. Smyth, "Postfeminism."
49. Jean-Luc Godard, cited in Deleuze, *Cinema 2*, 22.
50. Epstein, "Mothering to Death," 257.
51. Beauvoir, "Pyrrhus and Cineas," 138.
52. LaChance Adams, *Mad Mothers*, 181.
53. Rose, *Mothers*, 1.
54. The film only hints at this given the material conditions under which Eva lives in the present compared to before the massacre and her brief conversation with her lawyer; however, Shriver's novel offers more detail. In the aftermath of the event, there were both a criminal trial and a civil case against Eva, in the wake of which she is forced to sell her house. However, the novel suggests that her decision to move into the rundown clapboard house is also a form of self-punishment rather than a consequence of significant material loss given that she fetched a near fortune from the sale of her previous house. See Shriver, *We Need to Talk*, 8–10.
55. Muller, "Good and Bad," 39.
56. Shriver, *We Need to Talk*, 39.
57. Arnold, *Maternal Horror Film*, 68.
58. Fuery, *Ambiguous Cinema*, 191.
59. Ladd-Taylor and Umansky, *"Bad" Mothers*, 2.
60. Although the film's historical setting is unclear, in the novel Eva's pregnancy begins in the 1980s, during the conservative period of Ronald Reagan's presidency.
61. Ladd-Taylor and Umansky, *"Bad" Mothers*, 2, original emphasis.
62. Monique Plaza cited in Ruddick, *Maternal Thinking*, 34.
63. E. Walker, "Bringing Along Baby."
64. Almond, *Monster Within*, 10.
65. Heffernan and Wilgus, "Introduction," 4.
66. Smyth, "Postfeminism"; Berlant, "Structures," 193.
67. A. Rich, "Motherhood," 112.
68. Moya, "De Madres incorregibles."
69. Dolan, "At Its Core."
70. Bourdeau, "Politics and Motherhood," 179.
71. Bourdeau, "Politics and Motherhood," 169–79. See also Massimi, "Boy's Best Friend."
72. Bradshaw, "*Mommy* Review."
73. "Joual" is a dialect or argot of French spoken in Quebec. It incorporates a lot of slang, English words, and older vocabulary not standardized into French of the l'Académie française. It is a dialect typically linked to working-class francophone Quebecers.

74. See Bruckner, "Lost Time"; Beckman [Redrobe], *Crash*; Landry, *Movement and Performance*.
75. Bourdeau, "Politics and Motherhood," 180.
76. Arnold, *Maternal Horror Film*, 68–114; Ladd-Taylor and Umansky, *"Bad" Mothers*, 2.
77. Motherhood and sexuality, not to mention sex appeal, are seldom brought into conversation in most, if not all, cultures. See Montemurro and Siefken, "MILFS and Matrons."
78. Linda Williams elaborates on Stella's exaggerated style and the ultimate conflict of her body and dress in "Something Else besides a Mother."
79. Brooks, *Melodramatic Imagination*, 56–80; see esp. 56–57.
80. Bourdeau, "Politics and Motherhood," 183.
81. As Hays also indicates, the phenomenon of the "guilt gap" was actually first identified by Ellen Goodman in a 1990 article for the *Los Angeles Times*. Hays, *Cultural Contradictions*, 104.
82. A. Rich, *Of Woman Born*, 288.

Chapter 6. Disgust

1. Ngai, *Ugly Feelings*, 335.
2. Kristeva, *Powers*, 4.
3. Kristeva, *Powers*, 13, original emphasis.
4. Creed, *Monstrous-Feminine*, 10.
5. See Williams, "Film Bodies."
6. Carroll, *Philosophy of Horror*, 17.
7. Arnold, *Maternal Horror Film*, 68–114.
8. Doane, *Bigger Than Life*, 60.
9. Kristeva, *Powers*, 2–3.
10. Menninghaus, *Disgust*, 7.
11. Menninghaus, *Disgust*, 5, 7, 6.
12. Kolnai, *On Disgust*, 6, 40, 34.
13. Brinkema, *Forms*, 161.
14. Brinkema, *Forms*, 161; Menninghaus, *Disgust*, 178; Kolnai, *On Disgust*, 30, 45.
15. Kristeva, *Powers*, 47.
16. Tyler, "Against Abjection," 78.
17. Baraitser, *Maternal Encounters*, 7.
18. Miller, *Anatomy of Disgust*, 11.
19. McGinn, *Meaning of Disgust*, 101.
20. Kristeva, *Powers*, 53.
21. Kristeva, *Powers*, 73.
22. The official English title is *The Stranger in Me*, but the direct translation of the German is "the strange or foreign object in me."
23. Rose, *Mothers*, 139–40.

Notes to Chapter 6

24. Tyler and Baraitser, "Private View," 7.
25. Tomar, "EXBlicks."
26. Kant, *Observations*, 83.
27. Kant, *Critique of Judgment*, 116.
28. Menninghaus, *Disgust*, 7.
29. Kristeva, *Powers*, 3.
30. Kristeva, *Powers*, 108.
31. Creed, *Monstrous-Feminine*, 10.
32. Kristeva, *Powers*, 1.
33. A. Rich, *Of Woman Born*, 3.
34. McGinn, *Meaning of Disgust*, 101.
35. Kristeva, *Powers*, 71.
36. Žižek, "Architectural Parallax," 274.
37. Ahmed, *Cultural Politics*, 89.
38. Menninghaus, *Disgust*, 1.
39. Doane, *Bigger Than Life*, 33, 60. See also Doane, "Close-Up."
40. Douglas and Michaels, *Mommy Myth*, 25. See also Petersen, *Momfluenced*.
41. McRobbie, "Notes," 7.
42. Berlant, *Cruel Optimism*, 1–2.
43. A. Rich, *Of Woman Born*, 5.
44. Ngai, *Ugly Feelings*, 354.
45. Ahmed, *Cultural Politics*, 91.
46. Milkova, "Mothers, Daughters, Dolls," 92.
47. *La figlia oscura* (*The Lost Daughter*, 2008) stands out as the most apparent exploration of maternal disgust, but we might also consider her novel *I giorni dell'abbandono* (The days of abandonment, 2002) about the inner struggles of a stay-at-home mother. Finally, Ferrante's *L'amore molesto* (Troubling love, 1991) and the later *Storia della bambina perduta* (Story of the lost child, 2014) are both keenly attuned to mother-daughter relationships and viscerally explore the daughter's disgust with the maternal body.
48. Milkova, "Mothers, Daughters, Dolls," 92.
49. See Rose, *Mothers*, 162.
50. Kolnai, *On Disgust*, 59.
51. Kristeva, *Powers*, 2.
52. Ferrante, *Lost Daughter*, 14.
53. Brinkema, *Forms*, 164.
54. Milkova, "Mothers, Daughters, Dolls," 98.
55. Berger, *Caterpillage*, 1; Milkova, "Mothers, Daughters, Dolls," 99.
56. Milkova, "Mothers, Daughters, Dolls," 100.
57. Kristeva, *Powers*, 53.
58. Menninghaus, *Disgust*, 8; Kristeva, *Powers*, 13.
59. Miller, *Anatomy of Disgust*, 27.
60. Ferrante, *Lost Daughter*, 123.
61. Menninghaus, *Disgust*, 6.

62. Kolnai, *On Disgust*, 42.
63. Williams, "Film Bodies," 6–7.
64. Brinkema, *Forms*, 166.

Conclusion. Warning: Mothering Can Crush!

1. As I was in the midst of copyediting the manuscript, Lori Jo Marso's *Feminism and the Cinema of Experience* (2025) appeared. Unable to engage with it here, I still want to point to it as a critical new and contemporaneous study on feminist cinema that focuses, inter alia, on the good and bad feelings of the viewer.
2. Butler, *Women's Cinema*, 1.
3. Lesage, "Political Aesthetics," 507.
4. White, *Women's Cinema*, 8.
5. C. Johnston, "Women's Cinema," 188.
6. White, *Women's Cinema*, 12–13.
7. This question was posed during a related panel on motherhood at the Society for Cinema and Media Studies in Boston, Massachusetts, in 2024.
8. US Department of Health and Human Services, "U.S. Surgeon General."

Filmography

The Arbor. Director Clio Barnard, United Kingdom, 2010. Color film, 94 min. Artangel.
The Babadook. Director Jennifer Kent, Australia, 2014. Color film, 94 min. Screen Australia.
The Baby. Creators Lucy Gaymer and Siân Robins-Grace, United Kingdom, 2022. Color cable television, 8 episodes. HBO.
Baby Ruby. Director Bess Wohl, United States, 2022. Color film, 93 min. Page Fifty-Four Pictures.
Cinco Lobitos (Lullaby). Director Alauda Ruiz de Azúa, Spain, 2022. Color film, 104 min. Encanta Films.
Das Fremde in mir (The stranger in me). Director Emily Atef, Germany/France, 2008. Color film, 99 min. NiKo Film.
Die allseitig reduzierte Persönlichkeit—Redupers (The all-round reduced personality—redupers). Director Helke Sander, West Germany, 1978. Black-and-white film, 98 min. Zweites Deutsches Fernsehen (ZDF).
Earth Mama. Director Savanah Leaf, United States, 2023. Color film, 101 min. A24.
Gelegenheitsarbeit einer Sklavin (Part-time work of a domestic slave). Director Alexander Kluge, West Germany, 1973. Black-and-white film, 91 min. Kairos Film.
Hereditary. Director Ari Aster, United States, 2018. Color film, 127 min. A24.
Ich war zuhause, aber . . . (I was at home, but . . .). Director Angela Schanelec, Germany, 2019. Color film, 105 min. Nachmittagfilm.
J'ai tué ma mère (I killed my mother). Director Xavier Dolan, Canada, 2009. Color film, 96 min. K Films Amerique.
Jeanne Dielman, 23 quai du Commerce, 1080 Bruxelles. Director Chantel Akerman, Belgium, 1975. Color film, 201 min. Paradise Films/Unité Trois.

The Lost Daughter. Director Maggie Gyllenhaal, United States, 2021. Color film, 121 min. Endeavor Content.

Madonnen (Madonnas). Director Maria Speth, Germany, 2007. Color film, 125 min. Pandora Film Produktion GmbH.

Mater Amatísima: Imaginaries and Discourses on Maternity in Times of Change. Director María Ruido, Spain, 2017. Color video, 55 min. Vimeo.

Mommy. Director Xavier Dolan, Canada, 2014. Color film, 138 min. Metafilms.

The Motherhood Archives. Irene Lusztig, United States, 2013. Black-and-white and color film, 91 min. Women Make Movies.

Nachrichten aus der ideologischen Antike—Marx/Eisenstein/Das Kapital (News from ideological antiquity—Marx/Eisenstein/The Capital). Director Alexander Kluge, 2008. Color film, 570 min. Suhrkamp.

Persona. Director Ingmar Bergman, Sweden, 1966. Black-and-white film, 84 min. AB Svensk Filmindustri.

Pieces of Her. Creator Charlotte Stoudt, director Minkie Spiro, United States, 2022. Color series, 8 episodes. Netflix.

Regretting Motherhood. Directors Merle Grimme and Felizitas Hoffmann, Germany, 2017. Color film, 18 min. DREIFILM.

Rosemary's Baby. Director Roman Polanski, United States, 1968. Color film, 137 min. William Castle Enterprises.

Saint Omer. Director Alice Diop, France, 2022. Color film, 122 min. Srab Films.

Stories We Tell. Director Sarah Polley, Canada, 2012. Color film, 109 min. National Film Board of Canada.

A Thousand and One. Director A. V. Rockwell, United States, 2023. Color film, 116 min. Sight Unseen.

Tully. Director Jason Reitman, United States, 2018. Color film, 95 min. Bron Studios.

Unsichtbare Gegner (Invisible adversaries). Director Valie Export, Austria, 1976. Color film, 104 min. Valie Export Filmproduktions GmbH.

Von wegen Schicksal (Is this fate?). Director Helga Reidemeister, West Germany, 1979. Color film, 121 min. Zweites Deutsches Fernsehen (ZDF).

We Need to Talk about Kevin. Lynne Ramsay, United Kingdom/United States, 2011. Color film, 112 min. Oscilloscope Laboratories.

Bibliography

Abel, Marco. *The Counter-Cinema of the Berlin School*. Rochester, NY: Camden House, 2013.
Ahmed, Sara. *The Cultural Politics of Emotion*. 2nd ed. New York: Routledge, 2015.
Ahmed, Sara. *Living a Feminist Life*. Durham, NC: Duke University Press, 2017.
Ahmed, Sara. *The Promise of Happiness*. Durham, NC: Duke University, 2010.
Almond, Barbara. *The Monster Within: The Hidden Side of Motherhood*. Berkeley: University of California Press, 2010.
Archer, Nandini Naira. "What Overturning Roe v Wade Could Mean for Abortion in the UK." *openDemocracy*, June 22, 2022. https://www.opendemocracy.net/.
Aristotle. *Nicomachean Ethics*. Translated by Roger Crisp. Cambridge: Cambridge University Press, 2004.
Arnold, Sarah. *Maternal Horror Film: Melodrama and Motherhood*. Basingstoke, UK: Palgrave Macmillan, 2013.
Austin, J. L. *How to Do Things with Words*. Cambridge, MA: Harvard University Press, 1962.
Baer, Hester. "Remediations of Cinefeminism in Contemporary German Film." In *Transnational German Film at the End of Neoliberalism: Radical Aesthetics, Radical Politics*, edited by Claudia Breger and Olivia Landry, 142–61. Rochester, NY: Camden House, 2024.
Balanzategui, Jessica. "The Babadook and the Haunted Space between High and Low Genres in the Australian Horror Tradition." *Studies in Australasian Cinema* 11, no. 1 (2017): 18–32.
Baraitser, Lisa. *Maternal Encounters: The Ethics of Interruption*. London: Routledge, 2009.
Barone, Matt. "The Year's Best Horror Movie? It's *This Australian Creepshow*, Hands Down." *Complex*, November 28, 2014. https://www.complex.com/pop-culture/2014/11/interview-the-babadook-jennifer-kent.

Bauer, Nancy. "Beauvoir's Heideggerian Ontology." In *The Philosophy of Simone de Beauvoir*, edited by Margaret A. Simons, 65–91. Bloomington: Indiana University Press, 2006.

Bazin, André. *What Is Cinema?* Vol. 2. Translated by H. Gray. Berkeley: University of California Press, 1959.

Beauvoir, Simone de. *The Ethics of Ambiguity*. Translated by Bernard Frechtman. New York: Citadel Press, 1948.

Beauvoir, Simone de. "Pyrrhus and Cineas." In *Philosophical Writings*, edited by Margaret A. Simons, 77–158. Urbana: University of Illinois Press, 2004.

Beauvoir, Simone de. *The Second Sex*. 1949. Translated by Constance Borde and Sheila Malovany-Chevallier. New York: Vintage, 2011.

Beckman [Redrobe], Karen. *Crash: Cinema and the Politics of Speed and Stasis*. Durham, NC: Duke University Press, 2010.

Benson-Allott, Caetlin. "Film and the Right to Privacy." *Film Quarterly* 75, no. 4 (2022): 58–63.

Berger, Harry, Jr. *Caterpillage: Reflections on Seventeenth-Century Dutch Still Life Painting*. New York: Fordham University Press, 2011.

Berlant, Lauren. *Cruel Optimism*. Durham, NC: Duke University Press, 2011.

Berlant, Lauren. *On the Inconvenience of Other People*. Durham, NC: Duke University Press, 2022.

Berlant, Lauren. "Structures of Unfeeling: *Mysterious Skin*." *International Journal of Politics, Culture, & Society* 28 (2015): 191–213.

Berlant, Lauren, and Lee Edelman. *Sex, or the Unbearable*. Durham, NC: Duke University Press, 2014.

Biss, Eula. "Of Institution Born." Preface to *Of Woman Born: Motherhood as Experience and Institution*, by Adrienne Rich, xi–xxvi. New York: Norton, 2021.

Bock, Gisela. "Racism and Sexism in Nazi Germany: Motherhood, Compulsory Sterilization, and the State." *Signs: Journal of Women in Culture and Society* 8, no. 3 (1983): 400–421.

Bordwell, David. *Figures Traced in Light: On Cinematic Staging*. Berkeley: University of California Press, 2005.

Bourdeau, Loïc. "Politics and Motherhood in Xavier Dolan's *J'ai tué ma mère* and *Mommy*." In *Horrible Mothers: Representations across Francophone North America*, edited by Loïc Bourdeau, 169–94. Lincoln: University of Nebraska Press, 2019.

Bradshaw, Peter. "*Mommy* Review—Outrageous and Brilliant, a Daytime Soap from Hell." *London Guardian*, March 19, 2015. https://www.theguardian.com/.

Bradshaw, Peter. "Tully Review—Charlize Theron Pregnancy Drama Doesn't Quite Deliver." *London Guardian*, May 2, 2018. https://www.theguardian.com/.

Brady, Miranda J. *Mother Trouble: Meditations of White Maternal Angst after Second Wave Feminism*. Toronto: University of Toronto Press, 2024.

Brauerhoch, Annette. *Die gute und die böse Mutter: Kino zwischen Melodrama und Horror* [The good and the bad mother: Cinema between melodrama and horror]. Marburg, Germany: Schüren, 1996.

Briefel, Aviva. "Parenting through Horror: Reassurance in Jennifer Kent's *Babadook*." *Camera Obscura* 32, no. 2 (95) (2017): 1–27.

Brinkema, Eugenie. *The Forms of the Affects*. Durham, NC: Duke University Press, 2014.

Brody, Richard. "'Earth Mama' Reinvigorates the Closeup, the Heart of the Cinema." *The New Yorker*, July 13, 2023. https://www.newyorker.com/.

Brooks, Peter. *The Melodramatic Imagination: Balzac, Henry James, Melodrama, and the Mode of Excess*. New Haven, CT: Yale University Press, 1976.

Bruckner, René Thoreau. "Lost Time: Blunt Head Trauma and Accident-Driven Cinema." *Discourse* 30, no. 3 (2008): 373–400.

Butler, Alison. *Women's Cinema: The Contested Screen*. London: Wallflower, 2002.

Carroll, Noël. *The Philosophy of Horror, or Paradoxes of the Heart*. New York: Routledge, 1990.

Carruthers, Anne. *Fertile Visions: The Uterus as a Narrative Space in Cinema from the Americas*. New York: Bloomsbury, 2021.

Cartwright, Lisa. *Moral Spectatorship: Technologies of Voice and Affect in Postwar Representations of the Child*. Durham, NC: Duke University Press, 2008.

Casarino, Cesare. "Images for Housework: On the Time of Domestic Labor in Gilles Deleuze's Philosophy of the Cinema." *differences: A Journal of Feminist Cultural Studies* 28, no. 3 (2017): 67–92.

Catsoulis, Jeannette. "'The Lost Daughter' Review: The Parent Trap." *New York Times*, December 30, 2021, https://www.nytimes.com/.

Cherry, Myisha. *The Case for Rage: Why Anger Is Essential to Anti-Racist Struggle*. Oxford: Oxford University Press, 2021.

Chion, Michel. *The Voice in Cinema*. Translated by Claudia Gorbman. New York: Columbia University Press, 1982.

Chodorow, Nancy. *The Reproduction of Mothering: Psychoanalysis and the Sociology of Gender*. Berkeley: University of California Press, 1978.

Chodorow, Nancy, and Susan Contratto. "The Fantasy of the Perfect Mother." In *Rethinking the Family: Some Feminist Questions*, edited by Barrie Thorne and Marilyn Yalom, 54–75. New York: Longman, 1982.

Clover, Carol. *Men, Women, and Chainsaws: Gender in the Modern Horror Film*. Princeton, NJ: Princeton University Press, 1992.

Collins, Patricia Hill. "The Meaning of Motherhood in Black Culture and Black Mother-Daughter Relationships." *Sage* 4, no. 2 (1987): 3–10.

Collins, Patricia Hill. "Shifting the Center: Race, Class, and Feminist Theorizing about Motherhood." In *Mothering: Ideology, Experience, and Agency*, edited by Evelyn Nakano Glenn, Grace Chang, and Linda Rennie Forcey, 45–65. Abingdon, UK: Routledge, 2016.

Columpar, Corinn, and So Mayer, eds. *There She Goes: Feminist Filmmaking and Beyond*. Detroit, MI: Wayne State University Press, 2009.

Cooper, Brittney. *Eloquent Rage: A Black Feminist Discovers Her Superpower*. New York: St. Martin's, 2018.

Copjec, Joan. "The Object-Gaze: Shame, *Hejab*, Cinema." *Gramma: Journal of Theory and Criticism* 14 (2006): 163–82.

Cormican, Muriel, and Jennifer Marston William, eds. *The Tender Gaze: Compassionate Encounters on German Screen, Page, and Stage*. Rochester, NY: Camden House, 2021.

Creed, Barbara. *The Monstrous-Feminine: Film, Feminism, Psychoanalysis*. Abingdon, UK: Routledge, 1993.

Curtis, Robin, and Angelica Fenner, eds. *The Autobiographical Turn in Germanophone Documentary and Experimental Film*. Rochester, NY: Camden House, 2014.

Deleuze, Gilles. *Cinema 2: The Time-Image*. Translated by Hugh Tomlinson and Robert Galeta. Minneapolis: University of Minnesota Press, 1985.

Deleuze, Gilles. "The Exhausted." In *Essays Critical and Clinical*, edited by M. A. Greco and D. W. Smith, 152–74. Minneapolis: University of Minnesota Press, 1992.

Deuber-Mankowsky, Astrid. "Cinematographic Aesthetics as Subversion of Moral Reason in Pasolini's Medea." In *The Scandal of Self-Contradiction: Pasolini's Multistable Subjectivities, Traditions, Geographies*, edited by Luca Di Blasi, Manuele Gragnolati, and Christoph F. E. Holzhey, 255–66. Cultural Inquiry, 6. Vienna: Turia + Kant, 2012.

Diop, Alice. "Entretien avec Alice Diop." *Cineworx gmbh*. 2023. https://cineworx.ch/cargo/uploads/SOM-Presseheft-D-CH-_mg_compressed.pdf.

Doane, Mary Ann. *Bigger Than Life: The Close-Up and Scale in Cinema*. Durham, NC: Duke University, 2021.

Doane, Mary Ann. "The Close-Up: Scale and Detail in the Cinema." *differences: A Journal of Feminist Cultural Studies* 14, no. 3 (2003): 89–111.

Doane, Mary Ann. *Desire to Desire*. Bloomington: Indiana University Press, 1987.

Dolan, Xavier. "At Its Core, Warped Family Drama 'Mommy' Is 'a Story of Love.'" *NPR*, January 25, 2015. https://www.npr.org/.

Donath, Orna. *#regretting motherhood. Wenn Mütter bereuen* [When mothers regret]. Translated by Karlheinz Dürr and Elsbeth Ranke. Munich: Knaus, 2016.

Donath, Orna. "Regretting Motherhood: A Sociopolitical Analysis." *Signs: Journal of Women in Culture and Society* 40, no. 2 (2015): 343–66.

Donath, Orna. *Regretting Motherhood: A Study*. Berkeley, CA: North Atlantic, 2016.

Douglas, Susan J., and Meredith W. Michaels. *The Mommy Myth: The Idealization of Motherhood and How It Has Undermined Women*. New York: Free Press, 2004.

Dubin, Minna. "The Rage Mothers Don't Talk About." *New York Times*, April 15, 2020. https://www.nytimes.com/.
Eichhorn, Kate. *The Archival Turn in Feminism: Outrage in Order*. Philadelphia: Temple University Press, 2013.
Epstein, Su. "Mothering to Death." In *"Bad" Mothers: The Politics of Blame in Twentieth-Century America*, edited by Molly Ladd-Taylor and Lauri Umansky, 257–62. New York: New York University Press, 1998.
Euripides. *Medea: A New Translation*. Translated by Charles Martin. Berkeley: University of California Press, 2019.
Federici, Silvia. *Wages against Housework*. Montpelier, UK: Power of Women Collective and the Falling Wall Press, 1975.
Ferrante, Elena. *The Lost Daughter*. Translated by Ann Goldstein. New York: Europa Editions, 2006.
Fischer, Lucy. *Cinematernity: Film, Motherhood, Genre*. Princeton, NJ: Princeton University Press, 1996.
Fischer, Sarah. *Die Mutterglück-Lüge: Regretting Motherhood—Warum ich lieber Vater geworden wäre* [The maternal happiness lie: Regretting motherhood—why I would prefer to be a father]. Munich: Ludwig Verlag, 2016.
Flynn, Andrea. "The 'All-Consuming' Emotional Labor Caused by Coronavirus—and Shouldered by Women." *Ms.*, March 31, 2020. https://msmagazine.com/2020/03/31/op-ed-the-all-consuming-emotional-labor-caused-by-coronavirus-and-disproportionately-shouldered-by-women/.
Friedan, Betty. *Feminine Mystique*. New York: Norton, 1997.
Frye, Marilyn. *The Politics of Reality: Essays in Feminist Theory*. Berkeley, CA: Crossing Press, 1983.
Fuery, Kelli. *Ambiguous Cinema: From Simone de Beauvoir to Feminist Film-Phenomenology*. Edinburgh: Edinburgh University Press, 2022.
Gill, Rosalind. "The Affective, Cultural and Psychic Life of Postfeminism: A Postfeminist Sensibility 10 Years On." *European Journal of Cultural Studies* 20, no. 6 (2017): 606–26.
Gledhill, Christine, and Julia Knight, eds. *Doing Women's Film History: Reframing Cinemas, Past and Future*. Urbana: University of Illinois Press, 2015.
Gleeson, J. J., and K. D. Griffiths. "Kinderkommunismus: A Feminist Analysis of the 21st-Century Family and a Communist Proposal for Its Abolition." *A New Institute for Social Research*, 2015. https://isr.press/Griffiths_Gleeson_Kinderkommunismus/index.html.
Göbel, Esther. *Die falsche Wahl: Wenn Frauen ihre Entscheidung für Kinder bereuen* [The wrong choice: When women regret their decision to have children]. Munich: Droemer, 2016.
Göbel, Esther. "Sie wollen ihr Leben zurück" [They want their lives back]. *Süddeutsche Zeitung*, April 5, 2015. https://www.sueddeutsche.de/gesundheit/unglueckliche-muetter-sie-wollen-ihr-leben-zurueck-1.2419449.
Gorfinkel, Elena. "Weariness, Waiting: Endurance and Art Cinema's Tired Bodies." *Discourse* 34, nos. 2–3 (2012): 311–47.

Guevara-Flanagan, Kristy, and Irene Lusztig. "How to Do Everything: A Conversation between Filmmakers." In *Mothers of Invention: Film, Media, and Caregiving Labor*, edited by So Mayer and Corinn Columpar, 61–79. Detroit: Wayne State University Press, 2022.

Gumbs, Alexis Pauline, China Martens, and Mai'a Williams, eds. *Revolutionary Mothering: Love on the Front Lines*. Binghamton, NY: PM Press, 2016.

Guttmacher Institute. "One Week Later, Women Denied an Abortion Feel More Regret and Less Relief Than Those Who Have One." *Guttmacher*, August 5, 2013. https://www.guttmacher.org/.

Hamacher, Sophie, and Irene Lusztig. "A Conversation with Irene Lusztig." In *Supervision: On Motherhood and Surveillance*, edited by Sophie Hamacher and Jessica Hankey, 64–70. Cambridge, MA: MIT Press, 2023.

Hartman, Saidiya. *Lose Your Mother: A Journey along the Atlantic Slave Route*. New York: Farrar, Straus, and Giroux, 2007.

Hartman, Saidiya. *Wayward Lives, Beautiful Experiments: Intimate Histories of Riotous Black Girls, Troublesome Women, and Queer Radicals*. New York: Norton, 2019.

Hays, Sharon. *The Cultural Contradictions of Motherhood*. New Haven, CT: Yale University Press, 1996.

Heffernan, Valerie, and Gay Wilgus. "Introduction: Imagining Motherhood in the Twenty-First Century—Images, Representations, Constructions." *Women: A Cultural Review* 29, no. 1 (2018): 1–18.

Heffernan, Valerie, and Katherine Stone. "International Responses to Regretting Motherhood." In *Women's Lived Experiences of the Gender Gap: Gender Inequalities from Multiple Global Perspectives*, edited by Angela Fitzgerald, 121–33. Singapore: Springer, 2022.

Heffernan, Valerie, and Katherine Stone. "#regrettingmotherhood in Germany: Feminism, Motherhood, and Culture." *Signs: Journal of Women in Culture and Society* 46, no. 2 (2020): 337–60.

Heidegger, Martin. *Being and Time*. Translated by John Macquarrie and Edward Robinson. New York: Harper & Row, 1927.

Hess, Amanda. "When Motherhood Is a Horror Show." *New York Times*, May 13, 2022. https://www.nytimes.com/.

Hirsch, Marianne. *The Mother/Daughter Plot: Narrative, Psychoanalysis, Feminism*. Bloomington: Indiana University Press, 1989.

Hoffmann, Felizitas, and Merle Grimme, dirs. *Regretting Motherhood*. Dreifilm, 2017. 18 min. http://www.dreifilm.de/portfolio/regretting-motherhood.

Hornaday, Ann. "'A Thousand and One': A Film Worth Not Just Seeing—But Celebrating." *Washington Post*, March 29, 2023. https://www.washingtonpost.com/.

Horton, Adrian. "How the Lost Daughter Confronts One of Our Most Enduring Cultural Taboos." *US Guardian*, January 5, 2022. https://www.theguardian.com/.

Howell, Amanda, and Lucy Baker. *Monstrous Possibilities: The Female Monster in 21st Century Screen Horror.* Cham, Switzerland: Palgrave, 2022.

Hussing, Kira. "Regretting Motherhood in Maria Speth's *Madonnen* (2007)." *NPPSH Reflections: Dialectics* 1 (2017): 78–82.

"Ich war zuhause, aber." *Filmportal.de*. https://www.filmportal.de/. Accessed January 19, 2025.

Irigaray, Luce. *Between East and West: From Singularity to Community.* Translated by Stephen Pluháček. New York: Columbia University Press, 1999.

Johnston, Claire. "Women's Cinema as Counter-Cinema." In *Film Theory: Critical Concepts in Media Cultural Studies*, edited by Philip Simpson, Andrew Utterson, and K. J. Shepherdson, 183–92. London: Routledge, 2004.

Johnston, Sarah Iles. Introduction to *Medea*, edited by James J. Clauss and Sarah Iles Johnston, 3–20. Princeton: Princeton University Press, 1997.

Kaiser, Mareice. *Das Unwohlsein der modernen Mutter* [The uneasiness of the modern mother]. Hamburg: Rowohlt, 2021.

Kant, Immanuel. *Critique of Judgment.* Translated by J. H. Bernard. 1790. Mineola, NY: Dover, 2005.

Kant, Immanuel. *Observations on the Feeling of the Beautiful and the Sublime.* Translated by John T. Goldthwait. 1764. Berkeley: University of California Press, 1960.

Kaplan, E. Ann. "The Case of the Missing Mother: Maternal Issues in Vidor's *Stella Dallas*." In *Issues in Feminist Film Criticism*, edited by Patricia Erens, 126–36. Bloomington: Indiana University Press, 1990.

Kaplan, E. Ann. *Motherhood and Representation: The Mother in Popular Culture and Melodrama.* London: Routledge, 1992.

Karklin, Diana. *Undo Motherhood.* Amsterdam: Schilt, 2022.

Keltner, Stacy. "Beauvoir's Idea of Ambiguity." In *Philosophy of Simone de Beauvoir*, edited by Margaret A. Simons, 201–13. Bloomington: Indiana University Press, 2006.

Kerrigan, John. *Revenge Tragedy: Aeschylus to Armageddon.* Oxford: Oxford University Press, 1996.

Kiesling, Lydia. "Hollywood Loves a Monstrous Mommy: Can It Do Her Justice?" *New York Times*, December 7, 2021. https://www.nytimes.com/.

Kim, Sue J. *On Anger: Race, Cognition, Narrative.* Austin: University of Texas Press, 2013.

Knight, Julia. *Women and the New German Cinema.* London: Verso, 1992.

Kolnai, Aurel. *On Disgust.* Edited by Barry Smith and Carolyn Korsmeyer. Translated by Elizabeth Kolnai. Chicago: Open Court, 2004.

Kristeva, Julia. *Powers of Horror: An Essay on Abjection.* Translated by Leon S. Roudiez. New York: Columbia University Press, 1980.

Kristeva, Julia. "Stabat Mater." Translated by Arthur Goldhammer. *Poetics Today* 6, nos. 1–2 (1985): 135–52.

Kuzniar, Alice A. "Sublime Shame." *GLQ* 15, no. 3 (2009): 499–512.

LaChance Adams, Sarah. *Mad Mothers, Bad Mothers, & What a "Good" Mother Would Do: The Ethics of Ambivalence*. New York: Columbia University Press, 2014.
Ladd-Taylor, Molly, and Lauri Umansky, eds. *"Bad" Mothers: The Politics of Blame in Twentieth-Century America*. New York: New York University Press, 1998.
Landman, Janet. *Regret: The Persistence of the Possible*. Oxford: Oxford University Press, 1993.
Landry, Olivia. "A Gendered Suspension of Time: Waiting in the Cinema of Angela Schanelec." In *Between Ambivalence and Ambition: The Politics of (Post)Feminist Film Practice in Twenty-First Century German Cinema*, edited by Angelica Fenner and Barbara Mennel, 160–81. Special issue of *Feminist German Studies Yearbook*. Lincoln: University of Nebraska Press, 2022.
Landry, Olivia. "Motherhood That Is *Einfach anders*." *German Studies Review* 48, no. 1 (2025): 67–85.
Landry, Olivia. *Movement and Performance in Berlin School Cinema*. Bloomington: Indiana University Press, 2018.
Landry, Olivia. "Searching for a Storyteller, Remediating the Archive: Philip Scheffner's *Halfmoon Files*." *New German Critique* 46, no. 3 (138) (2019): 103–24.
Landry, Olivia. *Theatre of Anger: Radical Transnational Performance in Contemporary Berlin*. Toronto: University of Toronto Press, 2020.
Landry, Olivia, and Christinia Landry. "Torlasco's 'Philosophy in the Kitchen': Image, Domestic Labor, and the Gendered Embodiment of Time." *New Review of Film and Television Studies* 17, no. 4 (2019): 456–80.
Lawrence, Andrew. "'It's Incredibly Heavy': Behind a Tough Film about the US Foster Care System." *London Guardian*, July 7, 2023. https://www.theguardian.com/.
LeBeau, Claire S. "Ontological and Ethical Guilt: Phenomenological Perspectives on Becoming a Mother." *Humanistic Psychologist* 45, no. 4 (2017): 333–47.
Lesage, Julia. "The Political Aesthetics of the Feminist Documentary Film." *Quarterly Review of Film Studies* 3, no. 4 (1978): 507–23.
Lesage, Julia. "Women's Rage." In *Marxism and the Interpretation of Culture*, edited by Cary Nelson and Lawrence Grossberg, 419–28. Urbana: University of Illinois Press, 1988.
Levinas, Emmanuel. *Entre Nous: Thinking-of-the-Other*. Translated by Michael B. Smith and Barbara Harshav. New York: Columbia University Press, 1991.
Levinas, Emmanuel. *On Escape*. Translated by Bettina Bergo. 1982. Stanford, CA: Stanford University, 2003.
Levinas, Emmanuel. *Otherwise Than Being or Beyond Essence*. 1974. Translated by Alfonso Lingis. Berlin: Springer Science+Business Media, 1991.

Lewis, Sophie. *Abolish the Family: A Manifesto for Care and Liberation*. London: Verso, 2022.

Lewis, Sophie. *Full Surrogacy Now: Feminism against Family*. London: Verso, 2021.

Leyda, Jay. *Films Beget Films: A Study of the Compilation Film*. New York: Hill and Wang, 1964.

Li, Shirley. "The Movie That Understands the Secret Shame of Motherhood." *The Atlantic*, January 5, 2022. https://www.theatlantic.com/.

Lombardo, Palma. "Medeas. Interview with María Ruido." *Cinema Compart/ive Cinema* 4, no. 8 (2016): 24–27.

Lorde, Audre. *Sister Outsider*. New York: Crossing Press, 2007.

Lubecker, Nikolaj. *Feel-Bad Film*. Edinburgh: Edinburgh University Press, 2015.

MacInnes, Paul. "The Babadook: 'I Wanted to Talk about the Need to Face the Darkness in Ourselves.'" *London Guardian*, October 18, 2014. https://www.theguardian.com/.

Mangan, Lucy. "The Baby Review—Post-Roe, This Comedy-Horror Is Truly Terrifying." *London Guardian*, July 7, 2022. https://www.theguardian.com/.

Marso, Lori Jo. *Feminism and the Cinema of Experience*. Durham, NC: Duke University Press, 2025.

Marso, Lori Jo. "Phenomenology in the Kitchen: Feeling Time like a Feminist." In *Film Phenomenologies: Temporality, Embodiment, Transformation*, edited by Kelli Fuery, 41–60. Edinburgh: Edinburgh University Press, 2024.

Marston, Kendra. *Postfeminist Whiteness: Problematising Melancholic Burden in Contemporary Hollywood*. Edinburgh: Edinburgh University Press, 2018.

Marx, Karl, and Friedrich Engels. "Manifesto of the Communist Party." In *The Marx and Engels Reader*, edited by Robert C. Tucker, 469–500. Translated by Martin Nicolaus. 1848. New York: Norton, 1978.

Massimi, Fulvia. "'A Boy's Best Friend Is His Mother': Québec's Matriarchy and Queer Nationalism in the Cinema of Xavier Dolan." *Synoptique* 4, no. 2 (2021): 13–36.

Mayer, So, and Corinn Columpar, eds. *Mothers of Invention: Film, Media, and Caregiving Labor*. Detroit, MI: Wayne State University Press, 2022.

McGinn, Colin. *The Meaning of Disgust*. New York: Oxford University Press, 2011.

McHugh, Kathleen. "Prolegomenon: Anger, Aesthetics, and Affective Witness in Contemporary Feminist Cinema." *Film Quarterly* 75, no. 1 (2021): 10–22.

McRobbie, Angela. *The Aftermath of Feminism: Gender, Culture, and Social Change*. Los Angeles: Sage, 2009.

McRobbie, Angela. "Notes on the Perfect: Competitive Femininity in Neoliberal Times." *Australian Feminist Studies* 30, no. 83 (2015): 3–20.

Mennel, Barbara. *Women at Work in Twenty-First-Century European Cinema*. Urbana: University of Illinois Press, 2019.

Menninghaus, Winfried. *Disgust: Theory and History of a Strong Sensation*. Translated by Howard Eiland and Joel Golb. Albany: State University of New York Press, 2003.

Merleau-Ponty, Maurice. *Phenomenology of Perception, 1945*. Translated by Colin Smith. London: Routledge, 1996.

Meyer, Cheryl L., and Michelle Oberman. With Kelly White, Michelle Rone, Priya Batra, and Tara C. Proano. *Mothers Who Kill Their Children: Understanding Acts of Moms from Susan Smith to the "Prom Mom."* New York: New York University Press, 2001.

Milkova, Stiliana. "Mothers, Daughters, Dolls: On Disgust in Elena Ferrante's *La figlia oscura*." *Italian Culture* 31, no. 2 (2013): 91–109.

Miller, William Ian. *The Anatomy of Disgust*. Cambridge, MA: Harvard University Press, 1999.

Milton, John. *Paradise Lost*. London: Routledge, 1905.

Modleski, Tania. *The Women Who Knew Too Much: Hitchcock and Feminist Theory*. New York: Routledge, 2005.

Montemurro, Beth, and Jenna Siefken. "MILFS and Matrons: Images and Realities of Mothers' Sexuality." *Sexuality & Culture* 16, no. 4 (2012): 366–88.

Moya, Tamara. "De Madres incorregibles e hijos imposibles: El conflicto materno-filial ante la Muerte de la figura paterna en el cine de la postmodernidad" [Of incorrigible mothers and impossible sons: The mother-son conflict before the death of the father figure in postmodern cinema]. *La omnipresencia de la imagen: estudios interdisciplinares de la cultura visual*, 443–59. Dialnet, 2017. https://dialnet.unirioja.es/servlet/articulo?codigo=8185227.

Muller, Vivienne. "Good and Bad Mothering: Lionel Shriver's *We Need to Talk about Kevin*." In *Theorising and Representing Maternal Realities*, edited by Marie Porter and Julie Kelso, 38–53. Cambridge: Cambridge Scholars, 2008.

Mulvey, Laura. "Visual Pleasure and Narrative Cinema." In *Issues in Feminist Film Criticism*, edited by Patricia Erens, 28–40. Bloomington: Indiana University Press, 1990.

Mulvey, Laura. "Women Making History: Gleaning and the Compilation Film." In *Where Is History Today? New Ways of Representing the Past*, edited by Marcel Arbeit and Ian Christie, 27–38. Olomouc, Czech Republic: Palacký, 2015.

Mundlos, Christina. *Mütterterror: Angst, Neid und Aggressionen unter Müttern* [Mother terror: Fear, jealousy, and aggression among mothers]. Marburg, Germany: Tectum, 2013.

Mundlos, Christina. *Wenn Mutter sein nicht glücklich macht. Das Phänomen Regretting Motherhood* [When being a mother doesn't make you happy: The phenomenon of regretting motherhood]. Munich: mvg, 2015.

Nancy, Jean-Luc. *The Fall of Sleep*. Translated by Charlotte Mandell. New York: Fordham University Press, 2007.

Nash, Jennifer C. *Birthing Black Mothers*. Durham, NC: Duke University Press, 2021.

Nash, Jennifer C. "The Political Life of Black Motherhood." *Feminist Studies* 44, no. 3 (2018): 699–712.

Ngai, Sianne. *Ugly Feelings*. Cambridge, MA: Harvard University Press, 2005.

Nichols, Bill. *Introduction to Documentary*. Bloomington: Indiana University Press, 2017.

Nichols, Bill. "Remaking History: John Leyda and the Compilation Film." *Film History* 26, no. 4 (2014): 146–56.

Nicodemus, Katja. "Mama geht weg." *Die Zeit*, December 5, 2007. https://www.zeit.de/2007/50/Madonnen?utm_referrer=https%3A%2F%2Fwww.google.com%2F.

Nietzsche, Friedrich. *Beyond Good and Evil/On the Genealogy of Morality*. Translated by Adrian Del Caro. Stanford, CA: Stanford University Press, 2014.

O'Brien, M. E. *Family Abolition: Capitalism and the Communizing of Care*. London: Pluto, 2023.

O'Reilly, Andrea. "Mothering against Motherhood and the Possibility of Empowered Maternity for Mothers and Their Children." In *From Motherhood to Mothering: The Legacy of Adrienne Rich's* Of Woman Born, edited by Andrea O'Reilly, 159–74. Albany: State University of New York Press, 2004.

O'Reilly, Andrea. "'Trying to Function in the Unfunctionable': Mothers and COVID-19." *Journal of the Motherhood Initiative* 11, no. 1 (2020): 7–24.

Parker, Rozsika. *Torn in Two: The Experience of Maternal Ambivalence*. London: Virago, 1995.

Pérez Nieto, Esther. "Motherhood: Between Ambivalence and Regret. An Analysis of the Essay Film *Mater Amatísima* (2017) by María Ruido." In *Beyond Identities: Interdisciplinary Perspectives on Gender*, edited by Emma Domínguez-Rué, 198–214. London: Interdisciplinary Discourses, 2021.

Petersen, Sara. "'Burn It Down': The Importance of Female, and Maternal, Rage." *Washington Post*, October 3, 2019. https://www.washingtonpost.com/.

Petersen, Sara. *Momfluenced: Inside the Maddening, Picture-Perfect World of Mommy Influencer Culture*. New York: Beacon, 2023.

Pethö, Ágnes. "Between Absorption, Abstraction and Exhibition: Inflections of the Cinematic Tableau in the Films of Corneliu Porumboiu, Roy Andersson, and Joanna Hogg." *Acta Univ. Sapientiae, Film and Media Studies* 11 (2015): 39–76.

Peucker, Brigitte. *The Material Image: Art and the Real in Film*. Stanford, CA: Stanford University Press, 2007.

Pilarczyk, Hannah. "Schultern hängen, Augen lauern." *TAZ*, February 2, 2002. https://taz.de/Schultern-haengen-Augen-lauern/!317353/.

Price, Brian. *A Theory of Regret*. Durham, NC: Duke University Press, 2017.

Probyn, Elspeth. "Writing Shame." In *The Affect Theory Reader*, edited by Melissa Gregg and Gregory J. Seigworth, 71–90. Durham, NC: Duke University Press, 2010.

Puar, Jasbir. "Precarity Talk: A Virtual Roundtable with Lauren Berlant, Judith

Butler, Bojana Cvejić, Isabell Lorey, Jasbir Puar, and Ana Vujanović." *TDR: The Drama Review* 56, no. 4 (2018): 163–77.

Putnam, EL. *The Maternal, Digital Subjectivity, and the Aesthetics of Interruption*. New York Bloomsbury, 2022.

Pyles, Tess. "Centring Complex Maternal Emotion in *The Babadook*." *Journal of the Motherhood Initiative* 10, nos. 1–2 (2019): 161–73.

Quindlen, Anna. "Playing God on No Sleep." *Newsweek*, September 1, 2001. https://www.newsweek.com/playing-god-no-sleep-154643.

Quiney, Ruth. "Confessions of the New Capitalist Mother: Twenty-First-Century Writing on Motherhood as Trauma." *Women: A Cultural Review* 18, no. 1 (2007): 19–40.

Quinlivan, Davina. *The Place of Breath in Cinema*. Edinburgh: University of Edinburgh, 2012.

Rangan, Pooja. *Immediations: The Humanitarian Impulse in Documentary*. Durham, NC: Duke University Press, 2017.

Redrobe, Karen. See Beckman, Karen.

Rémy, Lola. "'Yours in Sisterhood': Rethinking the Feminist Archive at the 2018 Recontres Internationales du Documentaire de Montréal." *Synoptique* 8, no. 1 (2019): 138–58.

Reuben Muñoz, Lindsey. "The Biopolitics of Domesticity in Fernando León de Aranoa's Amador (2010)." *Bulletin of Spanish Studies* 96, no. 7 (2019): 1153–75.

Rich, Adrienne. "Motherhood and Daughterhood." In *Essential Essays: Culture, Politics, and the Art of Poetry*, 107–46. New York: Norton, 2018.

Rich, Adrienne. *Of Woman Born: Motherhood as Experience and Institution*. New York: Norton, 2021.

Rich, B. Ruby. *Chick Flicks: Theories and Memories of the Feminist Film Movement*. Durham, NC: Duke University Press, 1998.

Rich, B. Ruby, and Linda Williams. "Right of Re-Vision: Michelle Citron's *Daughter Rite*." In *Chick Flicks: Theories and Memories of the Feminist Film Movement*, by B. Ruby Rich, 212–19. Durham, NC: Duke University Press, 1998.

Roberts, Dorothy. *Torn Apart: How the Child Welfare System Destroys Black Families—and How Abolition Can Build a Safer World*. New York: Basic Books, 2022.

Rose, Jacqueline. *Mothers: An Essay on Love and Cruelty*. New York: Farrar, Straus, and Giroux, 2018.

Ruddick, Sara. *Maternal Thinking: Toward a Politics of Peace*. Boston: Beacon Press, 1989.

Ruido, Maria. "Mater Amatísima: Imaginaries and Discourses on Maternity in Times of Change." *Work and Words*. http://www.workandwords.net/en/projects/view/602. Accessed June 7, 2023.

Russell, Catherine. *Archiveology: Walter Benjamin and Archival Film Practices*. Durham, NC: Duke University Press, 2018.

Sartre, Jean-Paul. *Being and Nothingness*. 1943. Translated by Hazel E. Barnes. New York: Washington Square Press, 1956.

Saymed, Asma, ed. *Screening Motherhood in Contemporary World Cinema*. Bradford, ON: Demeter, 2016.

Schnelle, Josef. "Rabenmutter." *Deutschlandfunk*, December 6, 2007. https://www.deutschlandfunk.de/rabenmutter-102.html.

Schwartz, Marie Jenkins. *Birthing a Slave: Motherhood and Medicine in Antebellum South*. Cambridge, MA: Harvard University Press, 2010.

Sedgwick, Eve Kosofsky. "Queer Performativity: Henry James's *The Art of the Novel*." *GLQ* 1, no. 1 (1993): 1–16.

Sedgwick, Eve Kosofsky. *Touching Feeling*. Durham, NC: Duke University Press, 2003.

Sharpe, Christina. *In the Wake: On Blackness and Being*. Durham, NC: Duke University Press, 2016.

Shriver, Lionel. *We Need to Talk about Kevin*. New York: Harper, 2003.

Slobodin, Ortal. "Between the Eye and the Gaze: Maternal Shame in the Novel *We Need to Talk about Kevin*." *Feminism & Psychology* 29, no. 2 (2018): 214–30.

Smyth, Sarah Louise. "Postfeminism, Ambivalence, and the Mother in Lynne Ramsay's *We Need to Talk about Kevin* (2011)." *Film Criticism* 44, no. 1 (2020). https://quod.lib.umich.edu/f/fc/13761232.0044.106/—postfeminism-ambivalence-and-the-mother-in-lynne-ramsays-we?rgn=main;view=fulltext.

Sobchack, Vivian. *Carnal Thoughts: Embodiment and Moving Image Culture*. Berkeley: University of California Press, 2004.

Spelman, Elizabeth V. *Fruits of Sorrow: Framing Our Attention to Suffering*. Boston: Beacon, 1997.

Spelman, Elizabeth V. "Woman as Body: Ancient and Contemporary Views." *Feminist Studies* 8, no. 1 (1982): 32–41.

Speth, Maria. "Interview with Maria Speth." *Internationales Forums des Jungen Films*. Accessed February 27, 2023. https://www.peripherfilm.de/madonnen/interview.htm.

Speth, Maria. "Madonnen." *Berlinale Forum 2007*. Accessed February 27, 2023. https://www.berlinale.de/de/2007/programm/20073103.html.

Spillers, Hortense J. "Mama's Baby, Papa's Maybe: An American Grammar Book." *Diacritics* 17, no. 2 (1987): 65–81.

Still, Caitlin. "Abject Relations: Postmaternal Australia in *The Babadook*." *Hecate* 45, nos. 1–2 (2020): 23–42.

Sutherland, Jean-Anne. "Mothering, Guilt, and Shame." *Sociology Compass* 4–5 (2010): 310–21.

Tasker, Yvonne. *Working Girls: Gender and Sexuality in Popular Cinema*. London: Routledge, 1998.

Taylor, Erin N., and Lora Ebert Wallace. "For Shame: Feminism, Breastfeeding Advocacy, and Maternal Guilt." *Hypatia* 27, no. 1 (2012): 76–98.

Telò, Mario. "Medea in the Courtroom: Foucault, Alice Diop, and Abolition." *Arethusa* 56, no. 3 (2023): 413–39.

Thompson, Kristin, and David Bordwell. "Observations on Film Art." Accessed October 30, 2022. http://www.davidbordwell.net/blog/category/tableau-staging/.

Thornham, Sue. "Impossible Subjects? In Search of the Maternal Subject in *Stories We Tell* (Polley 2012) and *The Arbor* (Barnard 2010)." *Women: A Cultural Review* 31, no. 3 (2020): 259–82.

Tomar, Shagun. "EXBlicks: Baby Blues." *ExBerliner*, January 21, 2015. https://www.exberliner.com/film/exblicks-das-fremde-im-mir/.

Tomkins, Silvan. *Shame and Its Sisters: A Silvan Tomkins Reader*. Edited by Eve Kosofsky Sedgwick and Adam Frank. Durham, NC: Duke University Press, 1995.

Torlasco, Domietta. "Against House Arrest: Digital Memory and the Impossible Archive." *Camera Obscura* 26, no. 1 (76) (2011): 38–63.

Torlasco, Domietta. "Philosophy in the Kitchen." *World Picture* 11 (2016). http://worldpicturejournal.com/article/philosophy-in-the-kitchen/.

Tremblay, Jean-Thomas. *Breathing Aesthetics*. Durham, NC: Duke University Press, 2022.

Trister Grace, Karen, and Jocelyn C. Anderson. "Reproductive Coercion: A Systematic Review." *Trauma, Violence, & Abuse* 19, no. 4 (2018): 371–90.

Tyler, Imogen. "Against Abjection." *Feminist Theory* 10, no. 1 (2009): 77–98.

Tyler, Imogen, and Lisa Baraitser. "Private View, Public Birth: Making Feminist Sense of the New Visual Culture of Childbirth." *Studies in the Maternal* 5, no. 2 (2013): 1–27.

US Department of Health and Human Services. "U.S. Surgeon General Issues Advisory on the Mental Health and Well-Being of Parents." August 28, 2024. https://www.hhs.gov/about/news/2024/08/28/us-surgeon-general-issues-advisory-mental-health-well-being-parents.html.

Villarosa, Linda. "Why America's Black Mothers and Babies Are in a Life-or-Death Crisis." *New York Times Magazine*, April 11, 2018. https://www.nytimes.com/.

Wagner, Brigitta. "Vorschneider in Focus." *Film Quarterly* 63, no. 4 (2010): 62–64.

Walker, Alice. "A Writer Because of, Not in Spite of, Her Children." In *Mother Reader: Essential Writings on Motherhood*, edited by Moyra Davey, 99–102. New York: Seven Stories, 2001.

Walker, Esther. "Bringing Along Baby: Should We Talk about Kevin in Front of the Children?" *London Guardian*, November 4, 2011. https://www.theguardian.com/.

Walker, Janet, and Diana Waldman, eds. *Feminism and Documentary*. Minneapolis: University of Minnesota, 1999.

Weeks, Kathi. "Abolition of the Family: The Most Infamous Feminist Proposal." *Feminist Theory* 24, no. 3 (2023): 433–53.

Wellershaus, Elisabeth. "Rabenmutter." Translated by Jo Beckett. In *Zeitgeister: International Perspectives from Culture and Society*. Goethe-Institut e. V., September 2021. https://www.goethe.de/prj/zei/en/pos/22351887.html.

White, Patricia. "Documentary Practice and Transnational Feminist Theory: The Visibility of FGC." In *A Companion to Contemporary Documentary Film*, edited by Alexandra Juhasz and Alisa Lebow, 217–32. Hoboken, NJ: Wiley, 2015.

White, Patricia. *Women's Cinema, World Cinema: Projecting Contemporary Feminisms*. Durham, NC: Duke University Press, 2015.

Wildenthal, Lora. *German Women for Empire 1884–1945*. Durham, NC: Duke University Press, 2001.

Williams, Linda. "Film Bodies: Gender, Genre, Excess." *Film Quarterly* 44, no. 4 (1991): 2–13.

Williams, Linda. "'Something Else Besides a Mother': *Stella Dallas* and the Maternal Melodrama." In *Issues in Feminist Film Criticism*, edited by Patricia Erens, 137–62. Bloomington: Indiana University Press, 1990.

Zhang, Qian. "It's All about Repetition: Maternal Time in Horror from *Jeanne Dielman* (1975) to *The Babadook* (2014)." *Monstrum* 5, no. 1 (2022): 46–65.

Ziegler, Joanna E. "Michelangelo and the Medieval Pietà: The Sculpture of Devotion or the Art of Sculpture?" *Gesta* 34, no. 1 (1995): 28–36.

Žižek, Slavoj. "The Architectural Parallax." In *The Political Unconscious of Architecture: Re-opening Jameson's Narrative*, edited by Nadir Lahiji, 255–98. Surrey, UK: Ashgate, 2011.

Index

Note: Page numbers in *italics* denote figures.

abandonment, 4, 18, 90, 96, 103–4, 111, 136
abjection, 19, 130, 139, 146–47, 153, 158; "abject criticism," 142
abolition of the family, 10–13, 37, 41, 80, 161–62, 166n31
abortion, vii, 30, 78–81, 117
aesthetics, 16, 19, 40, 145, 160; of exhaustion, 46; of motherhood, 64, 144; of austerity, 98; of disgust, 141–42. *See also* interruption
affect studies, 13, 89, 91
Aftershock (Eiselt and Lee), 15, 101
Ahmed, Sara, 13, 153; anger as defined by, 17, 71, 73, 83–85; *Cultural Politics of Emotion*, 16; feminist snap, 18, 74, 85–86; guilt as defined by, 118; regret as defined by, 16, 28
alienation, 13, 22, 124
Almodóvar, Pedro, 123, 146
Almond, Barbara, 23, 77, 85, 130
ambivalence, 53, 83, 91, 152; definition of, 22–23; maternal ambivalence, 11, 14, 23, 41, 43, 72, 83–87, 123, 130
Angel of the House, 4; angel of the hearth, 123
Animal Locomotion (Muybridge), 5, *6–7*

Arbor, The (Barnard), 30, 166n20
archival turn, 9
Aristotle, 17, 69
Arnold, Sarah, 3, 5, 48, 72, 129, 134, 140
Austin, J. L., 84

Babadook, The (Kent), 16–17, 132, 170n23; anger, 72, 74–77, 85, 88; exhaustion, 43, 47–51, 54, 57, 66–67
Baby, The (Gaymer and Robins-Grace), 19, 72, 74, 78–83, 87, 152
Baby Ruby (Wohl), 19, 146, 147–53, 158
Bad Moms (Lucas and Moore), 4
bad mother, 3–4, 5, *7*, 52, 70, 81, 118, 129–30, 134; as disgusting mother, 19; blame, 18, 26, 89, 130, 138, 140; psychoanalysis, 124–25. See also *Rabenmutter*
Baer, Hester, 9
Baraitser, Lisa, 8, 43, 48, 50, 120, 143–44
Bataille, Georges, 141
Bazin, André, 45
Beauvoir, Simone de, 17, 43–47, 56–57, 108; alienation as defined by, 124, 144; ethics as defined by, 18, 108, 118–22, 129, 137–38; immanence as defined by, 17, 44, 46, 53, 121; motherhood as defined by, 13, 22, 82, 120–21, 128; "Pyrrhus and Cineas," 128; *The Second Sex*, 13, 22, 43, 82

being-for-itself, 46
being-for-the-Other, 18, 120–22, 137, 160
being-with-Others, 119–20
Beloved (Morrison), 84–85, 87
Berlant, Lauren, 23, 54, 92, 131, 151
Berlin School, 96, 174n20, 174n21
Black Lives Matter, 15, 69, 100
Bordwell, David, 62
Brauerhoch, Annette, 5
breastfeeding, 94, 117, 145–46
breath, 61, 109
Briefel, Aviva, 48, 170n21
Brinkema, Eugenie, 13, 62, 142, 154, 157
Brood, The (Cronenberg), 3, 48, 70, 79, 140
Brooks, Peter, 134. See also melodrama
Butler, Alison, 162

Campion, Jane, 74
car crash, 17, 47, 109, 133–34, 152, 157
care, 18, 41, 51, 76, 80, 118–19, 122; childcare, 3, 87, 95, 101; ethics of, 118–20, 122, 137–38; work, 48–49, 53, 111, 125–26. See also foster care
Carrie (De Palma), 3, 48, 70
Carroll, Noël, 139
Chion, Michel, 103
Chodorow, Nancy, 40, 76–77, 89
Cinco Lobitos (Lullaby), 18, 118, 122–27, 129, 131, 133
cinefeminism, 5, 166n20
cinematernity, 5, 8, 159–60
cinematography, 39, 96, 102, 108, 157
class, 11, 14–15, 57, 59, 80, 122, 130, 133, 167n49
Clover, Carol, 71–72
Collins, Patricia Hill, 14, 57–58
Communist Manifesto, The (Marx and Engels), 10, 37
compilation film, 17, 24, 29, 36, 113, 166n23; definition of, 35
confessional maternal memoirs, 167n49
Contratto, Susan, 40, 89
Conversation, The (Coppola), 148
Copjec, Joan, 92

COVID-19 pandemic, vii, 2–3, 43, 105, 125, 159, 162
Creed, Barbara, 70–72, 139, 147; monstrous feminine, 4, 76, 139
crushing, 1, 4, 12, 101, 105, 159–60; etymology of, 2

Das Fremde in mir (The stranger in me), 19, 143–47, 151–53, 178n22
Daughter Rite (Citron), 30
Davis, Angela, 58
Davis, Essie, 47, 49
Deleuze, Gilles, 17, 45–47, 55, 61–62; *Cinema 2*, 45; time-image, 17, 45–47, 49, 169n9
Die allseitig reduzierte Persönlichkeit-Redupers (The all-round reduced personality-redupers), 8
Diop, Alice, 109, 175n63
Doane, Mary Ann, 53; close-up as defined by, 140, 150
domestic labor, 3, 8, 44–45, 49, 121, 123
Donath, Orna, 10–11, 17, 25, 27–29, 40, 52–53, 121; *Regretting Motherhood*, xi, 24
Dubin, Minna, 69–70

Earth Mama (Leaf), 18, 98–104, 108, 111
Eichhorn, Kate, 9

failure, 18, 89–90, 105, 115, 118, 122, 132, 134, 138; temporality of, 46
fantasy, 55, 66, 92, 98, 101, 103, 109; as cruel optimism, 54, 151–52; of the perfect mother, 52, 54, 89–90
fatherhood, 108, 162
"feel-bad cinema," 4
feminism, 9–10, 73, 122; antifeminism, 26, 69, 86; Black feminist thought, 58, 69, 73–74, 88; postfeminism, 10, 151; second-wave, 44, 66
feminist cinema, 2, 5, 8, 49, 161, 180n1; feminist documentary, 29–32, 34; 168n38
femmes tondues, 109–10, 114
Ferrante, Elena, 1, 104, 153–55, 179n47

filicide, 4, 17, 37–40, 50, 77, 84–85, 88; infanticide, 79, 90, 109, 111
film philosophy, 160
Firestone, Shulamith, 11
Fischer, Lucy, 5, 8, 39, 82, 159
Fischer, Sarah, 11, 27
foster care, 30, 56–59, 99, 101–3, 174n28; child protective services (CPS), 99, 102
found footage, 8–9, 35
freedom, 18, 34, 37, 47, 64, 74, 99, 108, 158; as bad faith, 129; ethical, 121–22, 124; lack of, 33, 56–57, 59, 79–80, 101
Freud, Sigmund, 141
Friedan, Betty, 170n48
Frye, Marilyn, 17, 83–84
Fuery, Kelli, 127, 129

gaze, 18, 89–91, 96–97, 101–3, 105, 108 113; alien, 18, 90–91, 98, 102, 145; juridical, 112; male, 141; shaming, 89, 92, 94–95, 98, 102; tender, 102, 108
Gelegenheitsarbeit einer Sklavin (Part-time work of a domestic slave), 8
Germany, vii, 11, 16, 25–27, 29, 31, 34, 93, 99, 168n47
Gleeson, J. J., and K. D. Griffiths, 10–11
Göbel, Esther, 11, 25–26
Godard, Jean-Luc, 113, 128
good mother, 4–6, 6, 9–10, 18, 50, 52, 89, 134, 138; ideal, 130
Gorfinkel, Elena, 46, 62
Gumbs, Alexis Pauline, 14, 58
Guttmacher Institute, 117

happiness, 3, 19, 33, 92, 104, 114, 159
Hartman, Saidiya, 14, 59–60, 99
Hays, Sharon, 136, 178n81
Heart Still Hums, The (Leaf and Russell), 174n28
Heidegger, Martin, 18, 118–20, 137; *Being and Time*, 119
Hereditary (Aster), 3, 21, 48
Hirsch, Marianne, 54–55, 70; mother/daughter plot as defined by, 83; on anger, 84

Hiroshima mon amour (Resnais), 109–10
hooks, bell, 58, 70
horror cinema, 3–5, 17–18, 61, 70–72, 139–40, 157; maternal, 19, 48, 76; rape-revenge, 71–72
housewife-based model, 10–12, 80, 144, 161
housework, 5, 8, 44, 57; Wages for Housework, 165n5
Hüller, Sandra, 93

Ich seh, Ich seh (Goodnight Mommy), 3, 48
Ich war zuhause, aber . . . (I was at home, but . . .), 17, 43, 47, 60–66, 94
Imitation of Life (Sirk), 40
In den Tag hinein (The days between), 95, 174n21
Industrial Revolution, 25
interruption, 9, 43, 47–48, 50, 171n55; aesthetics of, 36
intersectionality, 74
Irigaray, Luce, 61

J'ai tué ma mère (Dolan), 132–33, 140
Jeanne Dielman (Akerman), 8, 49
Johnston, Claire, 161

Kant, Immanuel, 145
Kaplan, E. Ann, 4–5, 64–65, 72, 176n35; capitalism as defined by, 124–25; *Motherhood and Representation*, 78; psychoanalysis as defined by, 76–77
Kim, Sue J., 70
King, Tiffany Lethabo, 11
kinship, 12, 59–60, 80, 100, 161
Kluge, Alexander, 36–37; *Nachrichten aus der ideologischen Antike-Marx/Eisenstein/Das Kapital* (News from the ideological antiquity-Marx/Eisenstein/*The Capital*), 36
Kolnai, Aurel, 19, 142, 153, 157
Kristeva, Julia, 19, 139–44, 146–48, 153, 155–56; *Powers of Horror*, 139; *Stabat Mater* as defined by, 64–65

Index

LaChance Adams, Sarah, 23, 86, 119–20, 128
Lactatio Bernardi, 94
Landman, Janet, 11, 16, 27–28
La Passion de Jeanne d'Arc (Dreyer), 112–13
LeBeau, Claire S., 118–20
Lesage, Julia, 29, 87–88
Levinas, Emmanuel, 18, 90, 92, 94, 106; ethics and relationality as defined by, 118–20, 137–38
Leyda, John, 35. *See also* compilation film
Lewis, Sophie, 10–11, 166n31
lived experience, 13, 25, 44, 143
Lockman, Darcy, 69
Lost Daughter, The, 1, 16, 18–19; shame, 89–90, 103–9; disgust, 153–58
Lorde, Audre, 17, 58, 70, 73, 80
Louvart, Helene, 105, 108

Madonna del Latte, 93–94
Madonnen (Madonnas), 18, 89, 93–99, 102, 174n21
Madres parallelas (Parallel mothers), 146
Marso, Lori J., 169n4, 180n1
Mater Amatísima: Imaginaries and Discourses on Maternity in Times of Change (Ruido), 16, 24, 29, 34–42
McHugh, Kathleen, 71
McRobbie, Angela, 151
Medea, 36–40, 88, 114, 143; *Medea* (Pasolini), 38, 113–14; *Medea* (von Trier), 38
melodrama, 4–5, 19, 40, 57, 61, 122, 125, 134, 138
Mennel, Barbara, 123
Menninghaus, Winfried, 141, 145, 150, 156–57
Merleau-Ponty, Maurice, 18, 90–91
#MeToo, 69
Milkova, Stiliana, 153–55
Modleski, Tania, 71
momfluencer, 151
Mommy (Dolan), 18, 122, 132–38, 140
monstrous mother, 3–4, 40, 76. *See also* Creed, Barbara

Motherhood Archives, The (Lusztig), 8–9, 36
motherhood studies, 14
Mothers of Invention (Mayer and Columpar), 162
Mulvey, Laura, 39–40, 123; détournement as defined by, 9, 36, 168n54; gleaning as defined by, 9, 35–36; *Riddles of the Sphinx*, 39–40
Mundlos, Christine, 11, 27, 53, 81
Muybridge, Eadweard, 5–9

Nancy, Jean-Luc, 65–66
Nash, Jennifer C., 15, 58, 100–101, 114, 167n49, 171n55; *Birthing Black Mothers*, 100
National Socialism, 25
neoliberalism, 10, 124–25, 151
neorealism, 47, 169n9
New German Cinema, 8
new-momism, 10, 151
Ngai, Sianne, 13; irritation as defined by, 86; disgust as defined by, 139, 152; *Ugly Feelings*, 16
Nichols, Bill, 32, 35
Nietzsche, Friedrich, 18, 118–20, 137, 141–42; bad conscience as defined by, 119
Nightingale, The (Kent), 71–72, 74

O'Brien, M. E., 11, 37, 80. *See also* abolition of the family
O'Reilly, Andrea, 14, 125

Parker, Rozsika, 23
parturition, 82–83, 117, 130, 143–44, 147, 155, 158
Persona (Bergman), 21
Petersen, Sara, 69, 87
Peucker, Brigitte, 62
Pieces of Her (Stoudt), 18, 72, 74–75, 83–88
Pietà, 63, 65, 114
postpartum depression, 50, 55, 81, 87, 144, 147, 166n23; postpartum psychosis, 150, 152–53
postpartum mortality, 15
Prevenge (Lowe), 71–72
Price, Brian, 16, 27–28

Index

Psycho (Hitchcock), 3, 5, 48, 70, 76, 140
Putnam, EL, 43, 50. *See also* interruption

Quebec cinema, 132
Quindlen, Anna, 50–51

Rabenmutter, 26, 36, 93
race, 14–15, 87, 110, 115
Rangan, Pooja, 33–34
regretting motherhood, 10–13, 16–17, 24–27, 31–36, 161, 166n31; as filicide, 39–40; as international phenomenon, 169n74; as rejection, 41
Regretting Motherhood (Grimme and Hoffmann), 16, 24, 29–34, 40
relief, 45, 61, 76–77, 117
repetition, 17, 43–49, 56, 66
reproductive injustice, 15, 80, 83; obstetric negligence, 100
Revolutionary Mothering (Gumbs, Martens, Williams), 14–15
Rich, Adrienne, 14, 23, 25, 44, 52, 86, 108, 121, 159–60; on anger, 17, 69–70, 73–74; antiabortion as defined by, 82; on guilt, 117, 126, 131, 137; institution of motherhood as defined by, 1, 14, 23–24, 88; mask of motherhood, 152; natural mother as defined by, 107–8; *Of Woman Born*, 22, 58; on filicide, 77. *See also* ambivalence
Rich, B. Ruby, 8, 30, 166n20
Roberts, Dorothy, 11, 58–59, 99. *See also* foster care
Roe v. Wade, vii, 78
Rois, Sophie, 36–38, 175n62
Rose, Jacqueline, 121, 144
Rosemary's Baby (Polanski), 82, 130, 148
Ruddick, Sara, ix, 4, 122
Russell, Catherine, 35

Saint Omer (Diop), 18, 89–90, 109–15, 134
Sans toit ni loi (Vagabond), 95
Sartre, Jean-Paul, 18, 90–91, 98, 168n38; being-seen-by-the-Other, 18, 91, 112

Schuld, 18, 119, 122; debt, 118–20, 137–38
Sedgwick, Eve Kosofsky, 13, 18, 91–92, 112
self-narration, 9, 29, 33, 168n38
Shariat, Faraz, 79
Sharpe, Christina, 14, 100
Shriver, Lionel, 127, 177n54
slavery, 14, 99–100, 112, 174n33; afterlives of, 14
Spain, 16, 24, 34–35, 38–40, 123, 168n47; Francoist, 125
speech act, 28, 83–84
Spelman, Elizabeth, 16, 28; somatophobia, 55
Spillers, Hortense, 100
Stella Dallas (Vidor), 5, 134
Stories We Tell (Polley), 30, 166n20

tableau, 49, 62–65, 102, 130
temporality, 46
Theron, Charlize, 51, 55, 148
Thousand and On, A (Rockwell), 17, 43, 56–60, 66, 101, 121–22
thriller, 18, 21, 36, 83–84, 104, 127, 160
Till (Chukwu), 15
Töchter (Daughters), 95
Tod in Venedig (Death in Venice), 104, 154
Tomkins, Silvan, 18, 91, 94, 106, 112
Torlasco, Domietta, 9
tradwife, 10
Tully (Reitman), 17, 43, 51–56, 66, 146, 148, 152
Tyler, Imogen, 142, 144. *See also* abjection

Umberto D. (De Sica), 45
Undo Motherhood (Karklin), 12, 16
Unsichtbare Gegner (Invisible adversaries), 8
Us (Peele), 3, 48

Villarosa, Linda, 100–101, 114
voice, 9, 31, 32–34, 102, 148; acousmatic, 31, 98, 103
Von wegen Schicksal (Is this fate?), 8
Vorschneider, Reinhold, 96–97, 102

Wages for Housework, 165n5
waiting, 43, 45–46, 65
Walker, Alice, 58, 171n55
Weeks, Kathi, 11
Wellershaus, Elisabeth, 26
We Need to Talk about Kevin (Ramsay), 18, 48, 88, 127–32, 133
White, Patricia, 8, 31, 16–62, 168n38
whiteness, 25, 114
Williams, Linda, 5, 30; body genres, 61, 140

Witches (Sankey), 166n23
women's march, 85–87
women's movement, 5, 29, 34, 39, 41, 80, 161

Yates, Andrea, 50–51

Žižek, Slavoj, 149

OLIVIA LANDRY is an associate professor of German and chair of Gender, Sexuality, and Women's Studies at Virginia Commonwealth University and the author of *A Decolonizing Ear: Documentary Film Disrupts the Archive*.

The University of Illinois Press
is a founding member of the
Association of University Presses.

———————————————

Composed in 10.5/13 Mercury Text
with Avenir display
by Jim Proefrock
at the University of Illinois Press

University of Illinois Press
1325 South Oak Street
Champaign, IL 61820-6903
www.press.uillinois.edu